holiday IDEAS

THE ideas LIBRARY

FOR YOUTH GROUPS

THE IDEAS LIBRARY

holiday
IDEAS

THE *ideas* LIBRARY

FOR YOUTH GROUPS

Youth Specialties

ZondervanPublishing**House**

Grand Rapids, Michigan
A Division of HarperCollinsPublishers

Project editor: Vicki Newby
Cover and interior design: Curt Sell
Art director: Mark Rayburn

ISBN 0-310-22036-X

Printed in the United States of America

00 01 02 03 04 05 06/ /10 9 8 7 6

CONTENTS

OTHER HOLIDAYS

Super Bowl

April Fool's Day

Mothers Day

Fathers Day

Graduation ideas

So what holiday idea made your youth group so festive that your kids are still talking about it?

Youth Specialties pays $25 (and in some cases, more) for unpublished, field-tested ideas that have worked for you.

You've probably been in youth work long enough to realize that sanitary, theoretical, tidy ideas aren't what in-the-trenches youth workers are looking for. They want—*you* want—imagination and take-'em-by-surprise novelty in meetings, parties, and other events. Ideas that have been tested and tempered and improved in the very real, very adolescent world you work in.

So here's what to do:

• Sit down at your computer, get your holiday idea out of your head and onto your hard drive, then e-mail it to ideas@youthspecialties.com. Or print it off and fax it to 619-440-4939 (Attn: Ideas).

• If you need to include diagrams, photos, art, or samples that help explain your idea, stick it all in an envelope and mail it to our street address: Ideas, 1224 Greenfield Dr., El Cajon, CA 92021-3399.

• Be sure to include your name and all your addresses and numbers.

Let us have about three months to give your idea a thumbs up or down*, and a little longer for your 25 bucks.

---

*Hey, no offense intended if your idea isn't accepted. It's just that our fussy Ideas Library editor has these *really* meticulous standards. If the idea isn't creative, original, and just plain fun, she'll reject it (reluctantly, though, because she has a tender heart). Sorry. But we figure you deserve only the best holiday ideas.

NEW
YEAR

Dissolve those post-Christmas blahs with these fantastic ideas for New Year's Eve and New Year's Day. The weather outside may be frightful, but you'll find plenty of games and activities to warm up your kids' hearts.

PARTY IDEA
FUNFETTI

This idea gives a New Year's celebration or birthday bash a beautifully festive touch (as long as you can clean the floor easily). Fill medium-sized latex balloons with a handful of confetti per balloon. Inflate the balloons, tie them off, then attach them to (or suspend them from) the ceiling. When the clock hits midnight, puncture the balloons with pins or sharpened pencils, then watch out— confetti flies everywhere.

For real celebrating (and a real mess when it gets in hair), add glitter to the balloons. *Michael Capps*

EVENT
NEW YEAR'S DAY FOOTBALL MARATHON

For a wild and crazy day, and to give your kids something to do on New Year's Day, open your home for a Football Marathon. Have two televisions set up so you can watch two games simultaneously: the Fiesta and Cotton Bowls, then the Rose Bowl, then the Orange and Sugar Bowls. Make a poster with all five games listed, including team names, national rankings, and seasonal records. Allow the kids to pick winners ahead of time, and award a prize to the one with the best record of picks.

To help relieve some of the energy built up by sitting around for so long, organize a quick touch football game outside during halftimes or between games. Admission to the event can be a bag of chips or a six-pack of soda. For a simple meal, send out for pizza. *Ken S. Williams*

COLLAGE
THE YEAR-IN-REVIEW BANNER

This is a simple yet effective way to build group unity and to make some lasting memories. Take a long sheet of paper (butcher wrap or newsprint) and hang it on a smooth wall surface. Draw heavy vertical lines to divide the banner into 12 equal sections, and label each section with the names of the months in order. Then let the kids go to work decorating the banner, collage-style, to show what they did as a group each month of the preceding year. Use crayons and markers. Attach photos of group events, copies of the youth newsletter, movie posters, handouts, lesson outlines, letters, charts, publicity materials, ticket stubs—anything that would symbolize or remind them of what they did.

This activity is especially good for watch-night services or New Year's lock-ins. Just have the kids bring everything they've saved from youth group events over the previous 12 months, and add to their collection whatever you yourself have saved. It's also a good way to purge your office files! *Randy D. Nichols*

PARTY

NEW YEAR'S EVE EVE PARTY

With the holidays becoming more and more dangerous on New Year's Eve, why not have a New Year's Eve *Eve* Party instead? Celebrate New Year's Eve *Eve* at midnight. The kids can have all the fun of New Year's Eve and then stay home to babysit on the real New Year's Eve. *Dallas Elder*

DISCUSSION STARTER

NEW YEAR'S RESOLUTIONS

First discuss the meaning of the words *New Year's resolution*. Ask kids to share some resolutions they have made in the past and what happened to them. Did they last? How long? Next, introduce the word *covenant*, and ask kids to compare that word with the word *resolution*. What is the difference between the two? (One important difference is that a resolution is generally a private thing, and a covenant is a promise or agreement made publicly between two or among more people.)

After some discussion, have the kids form groups of three, preferably with friends they know fairly well. Then give them 10 minutes or so to write a few New Year's covenants. After they are completed, each person shares his or her covenants with other members of the small group and asks for feedback. Are they too vague? Impossible to keep? Too easy? Inappropriate? Kids are then allowed to rewrite their covenants based on the feedback they received. Last,

they share their rewritten covenants and perhaps discuss practical ways they plan to put them into practice. *J. Richard Short*

BIBLE STUDY

SCRIPTURE RESOLUTIONS

To create scriptural New Year's resolutions, have your kids go through the Bible and find their favorite verses. For those who claim they don't have a favorite verse, have them open their Bibles to Proverbs and start reading until they come to a verse they like. Make sure you have some extra Bibles on hand for this.

Tell the kids to paraphrase the verse they choose by putting it in their own words. Next they should personalize it by putting themselves in it. For example, Matthew 6:33 reads: "But seek first his kingdom and his righteousness, and all these things will be given to you as well." Someone who chooses that verse might paraphrase and personalize it this way: "I will always seek the things of God in all I do. And if I do this, all that I need here on this earth God will give me."

Let the kids write the paraphrase in large letters on a sheet of colored paper, then post it where they'll see it often. This personalized verses can then become their New Year's resolutions. *Ron Kostedt*

LESSON APPLICATION

TURN OR BURN

This idea works well at the first meeting of a new year or the last meeting of an old year. It involves the making of New Year's resolutions. Students are asked to "turn" (over a new leaf) or "burn" (an old habit).

Each person is given a few sheets of paper and an envelope along with a pencil. For effect you could print the shape of a leaf on one paper, and burn the edges of the other paper. Participants are then asked to write down on the leaf some resolutions for the new year (a good habit that you propose to begin doing). The papers are then folded and put into self-addressed individual envelopes and sealed. The envelopes are collected and will be mailed out to these people in June to remind them of their resolutions.

Next, the kids are asked to write on the "burn" paper a bad habit that they would like to discontinue. After some discussion on how one goes about ridding himself or herself of a bad habit, and after some prayer and mutual commitment to each other, each person brings their bad habit to the front and symbolically burns it in a little bonfire. You can probably build a fire inside a washtub, or use a small hibachi. Be sure to have adequate ventilation or just do this part of the meeting outside.

The best way to make a program like this effective over the long haul is to plan some ways to follow up on this during the year. It can prove to be a very meaningful way to approach on old idea.

Ed Skidmore

NEW YEAR'S PROPHECIES

This could be the funniest thing your group does all year! Get a copy of a sensational tabloid that makes predictions for the New Year. As you read it, circle the most outrageous predictions you can find.

Read aloud to your group what you find—this will be a scream in itself. Then have someone pass out index cards and pencils. Tell the group, "Anybody can do better than that," and let kids write down their own zany predictions for the next year. Then let everyone read them aloud. Some will tend to be about other members of the group, and they're guaranteed to be hilarious. *Todd Capen*

ST. VALENTINE'S DAY

Plan a memorable February 14th with these icebreakers, games, songs, activities, and Bible lessons—all about love, whether human or divine.

MIXER

LOVELY CONFUSION

Here's a Valentine's Day icebreaker for a party. Give everyone the list printed on page 20. Participants are on their own; the first person to accomplish all nine instructions is the winner. (They do not have to be accomplished in order, but they must all be done.) *Joe Snow*

GAME

FAMOUS SWEETHEARTS GAME

This game is great for Valentine parties. It is played just like the "Newlywed Game" on TV, except that participants take on the role of famous sweethearts—like these:
- Samson and Delilah
- Popeye and Olive Oyl
- Romeo and Juliet
- Adam and Eve
- Lucy and Ricky Riccardo
- Blondie and Dagwood
- George and Martha Washington
- Superman and Lois Lane
- Kermit the Frog and Miss Piggy

Make up pairs of name tags with names of famous people who were couples. Mix up the tags in a hat or bowl and have each person draw out a name tag. (Part of the fun of picking at random is that a guy may have to take on the role of Delilah or a girl that of Samson.) Teens then find their mates.

One at a time, the female characters leave the room. Their corresponding mates answer questions, trying to match what their famous sweethearts will say. (Have someone record the answers.) Questions should resemble these:
• What would you say your sweetheart is most famous for?
• Where would you say you and your sweetheart live?
• What color hair would you say your sweetheart has?

The female characters are brought back in and asked the same questions. Couples are awarded points if they match each other's answers. For the

Lovely Confusion

❤ Get 10 different autographs—first, middle, and last names.

❤ Unlace someone's shoe, lace it, and tie it again.

❤ Find two other people and have the three of you form a heart shape lying on the floor.

❤ Get a person of the opposite gender to kiss this paper five times and sign their name. _____

❤ Eat 10 red hots and show your red tongue to someone you do not know well. They sign here _____

❤ Recite this poem as loudly as you can:

How do I love thee
Let me count the ways
I love thee to the depth and
Breadth and height my soul can reach.
I love thee to the level of every day's most quiet need,
I love thee with the breath, smiles, tears of
All my life
And if God choose I shall but love thee
Better after death.

❤ Ask 10 people to be your valentine and record your score.
Yesses: _____ No's: _____

❤ Leapfrog over someone five times.

❤ You were given a piece of bubble gum at the beginning of the race. Chew it up and blow five bubbles. Find someone who will watch you do it and sign here when you finish:_____

second round, the male characters are taken out, and questions are asked of the female characters. The couples with the most points after two rounds wins.

A good way to begin the game is to award a certain number of points to the pair who find each other the quickest, one point less for the next pair to find each other, and so on. *Scott Pogue*

KISSING IN THE DARK

For this two-team relay, you'll need two identical bullseye targets 18 inches (or more) in diameter. Mark the targets' concentric circles with values like –10, 10, 25, 50, and 100. You'll also need two blindfolds, two tubes of lipstick, two tubes of Chapstick, and one adult with a marker for each target. (For larger groups, make more teams, adding one of the above items for each team added.) Post the targets on a wall 15 feet away from the starting line. Line up the two teams single file at the starting line, facing their target across the room.

Now announce the title of the game: "Kissing in the Dark." Explain that you will blindfold the first members of the teams, put Chapstick or lipstick (player's choice) on each one, and spin them around. Then, guided by their teammates shouts, the blindfolded players attempt to kiss the bull's-eye and then return to their own lines and blindfold the next player in line. Play continues until each player has had a chance to kiss in the dark.

It is helpful to have an adult circle each lip print immediately after it is made so that smearing from subsequent kisses doesn't confuse the scoring. For males who will put on the lipstick instead of the Chapstick, give their teams 10 bonus points. If play is too slow, add a time limit. *Doug Thorne and David Tohlen*

VALENTINE CANDY

Grab some of those Valentine candy conversation hearts (COOL KID, KISS ME, MY GAL, etc.) and try these ideas.

• **Valenteams.** Need to divide your group quickly—but with some Valentine fun—into teams? Determine before your party how many teams you want and how many on each team. Then pull that many sets of that many identical conversation hearts out of a bag.

When kids walk into the party, give them each one heart to hold onto—not eat! When the time comes to make teams, tell everyone to find others with their phrase. They can yell back and forth as much as they want until they all team up.

To divide for another team game, have everyone with the same *color* heart get together. *Tommy Baker*

• **Valentine Candy Charades.** Here's a good little game for your next Valentine's Day banquet. Put some candy conversation hearts in a bowl. One person from the group picks out one of the candies from the bowl and, using the regular rules for Charades, tries to pantomime the message. The person who correctly guesses the saying gets to eat that piece of candy. You can use teams, just like regular Charades, or you can do it like the game Password, where two partners on a team try to communicate with each other. It's hilarious to watch the participants try to do phrases like LOVER BOY, KISS ME, and all the other crazy sayings they put on those traditional candies. *Wayne Peterson*

• **Valentine Candy Bingo.** Make up a bunch of bingo cards—but instead of putting numbers in the squares, fill the squares with phrases from those little valentine candy hearts.

Buy enough candy hearts for all players to fill up all their bingo cards. Give players equal quantities of randomly selected candy hearts. On "Go!" players don't wait for a caller, but immediately try to cover their KISS ME squares with KISS ME candy hearts, their LOVER BOY squares with LOVER BOY hearts, etc. If they have a surplus of one kind of candy heart, they can trade with other players for hearts with phrases they need in order to cover every square on their card (or achieve a "bingo"—you make house rules).Players can eat the candy when the game is over.

• **Love Bingo.** This game is also suitable for a crowd breaker. Copy the bingo sheet on page 22. Make sure everyone has a pencil and a copy of the handout. The first person to get bingo wins a small prize. *Jeff Brown*

LOVE BINGO

Here is your Love Bingo card. Your mission: To be the first to get a bingo (across, down, or diagonal) by having persons sign the block that describes them.

Someone who was kissed today	A female friend	Someone who is 27 years old, 6'6", and 190 pounds	FREE FREE	The person you want to date but never have	Someone wearing red socks	Give someone a hug and have them sign here
The love of your life	The biggest female flirt	Your relative	Give someone a hug and have them sign here	The biggest male flirt	A close friend	FREE FREE
FREE FREE	A male with blue eyes	Your Sunday-school department director	Someone doing a lip sync tonight	Someone not wearing anything red	Someone kissed in 1991	"Sweet" describes this person
Give someone a hug and have them sign here	Someone wearing a red sweater	Someone with a charming personality	FREE FREE	Go up to some of the opposite sex, smile, and say, "Don't I know you from somewhere?" then have them sign here	Someone married	Your first boyfriend/girlfriend
Someone you want to get to know better	FREE FREE	A blonde	Someone who sleeps with a teddy bear	One of your closest friends	Give someone a hug and have them sign here	Someone wearing red shoes
The person you have a crush on	Your Sunday school teacher	FREE FREE	Someone wearing red	A brunette	A former boyfriend/girlfriend with whom you are still friends	A female with blue eyes
Someone who often encourages you or compliments you	Anyone at the party	Give someone a hug and have them sign here	Someone you really admire	Someone who has it all together	FREE FREE	A male friend

VALENTINE'S DAY SCAVENGER HUNT

Since it's too cold in most parts of the country to go outside on February 14, this scavenger hunt takes place indoors with magazines. Each team sits in a circle with a pile of magazines and the list found on page 24. The first team to find and tear out all 10 items is the winner. *Kathie Taylor*

VALENTINE CAROLS

You've probably gone Christmas caroling, but have you gone Valentine's Day caroling? Next Valentine's Day, have your group learn the songs on page 25 (or any love songs that you know) and serenade the people you love—parents, seniors, workers in the church, neighbors, etc. They will love it! If possible, dress everyone up in red and white—and maybe have one member of the group dress up like Cupid. You can also present a box of candy, cookies, or a Valentine's Day card to the people you sing for. You might also sing one or two Gospel songs that share the love of Christ as well. *Donn Williams*

PARENT VALENTINE BANQUET

Rather than the old Sweetheart Banquet, why not have your young people sponsor a Valentine Banquet for their parents? The young people prepare and serve the meal to their parents and then put on a program of skits and special music. Take lots of pictures and have lots of fun, and this may become an annual event. *David Butler*

LOVES ME, LOVES ME NOT

Kick off your Valentine's Day party—or your unit on dating and commitment—with this panel discussion.

Prior to your meeting ask four adults to each draft a short paragraph about their high school dating experiences, excluding any references that would identify them as male or female. Try to pick individuals who represent more than one kind of experience: married, unmarried, heavy high school daters, late

> Though I went steady with someone my entire eighth-grade year, in high school I was always getting dumped. I never had a relationship that lasted more than two weeks. It seemed the people I was attracted to were never attracted to me; and the people who were interested in me, I had no interest in. Thus, my love life in high school consisted of lots of dates but no steady. The same story continued on into college until I met my spouse-to-be in my first year. So other than the relationship I had in junior high, I've never gone steady with anyone but my spouse. Ironically, both the person I went with in eighth grade and the person I'm married to now have the same first name.

bloomers who didn't date until college, a woman who married her high school sweetheart, a man who married his wife a month after their first date, etc. Photocopy these paragraphs without naming the writers.

At the party or meeting, hand out the copies to the kids—while the four writers are seated up front. Students have to guess which story goes with which individual.

After the unveiling, kids jot down questions on index cards, then direct their questions to certain panel members or to panel members of a certain gender. *Deborah Carlson and Robert Malsack*

VALENTINE'S DAY SCAVENGER HUNT

FIND

1. A picture of a person you would like for a Valentine.

2. A picture of something people give for a Valentine's Day gift.

3. The word love.

4. A picture of something that rhymes with the word Valentine.

5. A picture of a romantic-looking couple.

6. A picture of a piece of clothing that is red.

7. A word or picture that describes your Valentine.

8. A picture of a red food.

9. A picture of anything that begins with the letter V.

10. A picture of a box of chocolates.

Valentine Carols

(to the tune of *Deck the Hall*)
Deck the hall with hearts of gladness
Fa, la, la, la ,la, la, la, la.
'Tis the day we don't want sadness
Fa, la, la, la ,la, la, la, la.
Don we now a big wide smile
Fa, la, la, la ,la, la, la, la.
Sing we love in every mile
Fa, la, la, la ,la, la, la, la.

(to the tune of *Mistletoe and Holly*)
Here we are, it's dandy
It's time for Valentines and candy
Big red presents
Val-en-tine cards
Saying we love you so.

Here we are and caring
It's time for loving
And for sharing
Kissing sweethearts
Big bright red cards
Spreading love wherever we go
(men) Happy Valentine's…
(women) Happy Valentine's…to you

(to the tune of *Jingle Bells*)
Chorus:
Big red hearts, flowered carts
Coming through the post
Valentines from someone who
You know will mean the most

Dashing through the snow
In a four-door or a coupe
We have come to you
To knock you for a loop
Our songs we bring today
To take away your blue
Oh, what fun it is to sing
A Valentine to you

Chorus:
Big red hearts, flowered carts
Coming through the post
Valentines from someone who
You know will mean the most

(to the tune of *O Christmas Tree*)
O Valentine, O Valentine
We bring you love from Jesus
O Valentine, O Valentine
We bring you love from Jesus
His love is true in summertime
But also in the wintertime
O Valentine, O Valentine
We bring you love from Jesus

(to the tune of *Jolly Old St. Nicholas*)
Jolly old St. Valentine
How'd you ever know
That we'd need a special day
To say, "We love you so!"?
Valentine's is here today
So we thought of you
We'll whisper how we love you so
That's just what we will do…

(whisper) "We love you!"

(to the tune of *We Wish You a Merry Christmas*)
We wish you a happy Val'tines
We wish you a happy Val'tines
We wish you a happy Val'tines
And a happy heart day.
Good tidings to you
We'll love you always
Good tidings on Val'tines
And a happy heart day.

ST. PATRICK'S DAY

No need to depend on the luck o' the Irish for your St. Patrick's Day programs. Other groups will be green with envy when they see the events you have planned around the memory and achievements of this very real and very influential Christian saint. Think of these ideas as the pot o' gold at the end of your March-programming rainbow.

MIXER

GREEN THANGS

When folks arrive, pin or tape on their backs an index card with the name of a green object written on it (in green marker, of course). Players may ask only yes-or-no questions of others in the group to determine what "green thang" they are. Players may ask only two questions of each person; then they must move on to question a new person.

When a player thinks she knows what she is, she tells her guess to a supervising sponsor. If the guess is correct, the sponsor removes the old card, gives it to the wearer, then attaches a new card to her back. Players hold on to the cards they correctly guessed until a final count at the end of the game. The person holding the most cards at the end of the time limit wins the game.

Some green thangs are avocado, green onion, cucumber, leprechaun, four-leaf clover, turtle, frog, grass, tree, ivy, lima bean, green pea, green apple, lettuce, paper money, artichoke, lime, kiwi fruit, Green Bay Packers, Green Hornet, green Jell-O,

pond scum, clover, spinach, pistachio ice cream, olive, mold, pickle, parrot, green parakeet, emerald, green underwear, envy.

Possible St. Patrick's Day prizes are Lucky Charms cereal; a can of green beans; green jelly beans; a green apple; a gold foil covered cup with candy in it (the pot of gold); green socks; green soda; green breath mints; and green mouthwash. *Jason Walker and Marcy Buford*

GAME

LEPRECHAUN SOFTBALL

Groups of 12 to 30 are perfect for celebrating St. Patrick's Day with this indoor or outdoor baseball variation.

Using a bathroom plunger for a bat and a small, lightweight rubber ball (such as a Squish Ball), play Leprechaun softball on a makeshift diamond:
• At first base is a table with paper cups and a pitcher full of green water (use food coloring).
• At second base is a bag of green balloons.
• At third base are two tubes of green lipstick.

• At home plate is the plunger, two wide-rim cups, and a box of Lucky Charms cereal. Place two empty cups about four to six feet behind home plate, either on the floor or on a table.

In addition to a pitcher and catcher, the fielding team has a baseman at each of the three bases. That's all—no shortstop and no fielders. At each

base is an umpire. Play is three to four innings.

Here's how to play:

• The batter tries to catch an underhand pitch in the plunger and toss the ball back into the field.

• Only the pitcher is allowed to field a ball that's been hit. The pitcher must catch the ball before it hits the ground in order to get the batter out on a hit. If the ball is immediately caught by the pitcher, the batter goes to the back of the batting line.

• If the pitcher cannot catch the ball, the batter runs to first base, where he races the first baseman in drinking a glass half-filled with green water. The first-base umpire calls the runner safe if he is the first one to set his empty glass upside down on the table. If the first baseman beats the runner at this drinking feat, the runner is called out.

• When a runner advances to second base, he must compete with the second baseman—this time to blow up a small green balloon, tie it, and sit on it until it pops. The second-base umpire determines the winner. If the runner wins, he stays on second base; if the second baseman wins, the runner is out.

• At third base, the runner and third baseman must each pick up a tube of green lipstick, apply it to their lips, close the lipstick, and lay the tube down. The third-base ump calls the runner safe or out, depending on if the runner won or lost the contest.

• The runner going home must compete with the catcher by tossing a handful of Lucky Charms piece by piece from home plate into the empty cup. The first person to get three pieces of cereal into the cup—with at least one piece being a marshmallow—wins. If the runner wins, his team scores 10 points. If

the catcher wins, the runner is out.

The team with the highest score wins the game. More bases with activities at each one may be added if you wish. *Jason Walker and Marcy Buford*

GAME

ST. PATRICK'S GOBBLE 'N' GIT

Divide your kids into teams for this relay race. Each team faces a table laden with the following fare: a green apple, a stick of celery, green jelly beans, a bowl of green gelatin, a bowl of pistachio pudding, and a large bowl of mint ice cream.

When the race begins, the first person on each team runs to her team's table, gobbles the first food, then races back to her team to tag the next player, who follows suit. The first team with an empty table wins.

Want a wilder, messier game? Try these variations: supply fewer jelly beans but add a spoon. Require players to flip the candies into their mouths. With the ice cream provide a container of green milk (use green food coloring) and a mixing spoon. The first player there must mix the ice cream and milk into a milkshake, and his teammates must each drink a glass of it during their turns. *Mark Christian*

GAME

LEPRECHAUN MAD LIB

In this holiday mad lib, give each of 24 people one of the slips on page 31. After the 24 players write their words or phrases on their slips, they come to the front and line up in the order of the numbers on their slips.

When the narrator reads the story on page 32, she pauses at each number so the corresponding answer can be read. Also, every time the word *leprechaun* is read, everyone in the audience stands up and shouts "Aye!" *Gwyn E. Baker*

GAME

ST. PADDY'S DAY QUIZ

Celebrate a St. Patrick's Day festival by taking the quiz on page 34 (print it on green paper, of course). The questions are designed to lead students into a discussion of who St. Patrick was, what he did, and

♣Leprechaun Mad Lib♣

1. Name one of your special treasures

_____

2. Noun (a thing)

_____

3. Adjective

_____

4. Part of the body

_____

5. Adjective

_____

6. Adjective

_____

7. Adjective

_____

8. Name of man in this room

_____

9. Name a place where you'd be afraid to walk (common noun)

_____

10. Name what you were wearing the last time your spouse or parent complained about the way you looked

_____

11. Name of person in the room

_____

12. Past-tense verb

_____

13. The most useless advice you've ever been given

_____

14. A catch phrase from a TV commercial you detest

_____

15. Name of a living thing

_____

16. Noun

_____

17. A tool

_____

18. Name or describe what you do when you get mad

_____

19. Plural noun

_____

20. Noun

_____

21. Plural noun

_____

22. Liquid

_____

23. Part of the body

_____

24. Part of the body

_____

story for
leprechaun mad lib

As tradition has it, if you catch a leprechaun, he must take you to the pot of _____, at the end of the _____. But you must beware! If you take your eyes off of him, he will disappear. These tricky little fellas are _____. Their _____ are _____. They wear a tiny _____ cobbler apron because they are in charge of making shoes for the fairies.

Once upon a time there lived a _____ Irishman named _____. One day he was strolling down the _____ wearing his _____. Then suddenly he spotted a leprechaun named _____ and _____ him and said, " _____," to which the leprechaun said, " _____." The Irishman threatened the leprechaun with his life if he didn't show him where the pot of _____ (same as #1) was. So

the leprechaun took the Irishman this way and that. Rough and hard ways they were, but the Irishman never took his eyes off the leprechaun. At long last they came to a place with large _____ trees. "Dig under the roots of this tree and you'll find your treasure," said the leprechaun. The Irishman thanked the little leprechaun and tied a _____ around the tree so he could mark the spot. He ran back to get his _____ to dig with, and when he came back there were (same as 16) around every tree. So he _____.

The moral of this story is: Love of _____ is the root of all _____; too many _____ spoil the _____; and the way to a man's _____ is through his _____.

how God can use bad or difficult circumstances for good—such as Patrick's six years in slavery. (During those six years, he learned to pray and depend on God, and his faith matured and was strengthened.)

To take a different direction, discuss luck. What things are lucky? What brings good luck? Compare the idea of luck with the Christian concept of God's blessing or of providence. Conclude the festival with green cake and punch.

Here are the answers:

1. green
2. Ireland
3. A.D. 389
4. Blarney Stone
5. pot of gold
6. Roman Catholic
7. leprechauns
8. pop quizzes
9. Ireland
10. Ireland
11. Blarney (in Britain)
12. Blarney
13. True
14. Blarney (used by the Irish to symbolize the Trinity)
15. Blarney
16. Blarney
17. True
18. Blarney (a deacon and alderman)
19. Blarney
20. True

Dianne Deming and Gary McCluskey

St. Patrick's Day Scavenger Hunt

Next St. Patrick's Day, give the following list to teams and give them 45 minutes or so to try to collect the following items from around town. The team with the most green items wins.

Green lettuce leaf	Green pear
Green piece of paper	Green lima bean
Green stamps	Four-leaf clover or shamrock
Green garter	One-dollar bill
Green pencil	Green turtle (live)
Green button	Green tennis shoe (left foot)
Green hair ribbon	Green toothpick
Green fingernail polish	Green bathing suit
Green toothbrush	Green palm leaf
Green hand soap	Green straw
Green dixie cup	Green shoelace
Green sweater	Green sucker
Green pickle	Green sock
Avocado	Seven-inch green string
Green ink	Green balloon, blown up
Green newspaper	Green flower
Green fish	Green key
Green onion	Green book
One pair green sunglasses	Green frog (live)
Green lipstick	Green lampshade
Green Ping-Pong paddle	Green gum
Green ticket stub	Jolly Green Giant picture
Green lime	Green stuffed animal

ST. PADDY'S DAY QUIZ

Circle the correct answer to each question.

1. What color is associated with St. Paddy's Day?

    green   red   mauve

2. Of which country is St. Patrick the patron saint?

    Ireland   England   Afghanistan

3. About which year was St. Patrick born?

    450 B.C.   A.D. 389   A.D. 1956

4. Which stone do the Irish kiss?

    Barney Stone   Barry Stone   Blarney Stone

5. What is found at the end of the rainbow?

    winter storm warnings   a bucket of coal   a pot of gold

6. What was Patrick's religion?

    Presbyterian   Roman Catholic   Jewish

7. Whom do the Irish call the Little People"?

    anyone under 5'3"   leprechauns   folks from Scotland

8. Which of the following are not associated with good luck?

    four-leaf clover   horseshoe   rabbit's foot   pop quizzes

9. Which country gives us the festival of St. Patrick?

    England   Ireland   Afghanistan

10. Patrick was called back into service in which country?

    England   Ireland   USA

Circle the correct answer for each statement, depending on whether it is true or blarney.

True   Blarney   11. St. Patrick was born in Ireland.

True   Blarney   12. St. Patrick chased all of the snakes out of Ireland.

True   Blarney   13. St. Patrick was poorly educated.

True   Blarney   14. St. Patrick first used the shamrock.

True   Blarney   15. Patrick's real name was Glockenspiel.

True   Blarney   16. St. Patrick wrote "When Irish Eyes Are Smiling" after a visit with Tip O'Neil in Boston.

True   Blarney   17. At a young age St. Patrick was a slave and received a divine call to work in the church.

True   Blarney   18. St. Patrick's father was a pagan soldier.

True   Blarney   19. St. Patrick drank green milkshakes at McDonald's.

True   Blarney   20. St. Patrick was a bishop.

SCORING

18-20 correct	You must be Irish.
14-18 correct	Your grandmother was probably Irish.
10-14 correct	You are full of blarney.
below 14 correct	You must be English.

Here are plenty of games, puzzles, craft projects, and scavenger hunt ideas—all tied to an Easter theme. But you'll also find service projects, worship activities, reenactments, Bible lessons, and meeting plans designed to commemorate the death and resurrection of Jesus Christ.

GAME

RECAPTURE THE KING

This twist on the classic game Capture the Flag is an entertaining way to demonstrate the impossibility of stealing Jesus' body from a heavily guarded grave. So you should realize from the outset (though you should let your students discover this fact gradually) that it's virtually impossible for the Disciples to recapture the King. For that reason, let each game go only five to 15 minutes; Romans and Disciples should switch roles with every new game.

Play Recapture the King with any size group from a dozen to 100. Choose a King and divide the rest of the group into Disciples and Romans (one Disciple for every three to five Romans). Lay out the borders of your playing field and let the Romans pick out a holding place for the King. (It can be wherever they wish, as long as the hiding place has at least one entrance.) The Romans must have a minimum of three guards around the holding place; there is no maximum. Also designate a safety zone for the Disciples and two jails: one for captured Disciples

and one for captured Romans.

The object of this game is for the Disciples to recapture their King from the Romans—who are guarding him (or her) in a holding place—and to return him to the Disciples' safety zone. To start the game, the Romans send a messenger to the Disciples, telling them exactly where the King is being held. Then the Roman returns to his team and they all stay in one place, giving the Disciples a chance to hide.

Once play begins, the Romans start searching for the hidden Disciples, capturing them by tagging them with a touch. The captured Disciples are taken to jail. Disciples can also capture Romans—but only if *three* (or more) Disciples tag one at (or about) the same time. Both Romans and Disciples can be freed by being tagged by a member of their own team.

For the Disciples to recapture their King, at least two Disciples must escort him to the safety zone. For the Romans to win decisively, they must capture all the Disciples. If the Disciples haven't recaptured their King within that time—and the odds are tremendously against them—they lose. *Bill Fry*

Bible-Clue Easter Egg Hunt

Have an Easter egg hunt using plastic eggs and Bible verses as clues for where to find them. Divide hunters into two teams, Reds and Blues. The first team will look for eggs with red numbers on them, and the second for eggs with blue numbers.

Get the teams started by giving each team leader an egg with the number 1 in the appropriate color. Inside the eggs they should find a slip of paper with a Bible reference that provides a clue to the where-abouts of egg #2. For instance, if the paper says "Isaiah 35:1," the kids will look up the Scripture in their Bibles and find that the verse mentions a rose. The logical place to look for the next egg, then, will be near a rose bush. Psalm 62:3 may be a clue for a fence; Ecclesiastes 11:3, a fallen tree; Numbers 24:7, an old bucket. Use your imagination.

No two eggs should be hidden in the same place. Hunters cannot move or otherwise disturb an egg that belongs to the other team. Eggs must be located in order by the clues—if one is discovered accidentally, it cannot be gathered until all previous eggs and their clues are found.

The team to find all its eggs first wins. Be sure the last egg contains a verse about victory! *Wilma Wyatt*

Egg-Citing Egg Hunt

The object of this game is to accumulate the most plastic eggs within the time limit.

Each team of at least five teenagers chooses a spy from among them. Switch all the spies around into other teams so that no spy is with his or her original team. The spy in each team makes sure the team ful-fills the instructions in one egg before finding anoth-er egg.

To prepare for the game, print out the "Challenges for Egg-Citing Egg Hunt" sheet found on page 39, cut apart the challenges (or create your own), and put each one in a plastic egg. Also include some edible tidbits. Then hide the eggs shortly before your meeting.

If you want, play the game at night with flash-lights. When time is up, the spies must give the teams they've spied on a clean bill of health. The

team with the most eggs wins. *James L Pagan*

Easter Eggstravaganza

Here's a scavenger hunt for egg-related items. Give your teams an hour to find—or to make—as many as they can of the items listed on page 40, and instruct them to purchase as few items as possible. Provide each team with a vehicle (and a licensed driver), wait an hour for them to return, then award predetermined points for each of the following egg-things in their baskets. *Maurice Gillard*

Easter Scavenger Hunt

Divide your group up into carloads, provide each car with a dozen Easter eggs, and send them off with a list of signatures they must gather—one sig-nature per egg. See page 41 for a sample list; make your own, and be creative! This isn't only great fun, but—like many scavenger hunts—is also a lighthearted way to introduce your group to the community.

Time each group and give prizes for the first and last team home safe. Be sure to have a time, perhaps over refreshments, for them all to talk about their experiences.

Or try this variation: all the items on the list have to be living—a plant, pet, mold, someone (not on the scavenger hunt, that is), a wild flower, a palm leaf, and so on. Following the scavenger hunt, study Scripture about the living Christ. *Chris Foley* and *Bert Jones*

The Magic Egg

This is a good group participation game that can be used at Easter—or any time you want to liven up the group interaction. Decorate a large plastic egg beforehand. Write out on strips of paper different silly things to do, then place them inside the egg.

Have the group sit in a circle and pass the egg as music is played. When the music stops, the person holding the egg must take out a paper, read the instructions loudly, and proceed to do them. If some-one gets caught with the egg twice, they may pass it

CHALLENGES FOR EGG-CITING EGG HUNT

- Form a circle, facing inward. As a group, count to 40—the first person says "One," the teammate next to her says "Two," etc. When a team member comes to five or a multiple of five, he must clap instead of saying the number. If someone makes a mistake, the team must start the count again over again.

- Quickly choose a cheerleader to lead a simple cheer. Example: "Give me a B! Give me a U! Give me a N! Give me another N! Give me a Y! What does it spell? (BUNNY!) Can't hear you! (BUNNY!)"

- The next egg you find must be green.

- Find a tree. Circle it and sing "Ring Around the Rosy" three times. And everyone must fall down.

- Do the bunny hop to the next egg.

- The next egg must be found by the youngest person in your group.

- Make piggyback pairs to find the next egg.

- Determine whose birthday is the nearest, and sing a raucous version of "Happy Birthday" to him or her.

- Sit in a circle do The Wave (you must stand up when it's your turn).

- Build a pyramid and hold it for 10 seconds.

- Spell EASTER by each of you contorting your body to shape a letter.

EASTER EGGSTRAVAGANZA LIST

- Decorated egg
- Hard-boiled egg
- Eggshell
- Intact eggshell that's been drained
- Scrambled egg
- Chocolate egg (extra points for smallest and largest)
- Cream-filled egg (extra points for most unusual flavor)
- Picture of egg
- Egg carton
- Egg shampoo
- Easter-contest form with an egg to be colored (must be colored)

- Pickled egg
- Eggcup
- Egg timer
- Egg roll
- Egg flipper (spatula)
- Eggplant
- Egg-salad sandwich
- Egg slicer
- Ornamental egg, painted Ukrainian fashion
- Eggnog
- Egg separator
- Eggo frozen waffle
- Poached-egg cup
- Egg beater
- Lego building block

Easter Scavenger Hunt List

DIRECTIONS: All teams will be sent out at the same time and will gather the signatures—on your eggs, one signature per egg—of the people listed below. You can get them in any order.

Rule #1—NO SPEEDING!

Rule #2—Always identify yourself. For example, "We're from St. Michael's youth group and we..."

Rule #3—Enjoy yourselves!

Go get the signatures of...

- A service station attendant or cashier
- The manager or person in charge at three different restaurants (these three restaurants must be on different streets)
- A customer in any 7-Eleven store
- A dorm student at a college
- The manager or a visitor in a Holiday Inn
- The DJ in a local radio station
- The manager or cashier at a movie theater
- A resident of a retirement center or rest home (first ask at desk)
- A patient or nurse at a hospital (first ask at desk)
- A high school faculty member

Be polite and cheerful, and you'll be ahead of the rest!

to the next person. You might want to vary this procedure by continuing the music and having two or three kids perform at once.

Here a few suggestions for silly antics, but you can add some that are unique to your group:

• Run around the circle, yelling the name of your favorite meat 10 times.

• Lead the entire group in your favorite aerobic exercise for three minutes.

• Using the Magic Egg as a demonstrator, show the group how to crack, peel, and eat a boiled egg.

• Make a noise like an ostrich 10 times while flapping your arms.

• While pinching your nose, recite your full name 10 times.

• Pretending you are the Easter Bunny, hop around the circle on one foot and drop the egg under someone's chair or in a lap.

• Rave on for two minutes about your favorite new ice cream—"Eggs and Cream."

• Give a pep talk for three minutes in Pig-Latin.

Mary Kent

GAME

EASTER DINNER DILEMMA

Here's a logic puzzle (see page 43) that's a perfect addition to an Easter-season get-together.

The solution is below. *Lynne Hartke*

Miss Flopsy wore the Easter bonnet.

Mrs. April is allergic to Easter lilies

Mrs. Lamb likes jelly beans.

Ms. Peter Rabbit is the hostess.

Miss Cottontail has an egg-shaped head.

Mrs. Mopsy hates chocolate bunnies.

GAME

CROSS WORD PUZZLE

The theme of the crossword puzzle on page 44 is the crucifixion of Christ, making it a "cross" word puzzle

in the truest sense of the term. Use it around Easter or anytime you are dealing with the meaning of the cross. Duplicate copies of the puzzle and the clues for each person or put it up on an overhead projector and fill it in as a group exercise. *Adapted from an idea contributed by Peter A. Ernst*

Solution:

```
S A L V A T I O N       B L O O D
  I     H         P U R P L E   W
S U F F E R       I     L   S I N S
O   T     E L I J A H   L   E
    E     U       C A L V A R Y
G   D   J E S U S     T   M
O   L A M B     T     E   E L O I
L   R     T     I     H   C
G   K I N G O F T H E J E W S   R
T   L     I     L   N   S A V E
H O R N S     C   L   T   U     D
A   T O   E A S T   U   R G R E E K
  E   B   M     T   H   R     M
    R E C O N C I L I A T I O N   P
  E   N   N   E   O   N     T
A B B A     S O N   V       V E I L
  O         E       E       O
F O R G I V E N   S A T A N W O N
  N
```

GAME

EASTER CROSSWORD

Here's a crossword puzzle that tests a group's knowledge of the events leading up to Easter. It can be printed up and done individually, or it can be done as a group game.

Group game instructions: First, put the crossword puzzle found on page 46 on an overhead transparency so it can be easily seen by the entire group.

Then divide the group into two teams. Teams may elect (or be assigned) to go either "across" or "down." There are an equal number of clues, and it is doubtful that there would be any advantage to being either "across" or "down." There are two (possibly three) rounds in the game. During round one, read each team one of their clues (in order; clues are on page 47). Teams get 100 points for each correct answer. The questions (clues) can be given to individuals on the teams, or the entire team, whichever you decide. (But be sure not to give the teams the list of clues in advance.) Once the answer is given, it cannot be changed, but wrong answers are not written in the puzzle. Alternate questions between the "across" and "down" teams until you have gone through the entire puzzle one time.

During round two, the missed clues are given again in the same fashion, only this time correct

Easter Dinner Dilemma

A woman invited five guests to her Easter dinner. The names of the six people who sat down at the round table were Mrs. April, Miss Flopsy, Ms. Peter Rabbit, Mrs. Mopsy, Miss Cottontail, and Mrs. Lamb. One of them liked jelly beans, one wore an Easter bonnet, one had a head like an egg, one simply hated chocolate bunnies, one was allergic to Easter lilies, and one was the hostess.

Can you identify each of these ladies, as well as determine where around the table each woman sat?

• The woman who hated chocolate bunnies sat directly opposite Miss Flopsy.

• The lady who liked jelly beans sat opposite Ms. Peter Rabbit, who sat between the woman who was allergic to Easter lilies and the woman who hated chocolate bunnies.

• The woman who had a head like an egg sat opposite Mrs. April, next to the lady who liked jelly beans, and to the left of the woman who hated chocolate bunnies.

• The woman who was allergic to Easter lilies sat between Ms. Peter Rabbit and the woman who sat opposite the woman who hated chocolate bunnies.

• Mrs. Lamb, who was a good friend to everyone, sat next to the egg-head-shaped lady and opposite the hostess.

• The woman who sat across from the one who wore a bonnet was not Miss Cottontail.

CROSS WORD PUZZLE

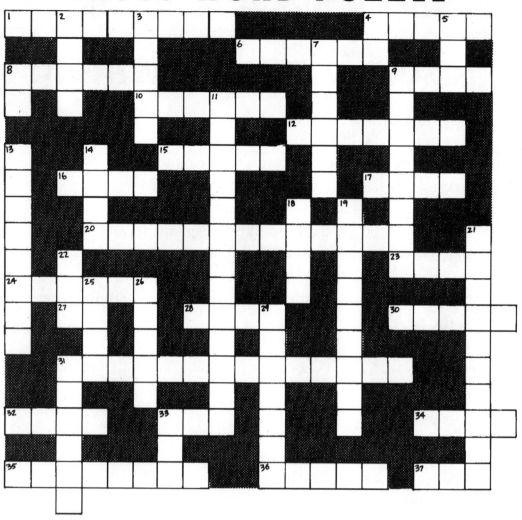

ACROSS

1. The result of the crucifixion. (Heb. 2:3)
4. Without it, there is no forgiveness of sin. (Heb. 9:22)
6. The color of Jesus' robe. (John 19:2)
8. What Jesus had to do on the cross. (Luke 24:26)
9. The reason for the crucifixion. (Acts 2:38)
10. Some thought Jesus was calling for help. (Matt. 27:47)
12. The mountain of the crucifixion.
15. The one who made salvation possible. (Rom. 5:8)
16. Jesus was a _____ without blemish. (1 Pet. 1:19)
17. Jesus cried "_____, _____, lama sabachthani?" (Matt. 27:46 NIV)
20. Pilate placed this written title over Christ's head. (Luke 23:38)
23. Jesus came to seek and to _____ . (Luke 19:10)
24. Jesus wore them on the cross. (Matt. 27:29)
27. Jesus came ___ die for us.
28. For his robe, the soldiers _____ lots. (John 19:24)
30. The sign above Jesus' head was written in Latin, Aramaic, and _____. (John 19:20, NIV)
31. Renewal of a once-lost relationship. (2 Cor. 5:18-19)
32. A word Christ used to address God. (Mark 14:36)
33. What God gave on the cross. (John 3:16)
34. It was "rent in twain." (Mark 15:38, KJV)
35. Because of the cross, our sins are _____. (Acts 2:38)
36. The cross defeated him. (Acts 5:3)
37. On the cross, the victory was _____.

DOWN

2. On the cross, Jesus was _____-ed up. (John 12:34)
3. Denied _____ times; _____ crosses; raised in _____ days. (John 2:20; 13:38)
4. He said, "If I ____ lifted up." (John 12:34)
7. He tried to set Jesus free. (John 19:12)
8. "For God ____ loved the World...." (John 3:16)
9. Characteristic of Christ's garment. (John 19:23)
11. A word that means "satisfaction"; the result of faith. (1 John 2:2; Rom. 3:25; Heb. 9:5)
13. The place of the skull. (Mark 15:22)
14. Condition of the sun when Jesus died. (Luke 23:45)
18. When Jesus died, he descended into _____. (The Apostles' Creed)
19. This man saw and believed. (Luke 23:47)
21. To be released and gain freedom through an act of purchase, by payment. (Heb. 9:15; Eph. 1:14)
22. Similar to a "die." (John 19:24)
25. What the soldiers gambled for. (John 19:24)
26. He carried Jesus' cross. (Mark 15:21)
29. They were crucified with Jesus. (Luke 23:32)
31. To be given new life. (Titus 3:5)
33. When Jesus was buried, Mary Magdalene and Mary the Mother of Jesus went to _____ where he was laid. (Mark 15:47)

answers are worth 50 points. If there are still empty spaces on the puzzle, then go ahead with round three, awarding 25 points for correct answers this time. Also, Scripture references and Bibles may be provided during this round. *Barbara Martin*

COLLAGE

EASTER COLLAGE

During Lent involve youths in a study of a character in the crucifixion as recorded in Luke 23 by creating a giant collage of the story. Divide Luke Chapter 23 into several sections, one for each study meeting. Have kids read the current section. Then choose a key verse that gives some insight into the life, attitude, and feelings of one of the characters. Give each kid a magazine with lots of photos in it. Each must find a picture portraying the attitude or feeling of the character as revealed in the passage. Have youths explain their pictures to the group. Keep the pictures for each character separate to build a giant horizontal collage, writing out the key verse under the character's picture cluster. When complete, the collage tells the Easter story. Display the collage during Easter week.

Suggested passages, characters, and key verses are as follows:

Luke 23:13-23	The Crowd	v. 21
Luke 23:13-25	Pilate	v. 24
Luke 23:26	Simon	v. 26
Luke 23:27-34	Jesus	v. 34
Luke 23:35-38	Mockers	v. 35-37
Luke 23:39	Criminal 1	v. 39
Luke 23:40-43	Criminal 2	v. 43
Luke 23:46-48	Centurion	v. 47
Luke 23:50-56	Joseph	v. 50-53

Donald Musser

OUTING

BACK TO THE GARDEN

This is a youth program/outing designed to improve the basic understanding of young people about the Crucifixion and Resurrection events. First, develop short scripts (scenarios) based on the following scenes:

- Preparations for Passover (Matt. 26:17-19)
- In the Upper Room (John 13:1-14: 27)
- Institution of the Lord's Supper (Matt. 26:26-30)
- At Gethsemane (Matt. 26:36-46)
- Jesus Arrested (Matt. 26:47-56, Luke 22:29, John 18:10-11)
- Trial by Caiaphas (Matt. 26:69-74, Mark 14:66-71, Luke 22:55-59, John 18:15-26)

Select a site with a large open room, a meandering path, and several spots along the path where a group can stop and sit. Organize a group of actors (adults and kids) to memorize the scripts and to create costumes that reflect the period. The people then arrive in groups and begin their walk to the Garden to live the Easter events all over again.

1. Near the area where people are unloaded, present a scene where the disciples are instructed to set up the Lord's Supper.

2. Take the group to the Upper Room for a reenactment of the Last Supper. (At the close of this scene have everyone in the audience also participate in the Lord's Supper.)

3. Continue down the path stopping for the Jesus' prayer at Gethsemane, Jesus' arrest, and the Trial.

4. End the evening by having the group assemble around a large cross (heavy enough so that it takes a number of people to lift it). Give a brief devotional about the cross and then close with the entire group attempting to lift the cross together. *Mike Turner*

MUSIC

EASTER CAROLING

Everyone goes caroling at Christmas, so why not at Easter as well? Decide where you are going and be sure to tell shut-ins or the staffs at institutions you

EASTER CROSSWORD

EASTER
CROSSWORD
CLUES

ACROSS

6. Luke's gospel emphasizes Jesus' humanity by calling him the "_____ of man."

9. This Jewish leader helped prepare Jesus' body for burial (John 19:39).

11. High Jewish priest at the time of the crucifixion (Matthew 26:3).

12. The Jews also wanted to kill this man because he'd been risen from the dead (John 12:10).

13. The man who carried Christ's cross (Luke 23:26).

14. This ripped from top to bottom upon Jesus' death (Matthew 27:51).

18. High council of Jewish leaders (Mark 15:1, NASV, cross-referenced).

19. Natural disaster which occurred when Jesus died (Matthew 27:54).

22. Jesus was his only begotten son (John 3:16).

23. Wealthy Jewish leader who gave his own tomb to Jesus (Matthew 27:59, 60).

26. The "blood money" paid to Judas was eventually used to purchase this burial place for strangers (Matthew 27:6-10).

27. Woman who anointed Jesus with expensive perfume (John 12:3).

28. He caused Judas to betray Christ (Luke 22:3).

29. The disciple who doubted Christ's resurrection (John 20:24, 25).

31. Jesus said he would rebuild this in three days (Mark 14:58).

35. This Old Testament prophet foretold the sufferings of Christ (Isaiah 53).

37. These were fashioned into a crown for Jesus by Roman soldiers (John 19:5).

38. Roman governor who passed the death sentence on Christ (Mark 15:15).

40. The day of Jesus' resurrection.

42. Jesus died for _____.

45. Peter was observed in this location when Jesus was taken by the mob (John 18:26).

46. Notorious prisoner released to the Jews by Pilate (Mark 15:7-11).

49. Animal that signaled Peter's denial of Jesus (John 18:27).

50. Jesus performed this service for the disciples in the Upper Room (John 13).

51. Gospel writer who devotes the greatest number of chapters to Jesus' last days (John 12-21).

52. Jesus compared his three days in the tomb to the plight of this Old Testament character (Matthew 12:40).

53. He was chosen by lot to replace Judas among the 12 (Acts 1:26).

54. This is a symbol of Christ's body, broken for us (1 Corinthians 11:24).

55. The crime which was Jesus was accused by the Jews (Matthew 26:65).

DOWN

1. The cry of the multitude during Jesus' triumphal entry to Jerusalem (Matthew 21:9).

2. Jesus' purpose in going to the Mount of Olives after the Last Supper, to _____ (Luke 22:40, 41).

3. "This is my _____ which is given for you; this do in remembrance of me." (Luke 22:19).

4. Roman soldier at the crucifixion who became convicted of Christ's deity (Mark 15:39).

5. In Gethsemane, Jesus prayed to have this taken from him (Mark 14:36).

7. Signal used by Judas to betray Christ (Matthew 26:49).

8. Occupation of the two men hung with Jesus (Matthew 27:38).

10. Type of branches cast before Jesus as he entered Jerusalem (John 12:13).

11. Christian sacrament which began with the Last Supper.

15. These were cast by soldiers to divide Christ's clothes (Mark 15:24).

16. First person to see the resurrected Christ (Mark 16:9, John 20:11-18).

17. _____ pieces of silver, the price paid to Judas (Matthew 26:15).

20. "The place of a skull" (where Jesus was crucified) (Mark 15:22).

21. Peter cut an ear off this slave of the high priest (John 18:10).

24. Disciple who denied Christ three times (Luke 21:61).

25. Book of the Bible which records Jesus' ascension to heaven (Acts 1:9).

26. The "Feast of Unleavened Bread" (Mark 14:1)

30. Jesus was made to be this for us, that we might become righteous (2 Corinthians 5:21).

32. Jesus' crucifixion was part of God's _____ of salvation.

33. The resurrected Jesus appeared to two men on the way to this village (Luke 24:13-15).

34. Christ did this for the bread and wine (Luke 22:17, 19).

36. Setting of the Last Supper (Luke 22:12).

39. Animal that was sacrificed at the Feast of Unleavened Bread (Mark 14:12).

41. Roman soldiers dressed Jesus in this garment of scarlet and mocked him (Matthew 27:28).

42. Young follower of Jesus (later a Gospel writer) who ran away without his clothes when he was seized by the mob in the garden (Mark 14:51,52).

43. The king of Judea who was in Jerusalem at the time of the crucifixion (Luke 23:8-12).

44. Jesus entrusted the care of his mother to this man (John 19:26, 27).

47. Animal that carried Jesus on his entry to Jerusalem (John 12:15).

48. Name for Jesus which means "teacher" or "master" (Mark 14:45).

plan to visit that you'll be coming. Meet an hour or so early to make sure everyone knows the songs you will be singing. You might invite the pastor to come and administer communion to the shut-ins and others. Another good idea is to have a group of older folks bring flowers to give to those you sing to.

Be creative with the songs and vary them—use solos, quartets, harmony, unison, and narration. Use familiar songs so that those being sung to can join in. If you carol all afternoon, you may want to have a party or supper or food and fellowship get together afterwards. *Robin Hoefer*

EASTER I.Q. TEST

This is a fun yet educational quiz (see pages 49-51) that you can use to usher in Lent and the Easter season. Read and discuss the answers when your group finishes with the test. *Howard Nielsen*

Answers:

1. False—The statement is true only since the ninth century for the Western churches. The Council of Nicaea (A.D. 325) had fixed the equinox on March 21, but the Easter date was disputed until the time of Charlemagne.

2. True—Easter was celebrated as a festival of spring at the vernal equinox in ancient times.

3. c

4. c

5. e

6. c

7. c

8. c (Mark 16)

9. Two (John 20)

10. c (John 20:11-18)

11. f

12. e (also Egyptian)

13. c

14. c

15. b (Matt. 27:38)

16. b

17. d (Acts 12:4)

18. c

19. c

20. e (Matt. 27:57)

21. c (Matt. 28:2)

22. c (1 Cor. 15:6)

23. d (John 20:11-18; Luke 24:13-32)

24. b

25. d

26. a

27. c

28. f

29. c

30. d

31. a—A jeweled egg made by the Russian jeweler Fabergé was given by Czar Alexander to his wife (*World Book Encyclopedia*, Vol 6, p. 26)

32. e (*World Book Encyclopedia*, Vol 6, p. 25)

33. b—These are holy days during Holy Week.

34. a (Job 19:25-26)

35. True

36. b (Gal. 5:11)

37. c—In the apocryphal book of the Epistle of Barnabas (A.D. 130-160) it is noted that Abraham had 318 servants. In the Greek alphabet where letters also represented numbers, 318 is expressed as IHT. IH are the first two letters of Jesus' name, while T is a picture of the cross—so there you are (according to Barnabas 9:8).

38. a (Luke 23:2)

39. b

40. Any answer is appropriate.

EASTER QUIZ

On page 52 you'll find a great short quiz that can be used in conjunction with a Bible study on Easter or simply to test a group's knowledge of the Easter story as it is presented in Scripture.

The answers are found in Matthew 28, Mark 16, Luke 24, John 20-21, and Acts 1. In questions 1 through 9, all of the choices are correct, and in question 10, none are correct, since none of the Gospels describe the actual resurrection of Christ; only what happened afterward. This quiz can open up some good discussion on the differences between the four Gospel accounts and how they can be reconciled to each other. *Tim Spilker*

EASTER I.Q. TEST

40 QUESTIONS FOR THE 40 DAYS OF LENT

INSTRUCTIONS

In the spaces provided on the left, mark the correct answers. Most of the questions are multiple-choice; a few are true/false; a couple are fill-in.

_____ 1. As long as Easter has been celebrated, it has been held on the first Sunday after the date of the first full moon that occurs on or after March 21.

_____ 2. Easter was originally a pagan festival.

_____ 3. Ash Wednesday, the beginning of Lent, is always 40 days before Easter, not counting
a) the pastor's day off.
b) the Sabbath.
c) Sundays.
d) Holy Week.
e) Ash Wednesday.

_____ 4. Jesus grew up in
a) Bethlehem.
b) Jerusalem.
c) Nazareth.
d) Oberammergau.
e) none of these.

_____ 5. When Jesus came into Jerusalem on Palm Sunday, he entered by
a) walking.
b) limousine.
c) riding a white horse.
d) walking a donkey.
e) riding a donkey.

_____ 6. With no room in Jerusalem during Holy Week, Jesus had to stay in
a) Bethlehem.
b) the Garden of Gethsemane.
c) Bethany.
d) the YMCA.
e) a stable.

_____ 7. When Jesus rose from the grave on Easter morning, he
a) got even with those who crucified him.
b) saw his shadow and went back inside for 40 more days of winter.
c) left the angels in charge of the tomb.
d) had breakfast with Moses and Elijah on the Mount of Transfiguration.
e) went straight to Galilee and appeared to the disciples.

_____ 8. According to the Gospel of St. Mark, how many women came to the tomb Sunday morning?
a) one
b) two
c) three
d) four
e) five or more

_____ 9. According to the Gospel of St. John, how many men came to the tomb Sunday morning? (Write in the correct number.)

_____ 10. Who was the first person Jesus talked to after he arose?
a) the gardener
b) the soldiers on guard
c) Mary Magdalene
d) Mary his mother
e) an Amway distributor
f) no one

_____ 11. Easter eggs are a part of Easter because
a) Jesus enjoyed eggs for breakfast.
b) Jesus was a good egg.
c) the disciples put all their eggs in one basket.
d) eggs are a symbol of new life.
e) rabbits lay eggs.
f) none of these reasons

_____ 12. Why is the Easter Rabbit a part of Easter?
a) A rabbit's foot is good luck.
b) Welsh rabbit was a favorite dish of the disciples.
c) The Bunny has nothing to do with anything.
d) The Easter Rabbit is just another commercialization of a religious holiday by Madison Avenue.
e) It's one of those old German customs.

_____ 13. Jesus was buried on Friday in
a) a pauper's grave.

b) a grave he and the family picked out before Holy Week.

c) a borrowed grave.

d) a mausoleum.

____ 14. Jesus was in the tomb for

a) three days.

b) an overnight stay.

c) between 30 and 35 hours.

d) a much-needed rest.

e) an unknown period of time.

____ 15. Jesus was crucified with two others who were

a) murderers.

b) thieves.

c) cutthroats.

d) blasphemers.

e) innocent victims like Jesus.

f) rock musicians.

____ 16. The Last Supper was held because

a) Jesus wanted a farewell party.

b) the Jewish Passover was to be celebrated.

c) Leonardo da Vinci thought it'd make a great painting.

d) Judas had to be exposed as a traitor.

e) none of these reasons.

____ 17. The word Easter appears in which version of the Bible?

a) RSV

b) TEV

c) MTV

d) KJV

e) all of these

____ 18. Lent is

a) something you find under your bed if you haven't cleaned for awhile.

b) past tense of loan.

c) a 40-day fast before Easter.

d) past participle of lental.

e) something I don't know because I'm not Jewish.

____ 19. How much was Judas paid to betray Jesus?

a) $100

b) two loaves and five fish

c) 30 silver coins

d) some gold, frankincense, and myrrh

e) 20 Roman coins.

____ 20. The Joseph who went to Pilate to ask for the body of Jesus was in fact

a) Jesus' father from Nazareth.

b) a rich man from Arimathea.

c) a secret disciple of Jesus.

d) none of these.

e) more than one of these.

____ 21. Who rolled the stone away from the grave Easter morning?

a) the 11 disciples

b) two men in white robes

c) an angel who sat on the stone

d) Gabriel who blew his horn

e) St. Peter

____ 22. How many people did Jesus visit after he rose from the dead?

a) the 11 disciples

b) the people of Emmaus

c) over 500

d) I don't know.

e) I wish I did.

____ 23. How did Jesus look after he arose?

a) same as always

b) like Moses

c) like Elijah

d) unrecognizable

e) I give up.

____ 24. The risen Jesus made breakfast one morning

a) in the upper room for the disciples.

b) on the shore of the Sea of Galilee.

c) at Burger King.

d) at his friends' home in Bethany.

e) to start the Easter breakfast tradition.

____ 25. In the beginning when God created the world, he also created the first computer. How do we know this?

a) Eve took a byte out of the Apple.

b) Adam and Eve were not compatible.

c) God monitored their every move.

d) It's known as a brain.

____ 26. One disciple was labeled "Doubting Thomas" because he

a) didn't believe Jesus rose.

b) missed the reunion party.

c) didn't believe in the Easter Bunny.

d) was from Missouri.

____ 27. The date of Easter in the Greek Orthodox tradition is

a) 12 days later than ours.

b) the 14th of the Jewish month of Nisan.

c) one, four, or five weeks later than ours.

d) the same as ours.

e) the same day as Passover.

f) Who knows?

28. Where do we find the Easter story in order to check up on all these ridiculous questions?
   a) Matthew
   b) Mark
   c) Luke
   d) John
   e) only a and c
   f) a, b, c, and d
   g) only b and d

29. The gospel writers devoted how much of their writings to Holy Week and Easter?
   a) the last chapters of each book
   b) half of their writings
   c) a third of their writings
   d) a quarter of their writings
   e) none of these

30. Easter is designated a holiday because
   a) it always falls on Sunday.
   b) the Easter Bunny lobby was successful in Washington.
   c) college kids needed a break so they could go to Florida.
   d) Easter is the focus of Christian theology.
   e) it comes four months after Christmas.

31. One of the most famous Easter eggs was
   a) given by a Russian Czar to his wife in 1880.
   b) laid by the original Easter Bunny in 1776.
   c) rolled on the White House lawn in 1952.
   d) a large chocolate egg that took three days to eat in 1967.

32. The custom of exchanging eggs at Easter comes from
   a) ancient Egypt.
   b) Persia.
   c) medieval Europe.
   d) People's Republic of China.
   e) a and b.
   f) b and d.

33. Palm Sunday is associated with what other holy days?
   a) Pentecost and Ash Wednesday
   b) Good Friday and Maundy Thursday
   c) Christmas and Epiphany
   d) Advent and Transfiguration

34. The biblical words "I know that my redeemer lives" were spoken by
   a) Job.
   b) Peter.
   c) Paul.
   d) Matthew.
   e) the Pope.
   f) Billy Graham.

35. True or False. The cross was the most common instrument of executing criminals in Roman times.

36. The cross was
   a) always made in the shape of a lowercase t.
   b) a stumbling block.
   c) used only by pagans and Gentiles.
   d) made with steel supports.
   e) burned after each use.

37. Genesis 14:14 has been interpreted as a prediction of Christ's death because
   a) Abraham's kinsmen were taken captive.
   b) Dan was a relative of Jesus.
   c) of the 318 servants.
   d) it was a mistake.
   e) Sorry—I don't know Hebrew.

38. Jesus was accused by the Jewish leaders before Pilate of
   a) tax evasion.
   b) taking over the temple.
   c) feeding the 5,000.
   d) being a Christian.
   e) selling Amway products.

39. Easter is
   a) time for parades.
   b) celebrated every Sunday of the year.
   c) an inspiration for Irving Berlin songs.
   d) the beginning of a new church year.
   e) the time of year to wear your best clothes.

40. I think this test was
   a) unbelievably simple.
   b) enlightening.
   c) thought-provoking.
   d) unnecessary.
   e) all of these.

Easter Quiz

INSTRUCTIONS

Place an X on the line if you think the answer is biblically correct.

1. The woman (or women) who went to the tomb was (or were):
  _____ a. Mary Magdalene and the other Mary
  _____ b. Mary Magdalene, Mary the Mother of James, and Salome
  _____ c. Mary Magdalene, Mary the Mother of James, Joanna, and others
  _____ d. Mary Magdalene

2. The time of early morning was:
  _____ a. when the sun had risen
  _____ b. while it was still dark

3. At the tomb was (or were):
  _____ a. an angel
  _____ b. a young man
  _____ c. two men
  _____ d. two angels

4. The reaction of the woman (or women) was one of:
  _____ a. amazement, astonishment
  _____ b. fear and trembling
  _____ c. great joy

5. After leaving the tomb, the woman (or women):
  _____ a. told the disciples
  _____ b. said nothing to anyone

6. The reaction of the disciples at first was that:
  _____ a. they did not believe the women, it seemed an idle tale
  _____ b. Peter and John went immediately and quickly to the tomb

7. Jesus first appeared to the disciples:
  _____ a. in Galilee, on a mountain
  _____ b. in an upper room in Jerusalem

8. Jesus seems to have last appeared to the disciples:
  _____ a. on a mountain in Galilee
  _____ b. on a mountain in Bethany (or just outside Bethany)
  _____ c. by the Sea of Tiberias

9. The gift of the Holy Spirit was given to the disciples:
  _____ a. before Jesus ascended; in the Upper Room he breathed on them
  _____ b. after Jesus ascended, on the Day of Pentecost

10. We have many details about the crucifixion and death of Jesus. Which Gospel writer gives the most details about the actual Resurrection of Jesus from the grave? Which one best describes what happened when Jesus rose from the dead?
  _____ a. Matthew
  _____ b. Mark
  _____ c. Luke
  _____ d. John

Easter Video

This is a great way to teach the Easter story (although it could work for any Bible story), have good fun and fellowship, and have a permanent video record of your youth group.

Have the youth group create a video presentation of the Easter Story. You could do it MTV-style and tape various scenes to music and/or narration. No need to create an entire dramatic production. The youth group itself will scout out the locations, find the props, make the costumes, and pose for the scenes. Make sure you include credits at the end; the video will turn into a keepsake.

Give yourselves plenty of time so you can achieve the desired effect and re-shoot if necessary. The video can be shown to the entire church, shut-ins, and many other groups. *Audrey J. Frank*

Easter Week in Review

On a table in the center of the room, arrange a number of objects named in the Scriptures that tell of Jesus' last week on earth. Like these:

PERFUME JAR (of alabaster)—Matt. 26:6-13
WINE BOTTLE—Matt. 26:26-30
WINE GOBLET—Matt. 26:26-30
WASH BASIN (hands and feet)—Matt. 26:36-46; John 13:1-11
SWORD—Matt. 26:47-54
WHIP—John 19:1-3
LARGE NAILS—Matt. 27:32-35
DICE—Matt. 27:32-35
PALM BRANCH (FROM FLORIST)—Mark 11:1-8
LOAF OF BREAD—Matt. 26:26-30
BAG OF SILVER (30)—Matt. 26:14-16
PRAYING HANDS (CERAMIC)—Matt 26:36-46
ROOSTER (CERAMIC)—Luke 22:60; Matt. 26:34-35
CROWN OF THORNS—Matt. 27:27-31
CROSS—Matt. 27:32-35
LINEN CLOTH—Matt. 27:57-61

Tell the young people that these objects (others can be used, too) were significant in Jesus' final week on earth. Then ask the group to write down the order in which the objects were used—from memory, without consulting their Bibles. After allowing some time, let them share their thoughts, questions, and the order of objects. Last of all, give them the specific Scripture and have them look up and read the passages.

This exercise will help give your young people a lasting visual impression of the events of Easter week. *Barbara D. Farish*

Good Friday Meditation

Read the Good Friday story from Matthew 27:27-66, or from a parallel passage. Then have the kids form small groups of two or three people and give each group an index card with one of the following phrases written on it:

THE ROPE THAT BINDS
THE FIST THAT STRIKES
THE ROBE
THE WHIP
THE CROWN OF THORNS
THE CROSS
THE NAILS
THE HAMMER
THE SPEAR
THE EARTH SUPPORTING THE CROSS
THE TOMB
THE ROCK SEALING THE TOMB

Have the kids write out thoughts about what it would have been like on Good Friday to have been the object identified on their card. For example: "If you had been the whip that was used on Jesus and could talk, how would you describe your feelings on Good Friday?" Allow 30 to 45 minutes for thought, then reassemble as a large group to share what was written. Dim the lights to provide a more serious setting, and end with reflective prayer that allows the kids' feelings to emerge. *David Washburn*

Easter Egg Hunt for Meaning

Give each student a plastic egg and ask them to fill the egg with something that to them represents or symbolizes the true Easter message. Have them bring the eggs back on Easter Sunday and exchange them with each other as Easter gifts. As the young people open them, allow each to perhaps share why they think the person chose that particular symbol of

Easter. The results can be very meaningful.

GOOD FRIDAY SCRAMBLE

For a Good Friday devotional, list each of the following events of that day (as recorded in Matthew 27) on an 8½ x 11 sheet of paper (the verse numbers are for your eyes only—they shouldn't be written on the sheets):

JESUS TAKEN TO PILATE *(vv. 1-20)*
JUDAS KILLS HIMSELF *(3-10)*
JESUS TRIED BY PILATE *(11-14)*
RELEASE BARABBAS OR JESUS? *(15-26)*
SOLDIERS MOCK AND BEAT JESUS *(27-31)*
SIMON OF CYRENE FORCED TO HELP CARRY THE CROSS *(32)*
CRUCIFIXION *(33-35)*
SOLDIERS GAMBLE FOR JESUS' CLOTHES *(35)*
ONLOOKERS MOCK JESUS AS HE HANGS *(39-44)*
DARKNESS FALLS AT NOON *(45)*
"MY GOD, MY GOD, WHY HAST THOU FORSAKEN ME?" *(46)*
JESUS' DEATH *(50)*
TEMPLE CURTAIN TEARS IN TWO *(51)*
JOSEPH OF ARIMATHEA BURIES JESUS *(57-60)*

Before you distribute the sheets to your kids, ask them if they can name some of the specific events that happened on that first Good Friday. Then ask for as many volunteers as you have sheets of paper to each take a sheet and stand in front of the group. Then let the volunteers attempt to arrange themselves in the proper sequence, with the help of the rest of the group. Some are obvious; others take real thought.

When kids feel as if they've got them all in order, read Matthew 27:1-61. As you read, let the kids correct out-of-order events. Follow up with a discussion of why Good Friday is called *good* when, after all, it was humanly such a dreadful day. Perhaps individuals could share what is special to them about Good Friday. The entire activity takes about 20 to 30 minutes. *Steve Allen*

MAUNDY THURSDAY EXPERIENCE

This is an excellent way to help make Easter week more meaningful for your young people. Have the kids meet on Maundy Thursday, the Thursday prior

to Easter, and participate in the following events:

• Begin with supper in small groups in homes. Prepare a discussion guide about what happened at the Last Supper. After the meal have one of the kids lead the discussion around the table, complete with leftover food and dirty dishes.

• Meet at the church (or elsewhere) with the entire group and have a communion service with all the members of the church, if possible.

• Take a short trip to "Gethsemane." This can be a nice park, isolated, with trees, brushes, hills, etc. Attempt to experience in some way the feelings and thoughts that Jesus must have had at Gethsemane. Sit together in a close group, and have someone relate the story of Gethsemane from the Bible. Someone can sing the Gethsemane song from the play *Jesus Christ, Superstar*, and perhaps another can do an interpretive dance to it.

• Point out that we, like Jesus, have our Gethsemanes. Have a few in the group share a time in their life when they felt something of what Christ must have felt. This can be very impressive.

• Close by joining hands in a large circle and singing Easter songs together.

Kenneth Dunivant

SEDER

The Seder is a meal of the Passover celebration that recalls the liberation of the Hebrews from slavery in Egypt. Your library should have a book on Jewish Festivals with an explanation of the meal and the symbolic foods used in the ceremony.

The Seder is an excellent way to help your youth group tie together our Judaic and Christian heritages. It is probably the meal that the disciples and Jesus celebrated in the upper room the night of Jesus' arrest. It should be done on Maundy Thursday. You can close with Communion in the Christian tradition. *Marge Clark*

GOOD FRIDAY SERVICE

As the youths enter the building for your Good Friday service, group them together in several clusters and take instant-developing photos. Then have each person cut out his or her face from the photo, glue it onto a small piece of black paper with rough edges, and tape a piece of red yarn to the back.

Have a cross made of scrap lumber and full of nails hung in the front of the room. When it's time for reflection, let the kids gather around the cross and tie their pictures to the nails. Talk about how the black paper represents our sins—the times when we've been selfish, held a grudge, failed to be loving. The photo shows us that despite how we look right now, Christ sees us as we will become in him. The red yarn represents his blood—shed on Good Friday—our salvation, and his invitation to be transformed. Allow kids to respond with their own thoughts. You may also want to heighten the effect of the cross with colored lights and a reading of the passion story.

An additional idea is to include photos of kids who aren't present as a reminder that Christ died for all—even those who aren't walking closely to him just now. *David Washburn*

WORSHIP

LAST SUPPER SIMULATION

This creative worship service is best with senior high youths at the beginning of Lent (or even Advent, with some adjustments).

• Leader Preparation

1. Become familiar with the general sequence of events of the Last Supper (study Matthew 26:17-35; Mark 14:12-31; Luke 22:7-34; and John 13:1 through 17:26).
2. Arrange to use a room (preferably an upstairs room) with little furniture. Make it a place where you will not be disturbed.
3. In the center of the room place a long, low table where everyone can sit on the floor on cushions; light the room with only candles or kerosene lanterns.
4. Ask parents to make a simple, thin soup and round loaves of bread. Bring grape juice. Set the table with no utensils, only a water glass and a bowl for each participant. Leave an empty space at the table for Jesus.
5. You dress in layered, loose-fitting garments. In other words, imitate Jesus' first-century attire. Prepare the students for the evening only by telling

them to dress casually and come ready for a light meal.

• Actual Reenactment

1. Before kids enter the room: All participants should remove their shoes. Ask them to imagine themselves as Jesus' closest friends about to share in his last meal on earth before his crucifixion.
2. When they enter the room, welcome them to the Passover Feast and explain about the place reserved for Christ. Pray together that Jesus will bless this time and invite the Holy Spirit to empower and guide everyone's thoughts. Ask that God's gift of Jesus will be made real to all.
3. As you eat, let students tell what they already know about the Passover Feast (when and why it started) and fill in background from the Old Testament story (in Exodus 12). Read Luke 22:7-16 and discuss who was present at the Passover meal we call the Last Supper.
4. Explore with them what Jesus was about to suffer. What do they think was felt by those who heard Jesus' words? Create a vivid picture.
5. After supper: Rise, take off your outer shawl or cape, and wrap a large, dark towel around your waist. Fill a large basin with warm water, then wash the feet of at least several of the youths. (Drop whatever hints you must ahead of time so they won't feel too embarrassed. Cue one student to, like Peter, refuse to let you wash her feet until you finally insist.)

Explore together Jesus' purpose in doing this and the significance of God's own Son choosing a lowly servant role.
6. Read aloud Luke 22:19-20 and Mark 14:22-24. Don't rush; let it sink in.
7. Take an unbroken, oval loaf of bread, wrap it in a rough cloth, and cradle it, reminding them of God's Son's coming to us. Pull the cloth from the bread, reviewing how the world refused the gift. While you hold the loaf up as if offering it as a sacrifice, break it in half and talk about how Jesus was willing to die—to be broken as a sacrifice for us.

Then pour a few drops of the grape juice into a cup. While holding half the bread, drip a few drops of juice from the cup onto the bread, reminding participants that Jesus' life blood was poured out for us. Finally, share the Lord's Supper by passing the broken bread and grape juice around the table.
8. Review the main message of Jesus to the disci-

ples—and to us—as found in John 13:31 to 17:26. Jesus said the following:

- He would be glorified.
- He was going away and couldn't be followed.
- Our most important new commandment is to love one another.
- We have a place in heaven.
- He sends us the Holy Spirit.
- We must be fruitful for God.
- He did all of this so that we can have his full joy. Get the group to explore what all this means. Ask how they think his friends responded.

9. Point out how Jesus prayed for his dearest friends—to be kept safe, united and one with God, dedicated to God's purpose, and entitled to all the resources and power that God has already given to Jesus. Ask what Jesus guaranteed to us through this prayer.

10. Lead the group to explore their experiences of the Last Supper. Help them think about God's gift of Christ to us. Furthermore, explore what talents and opportunities we have been personally given from God. How do we give back gifts to God? Does reliving this poignant Last Supper with Jesus cause you to think differently about how you do or don't give back your gifts to God?

11. Close with prayer, asking the Holy Spirit to continue to speak to each individual. Ask that the loving Lord Jesus' gifts be openly received by all and that we would be helped to discover new ways to give God's love outward to a needing world.

12. When your students leave the room, urge them to not speak in order to help the experience sink in.

• **Follow Up**

1. For several weeks following, pray for each participant by name. Ask that they will know the Holy Spirit's guidance and God's challenge from this experience.

2. Mail personal pledge cards to each youth, and follow up with a personal call.

3. Reenact the Parable of the Talents.

Connie Hewett

WORSHIP

EASTER BALLOON FEST

Since Easter's such a festive time, what better way to make your group feel the joy than to decorate the church, inside and out, with hundreds of balloons? Tie or tape them on chairs, windows, doors, and stair railings. Purchase the helium and balloons, then invite your kids to come and Easterize your church. The congregation will love the lift! *Chris Foley*

SERVICE

EASTER BASKETS FOR SHUT-INS

Decorate those green plastic containers that strawberries come in, using yarn, ribbon, lace, and so on. Place Easter grass in the baskets and fill with homemade candy. Make chocolate candy from molds and buy jelly beans to add color. Deliver to shut-ins or nursing home residents. *Deborah J. Nickel*

DRAMA

THE BLESSED BUNNY

The following story (see page 57) can be read to your youths (or adults) as an illustration of how secularized the Easter season has become. Follow up with appropriate discussion questions such as the following:

1. What is the point of the story?
2. How can Christians combat the intrusion of secular traditions which take away from the true meaning of Easter?
3. What are practical ways the resurrection of our Lord can be affirmed this Easter?

Donald Musser

DRAMA

EASTER ON THE NETWORK NEWS

Here is a drama (see page 59) that is an outline for a youth sunrise service or Easter program that can be conducted by the youth for the entire church body. Assign the character parts to various members of the youth group. The actors then study the scene(s) they are to participate in, study the appropriate Scripture, and then work out the necessary dialogue based on the facts in the Scripture. It is best to rehearse the entire service a few times before its presentation. The content can be refined during the rehearsal process. A songleader is needed to involve the congregation in singing between the newscasts. Some of the music, however, can be performed as solos,

the blessed bunny

It happened the week of March 26. Whoooosh! The spaceship swept low over the Planet Earth and quietly landed in a wooded city park at midnight. Disguised as earthmen, three visitors from outer space disembarked to begin a week's study of the religious practices of the third planet from the sun.

On April 1 the mysterious spaceship returned, and the three hurried on board with their sheaves of notes. Woooosh! Away they fled back to the Planet Mars.

The next Sunday the three read their report at the meeting of the religious study group that had sponsored their journey. This is what they said:

"Fellow Martians, it is apparent that a new religion is sweeping the United States of America on Planet Earth. We do not know the name nor origin of this religion, but we are certain that rabbits are the objects of worship. Do not laugh, brothers. It is true. Earthmen are not as advanced as previously believed. Hear out our evidence.

"Religious indoctrination in this belief in the 'Blessed Bunny' begins at birth. Earth babies learn early to positively identify with bunnies. They are dressed in cuddly sleepers which are shaped like bunnies and often have pictures of one or more of the furry animals on the chest. Their beds are painted with happy, playful bunnies and it is not uncommon for an earth baby to sleep with a stuffed bunny. During the early years further identification with bunnies is fostered through picture books and television programs.

"By age four mass religious instruction begins through Saturday morning television programs. Earth children huddle around the TV and watch animated cartoons of bunnies portrayed in many and varied roles. Bugs Bunny is an especially favored rabbit. His punch line is 'What's up, Doc?' We are not certain of the religious significance of this question. Occasionally a special program is seen in which a rabbit plays a special role. In Alice in Wonderland, for example, a crazy rabbit runs around panting, 'I'm late! I'm late! For a very important date!' We are impressed by the results of this mass education. Earth children receive a totally positive image of bunnies, and we did not find one child who thought rabbits were anything but good and cuddly and soft. They were 'blessed.'

"Worshippers of the Blessed Bunny observe a sacred week each year in the spring. It is called Easter. Even those who do not adhere to the faith go along with this festive celebration. Businesses promote their wares through the media gimmick of bunnies. One sign said, 'Hop on down to your florist.' Another advised, 'Our gas will keep your car hopping.' Bunny-shaped chocolate candy is sold everywhere. Balloons with bunny pictures stenciled on them fly gaily.

"We saw miniature villages populated by

the blessed bunny

stuffed bunnies in several shopping areas. These are apparently worship centers for children. The Blessed Bunny himself appears and sits on a regal throne. Children sit on his knee and hesitatingly talk with him. We felt that the children were awed by this experience and that it has much merit for religious educational purposes. Martians should take note of the fact that earthmen take their religion right into the marketplace where crowds observe the services.

"Song and dance accompany the festive sacred week. We heard many recordings of 'Here Comes Peter Cottontail.' It is also said that a religious dance is practiced by the most zealous adherents. It is called the bunny hop.

"One sidelight should be mentioned. Although worship of the Blessed Bunny in its several forms is widely tolerated, a small group of heretics take to the fields in the fall of the year to shoot and kill all bunnies they see. They hunt in groups and use vicious animals called 'dogs' to track down the defenseless creatures. The more zealous of these heretics eat the bunnies or make gloves of their soft fur. A growing number of earthmen believe the killing of bunnies should be stopped by the government.

"In conclusion let us say that we deeply appreciate the opportunity to make this study and to report it to you, our fellow members of the religious study group here on Mars. Our studies make us all the more convinced of the validity of our own religious faith. Friends, we need not fear that there is any better faith on Earth.

"For our faith in the Lord Jesus Christ, whom we worship here on Mars, was not challenged in any way by this new religion of the Blessed Bunny which is sweeping Planet Earth. Brother Gregor, who accompanied us, was so moved by the spiritual plight of earthmen that he bore personal witness to his faith in our Lord. A dozen times he initiated dialogue with earthmen, but they would have none of it. Especially did he find resistance to the belief in the Resurrection, that cornerstone of our faith. It is just as St. Paulinus said: 'Jesus is a scandal and offense to many.'

"When Brother Gregor shared the Good News with one earthman, he angrily told him, 'I go to church' and stomped off. We do not know what 'church' is, but whatever it is, this attender knew nothing of the living risen Lord.

"Friends, you know how we have often wondered if the Lord Jesus ever visited any of the other planets in the solar system besides Mars? Well, our study proves one thing. From the earthmen we met and talked with, it is highly unlikely that he ever visited the third planet from the sun."

Easter on the Network News

1 **TV Newsroom and Garden of Gethsemane.** Anchor presenting Thursday evening news. Among other items, he reports that..."Jesus Christ has just been arrested by a Roman battalion. For a report we go to the Garden of Gethsemane." There the reporter on the scene pieces together the story of the betrayal and arrest of Christ (which has just taken place). (Matthew 26:47-57) He reports back to the anchor. (Suggested songs: "Go to Dark Gethsemane," "Tis Midnight," and "On Olive's Brow")

2 **TV Newsroom and trial courtyard.** (Late Thursday night) Anchor breaks in with a late-breaking news development on the trial of Christ. "For a report we go to the High Priest's chambers." Reporter standing in the courtyard gives a report on the trial. (Matthew 26:59-68) Reporter then spots Peter and interviews him. (Matthew 26:69-75) He reports back to the anchor with the trial still in progress. (Suggested song: "Bold Peter Denied His Lord")

3 **TV Newsroom and Governor Pilate's courtyard.** (Friday morning) Anchor reports that the trial is over. Jesus has been condemned to die on the cross and is being led up the hill to Golgotha now. "For a report, we go to Governor Pilate's courtyard, where we have a reporter standing by." The reporter interviews Pilate concerning the trial, giving particular attention to his feelings. (Matthew 27:11-26) After interviewing Pilate, the reporter spots Barabbas, the criminal released in place of Christ. He interviews Barabbas. (Matthew 27:15-21) Then he reports back to the anchor. The anchor gives an update on Judas who betrayed Christ. (Matthew 27:3-5) (Suggested song: "The Old Rugged Cross")

4 **TV Newsroom and the crucifixion site.** (Friday afternoon) Anchor reports that Christ is on the cross. He reports and comments on some of the strange events associated with the crucifixion. (Matthew 27:45-53) "For a report on the crucifixion, we go to Golgotha." The reporter gives a brief account of what happened. (Matthew 27:27-50) Then he interviews the centurion (27:54) and Mary Magdalene (27:55-56). (A little more imagination is needed for these two interviews because of little Scriptural information.)

5 **TV Newsroom and burial site.** (Saturday morning) Anchor reports that Christ's body has been taken down from the cross and bound in the tomb of Joseph of Arimathea. (Matthew 27:57-60) "For a report we go to the tomb site." Reporter interviews some soldiers who are busy at the entrance of the tomb. (Matthew 27: 62-66) (Suggested song: "Christ Arose")

6 **TV Newsroom and burial site.** (Sunday morning) Anchor reports a rumor that the tomb in which Christ was laid is empty. "For an accurate report we go to the tomb site, where a reporter is standing by." He sums up what seems to be happening. Then he speaks with Mary, Mary Magdalene, Peter, and John standing in a group wondering what happened to the body of Christ. (Matthew 28:1-7, John 20:1-10) He also speaks with the guards, huddled in another group. (Matthew 27:4. 11-15) He reports back to the anchor. As the anchor is summarizing, another reporter cuts in with a report of two men who have seen and talked with Christ. (Luke 24:13-35) Almost immediately another reporter cuts in with a report from Mary Magdalene who has seen and talked with Christ. (John 20:11-18) (Suggested song: "Christ the Lord Is Risen Today")

7 **Final commentary on the weekend's events by the anchor.** (Suggested song: "Alleluia")

duts, or instrumentals.

Props do not have to be elaborate. People may use their imaginations. The dialogue is the most important part. You will want to set up a table-and-chair situation for the anchor, similar to a news broadcast on television. Since the idea is to recreate the Easter story as a current event, contemporary dress can be worn by everyone involved. The reporters who are on the scene may appear in various places around the room or platform. Since the anchor sets each scene, props are not necessary, but your own creativity and resources can dictate this.

The service may be introduced with remarks similar to these: "This morning's commemoration of this historical event is not one that fits with the usual sunrise service. But we trust that it will be used by God's Spirit to help you celebrate this joyous event. What we celebrate today happened many years ago...but what if these events had taken place today? What if God had chosen to reveal himself in Christ to our generation? How might these events have been reported through the news media? That is the setting for this service." *Douglas Swank*

DRAMA

LIVE FROM JERUSALEM

Presented as the talk show on a Jerusalem TV station, this 15-to-20-minute drama (starting on page 61) takes place shortly after Christ's resurrection. The single set is a talk-show set, cushioned chair for the host and perhaps a sofa for guests. *Steve Fortosis*

DRAMA

THE NIGHT BEFORE EASTER

Here's a short skit (see pages 65–66) developed as an opening for Easter morning Sunday school. It depicts a conversation between Peter and John in an upper room where they're hiding the night before the Resurrection. The dialogue focuses on Peter's grief over having denied Jesus, and how he cannot possibly make it right with the Lord now that he's gone.

The skit should be memorized for the best effect. It can be followed up with a Bible study on forgiveness, and on how Jesus is willing and able to forgive us when we feel we have let him down. Focus especially on John 21:15-19.
Brian Fullerton

DRAMA

THE TOMB REVISITED

Try a modern version of the Easter story, pages 67–68. Not very appropriate for a solemn morning service, but great as a creative way to introduce a story everyone seems overly familiar with. There are good discussion possibilities here. *Bill Calvin*

LIVE FROM JERUSALEM

CHARACTERS

(in either Middle Eastern or modern costuming; the cast can be cut as needed)

- Talk show host
- Ben Goldberg (formerly blind)
- Peter
- Lazarus
- Pontius Pilate
- Mary (mother of Jesus)
- Albert Rosenthal III (a Pharisee)
- Thomas
- Rashid (boy with the lunch)

Applause—either canned or live, prompted by APPLAUSE *sign—as host walks onstage.*

ANNOUNCER: *(unseen, over the sound system)* Live from Jerusalem, it's the Simeeeeeooooon Shavitz Show!

SHAVITZ: Hey, well, here we are again, sitting pretty here in Jerusalem, home of the blessed patriarchs and the not-so-blessed uniformed grunts that Caesar so kindly shipped over to us—hey, did I say that? Welcome anyway to a great lineup tonight.

We're broadcasting live from the Outer Courts up here on Temple Hill, and do we have a controversial lineup tonight! 10 days ago a rural laborer and sometime street preacher out of Nazareth was executed by the Romans. Shortly after his death came rumors that this Jesus of Nazareth was missing from his tomb. Stranger yet is the unsubstantiated report that he came alive again; in fact, some of his followers claim to have seen him, postdeath. We've gathered both supporters and skeptics tonight to interview—and just maybe we'll uncover the truth about this.

Welcome with me our first guest, the mother of yet one more in a long line of self-proclaimed, upcountry messiahs—Mary! *(Applause)*

SHAVITZ: Evening, ma'am.

MARY: Good evening, Simeon.

SHAVITZ: How does it feel to know you raised a son who turned out to be such an incredibly controversial figure?

MARY: I didn't teach him to be controversial—it just happened because he <u>is</u> who he is.

SHAVITZ: And, uh, just who <u>is</u> he?

MARY: The Son of God.

SHAVITZ: Whoa, I think ya lost me already. You saying that you, uh, got together somehow with, uh, the Man Upstairs, the Rabbi in the Sky, and, uh—

MARY: My husband's name was Joseph. But before we married, God gave me a son—his Son.

SHAVITZ: Sure, right, that clears everything up. *(Nervous laughter)* Well, to move on...at any rate, I am sincerely sorry that your son had to die the way he did. Our imported wannabe tyrants have no business laying a hand on any Jew, be he God or fraud.

MARY: Well, thank you for your sympathy. I do think, though, that he wanted it to be clear that he died so that we could live.

SHAVITZ: *(stares at Mary without speaking for a moment, then rises and ushers her offstage)* Ooookay. Well, we've got a lot of guests waiting tonight, so we'll have to cut off our pleasant chat right here. Thanks for joining us, Mary. *(applause)* Next we have a man who says he used to be blind, but no more. Jesus, he claims, healed him. Welcome with me Ben Goldberg! *(Applause as Goldberg walks on stage and seats himself)* So you say Jesus healed you.

GOLDBERG: Exactly.

SHAVITZ: How'd it all happen?

GOLDBERG: He spit on dirt and made a little mud. This is what my friends tell me—I couldn't see anything yet myself, of course. Then he smeared the dab of mud on my eyes and told me to wash it off in a pool.

SHAVITZ: Hey, my wife puts mud packs on her face, but I never knew one of those suckers could heal blindness! *(laughs)*

GOLDBERG: It can if Jesus applies it.

SHAVITZ: *(embarrassed pause)* We hear the Pharisees threw you out of the synagogue for believing in this Jesus.

GOLDBERG: You heard right. And that's not the only thing jealousy drove them to.

SHAVITZ: Well, we'll let them answer for themselves, because our next guests are two of the leading Pharisees in the Sanhedrin. *(Ben rises to leave; applause)* Let's bring on the big boy now—welcome Pharisee Albert Rosenthal III! *(Rosenthal enters; as he passes the exiting Goldberg, Rosenthal conspicuously walks widely around him. He is seated)*

SHAVITZ: So you weren't exactly bosom buddies with the naive Nazarene, huh?

ROSENTHAL: If you overlooked his heretical illusions of grandeur, his utopian teachings, and his deified death wish, you could probably get along with him okay.

SHAVITZ: Hey, you're forgetting what every Tom, Dick, and Harry on this end of the Mediterranean is talking about—his kindness, his miracles, his mercy.

ROSENTHAL: His kindness was only cunning, his miracles were merely magic, and his mercy only deceived the multitudes. Besides, the writings of the Prophets agree that the true Messiah will be born in Bethlehem. Jesus was from Nazareth. The Messiah will deliver us from our oppressors. Jesus went without a struggle to his own crucifixion. He couldn't fight his way out of a wet paper bag—not to mention a sealed granite tomb.

SHAVITZ: His followers say he's alive again.

ROSENTHAL: *(rolls his eyes and sighs loudly)* Another lie. His followers stole the body from the tomb and hid it.

SHAVITZ: You got some skeptics, Rosenthal. How did they get past the Roman guards, into a sealed tomb—you know as well as I do the size of a typical stone door—and out again, with the body, past the guards?

ROSENTHAL: Bribes, obviously.

SHAVITZ: Right, and we all know the millions of denari fishermen earn at their fragrant job. Well, thanks for being on the show, guy. *(applause as Rosenthal rises and leaves)* Speaking of fishermen, let's hope they left their occupational aroma at home—because here are two of Jesus' actual disciples—Peter and Thomas! *(Applause as Rosenthal leaves and Peter and Thomas walk on. After hearing who's following him, Rosenthal just shakes his head as he leaves the stage)*

SHAVITZ: Well, Pete—or should I call you Rocky?—you seem awfully happy, considering you just lost your rabbi. In fact, what is this stolen-body scenario, anyway?

PETER: Hard to believe, I know. But believe me anyway: Jesus isn't dead. I've seen him myself.

SHAVITZ: Okey dokey, Pete—confession's good for the soul. What else did you see at that opium party?

THOMAS: I doubted it too, Simeon. But then I saw Jesus with my own eyes. I even touched his scars.

SHAVITZ: Well for the love of Osiris...you guys are making this Jesus out to be some kind of god. Gimme a break.

PETER: If we hadn't been so dense at the time, we would have heard Jesus say himself that he'd be killed and then come back to life. Alive enough, in fact, to help break a week-long fishing slump that had put me behind on my mortgage. I'm caught up now, thanks to him.

SHAVITZ: So you're still fishing instead of hitting the speaking circuit? You know, "Disciple of Judean Messiah Tells You How to Stretch Your Loaves and Fishes"?

PETER: Fishing, but not the kind you have in mind.

SHAVITZ: Well, guys, gotta move on—but why don't you stick around? You know the next guy we're bringin' on. Come on in, Lazarus! *(applause as Lazarus enters)* We couldn't talk about a resurrection without talking with a recognized expert on the subject. Lazarus says he rose from the dead, too! You're one of a select few, Laz. Does this mean you're the Son of God, too?

LAZARUS: Heck, no. The difference is, I was a goner. There was no way I could have revived myself. If Jesus hadn't come along, I'd still be pushing up lilies. Jesus raised himself from the dead—by his own power—which I couldn't have done.

SHAVITZ: And the source of his power?...

LAZARUS: He's the Son of God, so he's got all of God's power.

SHAVITZ: *(leaning forward, looking hard at Lazarus, and momentarily getting serious)* You actually believe this guy is God?

LAZARUS: Yup. Proved it by his miracles, his perfect life, his teachings, his resurrection—

SHAVITZ: Hold on a minute. How did his resurrection prove he was God?

LAZARUS: If he was just a man, like you or me, he'd still be dead.

SHAVITZ: Whoa! It's getting a little thick in here. *(laughs nervously)* Anyway, we've got someone who may be Jesus' youngest follower waiting to come on. Welcome Rashid—the boy with the lunchbox. *(Applause as young Rashid joins the others onstage)*

SHAVITZ: So you're the boy who gave his lunch to Jesus.

RASHID: Uh-huh.

SHAVITZ: What happened? The Twelve ran out of peanut butter and jelly, and you came to the rescue?

RASHID: Jesus didn't have any food for this big crowd, so I gave him my lunch.

SHAVITZ: Exactly how big was this crowd?

RASHID: The grownups said there were more than 5,000 people.

SHAVITZ: I've heard about boys with hollow legs, but this is ridiculous. What does your mom give you for lunch, Meals on Wheels?

RASHID: All I had was five loaves of bread and two fish.

SHAVITZ: Jesus must have sliced that bread pretty thin, huh?

RASHID: Oh no, everybody was stuffed. In fact, they picked up a bunch of leftovers afterwards.

SHAVITZ: Well, kid, you're either one of the best little liars around, or this Jesus was a first-rate magician. Hey, I want to thank you and Laz here for appearing on the show. *(applause)* Our last guest is Caesar's toady in these parts—the man who couldn't bring himself to give a decisive sentence against

Jesus, so he just washed his hands of the whole deal and let the mob goad the soldiers into doing the dirty work. Sounds like a Roman to me. Hey, why doesn't this guy wash his hands of Judea itself and go home already? Just kidding. Let's give Pontius Pilate a big welcome. *(applause as the other guests leave and Pilate enters)*

PILATE: Watch it, Shavitz. Keep running at the mouth like that, and I'll have you arrested for treason. My personal guard is outside your studio doors at this moment.

SHAVITZ: Ratings, Governor Pilate, just ratings. No harm meant. Were you satisfied with the outcome of the Jesus scandal?

PILATE: *(getting comfortable, crossing his legs)* I'll tell you one thing: I've taken a cartload of sleeping pills since that crucifixion day. I can't seem to get the guy out of my mind. He still plagues me night and day.

SHAVITZ: Guilt, I suppose.

PILATE: Well, yeah, I do feel guilty—but there's nothing I can do about it now. Just the night before he was brought to trial, my wife had a terrible nightmare about the man and warned me to leave him alone. But I had to do what I did...I couldn't risk a full-scale riot.

SHAVITZ: We're almost out of time, governor. One last question: Do you put any credence in the rumor that Jesus has come back to life?

PILATE: *(pensive and troubled, almost as if talking to himself)* I don't know...Sometimes I think almost anything's possible with this man...I can still see him looking at me, still hear him saying that I have no real authority...I can't forget him. I just can't forget the man. *(bows his head and covers his face with his hands. Blackout)*

OFFSTAGE VOICE: I am the resurrection and the life; whoever believeth in me, though he were dead, yet shall he live. And whosoever liveth and believeth in me shall never die.

END

THE NIGHT BEFORE EASTER

CHARACTERS

Peter

John

Peter and John are lying on the floor sleeping. Peter suddenly begins tossing and turning, mumbling, "I'm sorry, Master, I'm sorry!" The more he tosses and turns, the louder he gets—until he snaps up to a sitting position, only half awake and sweating.

PETER: *(almost hysterical)* I'm sorry, Master! I'm sorry! *(buries his face in his hands and whimpers)* I'm sorry, so sorry...(John is awakened by the noise. He reaches over and touches Peter's arm.)*

JOHN: What is it, Peter? What's wrong?

PETER: I had a terrible nightmare. I'm sorry if I woke you.

JOHN: *(with a sleepy chuckle)* I'm afraid it wasn't much of a sleep to be awakened from. I'm tired, but sleep isn't coming easily tonight.

PETER: My sleep is fitful enough without nightmares.

JOHN: What are these nightmares you're having?

PETER: It's the same one over and over again. I'm standing in the courtyard of the high priest's house. As I look in the window, I can see the Master looking at me. He has the saddest look on his face I've ever seen. I know that I've denied him, but when I try to apologize, he turns his head away from me...(in a broken voice)* I denied him,

John. I swore that I didn't know him, when I promised that I would stand by him no matter what.

JOHN: I think I understand what you're feeling, Peter.

PETER: *(bewildered)* How can you understand what I'm feeling? You stood by him faithfully right up to the end. You stood at the cross with his mother; he spoke with you! How did you deny him?

JOHN: Isn't my hiding here in this room with you a form of denial? I may not have betrayed him with words, but what I do speaks loudly enough.

PETER: *(more relaxed)* Forgive me, John. I know this has been hard on all of us. It just seems that I was always giving the Master some kind of trouble. Remember when I tried to keep him from coming to Jerusalem in the first place? He called me Satan! And when I lashed out with my sword in the garden, he rebuked me. I swore that I would lay down my life for him if necessary; but when the time came, I denied him and ran. I've failed him again and again, John, and now he's dead and I can't make it right.

JOHN: I'm sure we all wish we had done differently. How do you think I'm feeling? He put me in charge of his mother—but how can I take care of her when soldiers are sure to be looking for us next?

PETER: The present doesn't concern me, John. It's the future that I'm thinking about. Remember what the Master said to us? That if anyone denied him before men, he would deny them before the Father. How can I go through life with the guilt that's mine because I betrayed him? I wanted to speak up for him, but I feared for my life. Now that fear may cost me eternity. *(Both sit quietly for a few moments.)*

JOHN: These past few days have left me confused. He was always telling us that he was going to die, but I never thought it would be so soon. What do you think will become of us now that he's gone?

PETER: He told us himself that we could expect the same treatment they'd give him. I fear we may soon join him.

JOHN: Maybe he'll rise from the dead as he promised. We saw him raise Lazarus—but could he possibly raise himself?

PETER: I hope that for your sake he does, John. But even if he did come back, I fear that our friendship would never be the same because of what I've done.

JOHN: He was a man of forgiveness and understanding, Peter. I'm sure he'd forgive you.

PETER: That may be true, John, but could I ever forgive myself? *(Both fall silent again. John stares off into space for a moment as if thinking. Then a smile grows across his face.)*

JOHN: It sure was a wonderful three years wasn't it, Peter? All that he said and did is so vivid in my mind—I'll never forget it. I remember best how much he loved us; how I could feel that love so strongly, even when he wasn't there. *(looking sadly at the floor)* I loved him so much. Never have I had a better friend.

PETER: Yes, he was some man—a good friend and teacher. Well, we really should try to get some sleep. Only God knows what tomorrow holds for each of us. *(Both lie back down, but neither closes his eyes. They are silent for a few moments.)*

JOHN: Peter, you once said he was the Messiah. Do you still believe that?

PETER: Yes, I do. But will believing it bring him back?

END

The Tomb Revisited

CHARACTERS

4 Tomb guards: Louie, Bernie, Marvin, and Norman
Chief Priest Caiaphas
Chief Priest Annas

Sleeping bags for guards
2 Sticks and some firewood
Box of matches
Box of cereal

PROPS

New tennis shoe
Desk
2 Chairs
Play money

SCENE ONE

Four guards are sleeping in front of the tomb of Jesus. They snore and awaken without paying any attention to the tomb.

LOUIE: *(wakes up, rubs eyes, yawns and stretches)* Man, is it cold out here! I'd better build up a fire. *(begins to rub two sticks, puts wood and leaves together, blows into it, etc.)*

BERNIE: Hey, wat'cha doing, Louie?

LOUIE: Oh, just putting my Boy Scout training to use.

BERNIE: Forgot the matches again, eh? *(gets up and goes over to a knapsack and finds a box of matches)* Here ya go. *(throws matches to Louie)*

MARVIN: *(awakening from sleep)* Hey what's going on with all the noise?

LOUIE: *(testily)* I'm trying to get a fire going for breakfast.

MARVIN: Never mind for me—I've got mine ready to go. *(shows a box of cereal and begins to prepare his own breakfast)*

NORMAN: *(who has by this time also awakened—sniffs in the air as if something is burning)* Hey, what's burning?

LOUIE: Probably wood.

NORMAN: *(walking toward fire)* No, no. It smells like something rotten is burning. *(pause)*

BERNIE: Oh it's just your imagination.

MARVIN: No—I smell something now, too.

LOUIE: What's that in the fire there? *(pokes a stick in the fire and pulls out a burned shoe)*

NORMAN: Those are my new Reeboks you've been using for kindling wood, you idiot. Why I ought to strangle you with my bare... *(this last line is said while chasing Louie around the fire; Louie falls at Norman's knees, wraps his arms around him, and begs for mercy)*

LOUIE: Please, Norman—have mercy on me.

BERNIE AND MARVIN: Yeah Norman, give him a break. *(just then Norman notices the empty tomb—his eyes bug out and he says)*

NORMAN: Look! The tomb! It's empty!

EVERYONE: We're in big trouble.

MARVIN: We're all gonna get fired.

LOUIE: *(crying)* I'm going to lose my pension—and I only had three more years to go until retirement.

BERNIE: Don't feel bad. I've got a house to pay for and a son attending Jerusalem State Medical School.

NORMAN: What are you guys talking about? It's not our fault the tomb is empty. Jesus must have really come back from the dead—just as he predicted.

LOUIE: What makes you say that, Norman?

NORMAN: Well, that rock. It's moved. Who do you think moved it, the tooth fairy?

MARVIN: *(glaring at Bernie)* I'm sure we would have slept through an earthquake.

BERNIE: Well don't look at me—I don't know where Jesus is.

LOUIE: Well, if it's not our fault he's gone, let's get down to headquarters and tell the chief priests to put out an APB.

EVERYONE: Right! *(pick up sleeping bags, put out fire, etc., as curtain closes)*

SCENE TWO

Chief Priest Caiaphas and Chief Priest Annas are in a room with a desk and chairs, depicting the place of the chief priests. The four guards come in.

CAIAPHAS: *(excitedly)* What are you guys doing here—you're supposed to be at the tomb!

LOUIE: *(nonchalantly)* There's nothing there to guard. Jesus is gone.

ANNAS: *(very excitedly)* Gone?! Where did he go?!

MARVIN: Norman thinks Jesus has risen from the dead—just like he predicted he would.

ANNAS: *(to all)* You nincompoops! We can't have people believing Jesus came back from the dead. Think what it will do to our religion and—more important—all of our jobs! Who's going to give to the Temple if they think there is a risen savior?

BERNIE: Well, what do you want us to do?

CAIAPHAS: *(coming back to the guards)* Look—who else knows about Jesus rising from the dead?

ALL THE GUARDS: Nobody.

CAIAPHAS: *(rubbing his hands together)* All right. This is what we're going to say to the press: Quote, "We do not know the whereabouts of Jesus of Nazareth's body—because while the guards were sleeping, his disciples stole him away."

NORMAN: That's no good. If we were sleeping, how would we know his disciples stole the body?

ANNAS: *(testily)* Look Norman, we're doing this for you as well as ourselves. This statement will not only save your job but will also make you rich.

NORMAN: *(sarcastically)* How?

ANNAS: *(pulls out a wad of money)* This money is for you—if you can keep our little secret. Do I have any takers, boys?

BERNIE: *(greedily stuffs money in pockets)* I've got a boy in medical school.

LOUIE: I need a little extra for my retirement. *(stuffs money into his pockets)*

MARVIN: Everybody likes money.

NORMAN: *(firmly)* Money never brought a man back from the dead though. *(exits right leaving the others standing in the room with a dumb look on their faces)*

HALLOWEEN

Why should the pagans have all the fun on October 31? (You may remember that October 31 is *also* Reformation Day and the eve of All Saint's Day—a pair of very distinguished days on the church calendar.) You want creepy effects, gross-out gags, wild costume parties, whacked-out games, and unusual craft projects? We've got 'em. We've also got more pumpkin activities than you can shake a black cat at—not to mention plenty of service project ideas and Bible lessons tied to Halloween themes.

MIXER

Costume Bingo

Here's a great mixer for a Halloween party, or any party in which all the players are in costume. Print up Bingo cards, like the one shown on page 72, and have kids get signatures of people who match the descriptive phrases. As in regular Bingo, five in a row wins. Keep playing until you have several winners. *Vernon Edington*

GAME

Bobbing for Pickles

Fill a large tub with ice water. Along with apples, add some smaller items such as pickles, olives, and grapes. Allow each person 30 seconds to bob for as many items as possible. They give their catches to a partner, who collects them on a paper plate. Use the following point system for scoring:

Apple	1
Pickle	2
Grape	3
Olive	4

Give prizes to the person with the highest score. *Marge Clark*

GAME

Jigsaw Jack-o'-Lanterns

Here's a great Halloween game for small teams (no more than two or three on a team). Give each team a pumpkin and a sharp knife. Then give each team only one minute to cut up the pumpkin any way they want. The pumpkin can be cut into no more than 10 pieces.

Then have the teams rotate to a different pumpkin. Have a supply of round wooden toothpicks available. Give each team two minutes to put the jigsaw puzzle pumpkin back together, using the toothpicks to hold the pieces in place. The first team to finish is the winner. Pumpkins must be able to stand alone to be considered. *Dan Scholten*

Costume Bingo

Sign your name in the blank marked "Your own name." Find other people who match the squares and get their signatures.

Your own Name	Someone whose mom told them how to dress for this party	Someone wearing facial make-up for the first time	Someone who waited until the last hour before deciding what to be
Someone who wishes Lady Godiva would have shown up	Someone who's giving up a favorite TV show to be here	Someone who's glad to have the chance to show off their legs	Someone who has to explain to everyone who they are
Someone whose hat keeps slipping off	Someone who plans to eat one of every dessert	Someone whose costume is uncomfortable	Someone who would rather not have their picture taken right now
Someone who wishes they could really be who they are dressed as	Someone who borrowed more than two items for their costume	Someone who wishes we had a costume party every year or so	Someone who can't get to where it itches

CREATIVE COSTUME SCAVENGER HUNT

Have your group go out begging on Halloween, not for treats, but for items to make a costume. Meet at the home of one of your staff or youths and divide the group into teams, assigning each one a different street in the surrounding neighborhood. Then let each team choose one of its members to be their

"model." Teams must go door to door, asking at each home for one or two items they can use in creating a costume for their model. At one place they may get an old hat, at another some lipstick, at another a wig, and so on. Set a time limit, and when teams report back to home base, hold a competition for the best costume. *Randy Lanford*

FIND THE PUMPKIN

All you need is a pumpkin for each team of three or four, a few flashlights, a dark and spooky place, and some advance planning. Hide the pumpkins well (don't ask your teenagers to do this, because they probably can't keep a secret when it means winning or losing). Then backtrack to the starting point in as obscure a manner as possible, writing up riddling clues on index cards as you backtrack. Hide the clues. Repeat the process for each pumpkin and team.

Give the youths the first clue, and—using logic and navigation—they should be able to locate the remaining clues. The prep time required is significant (do you have adult sponsors who could do it?),

but it's worth the unsurpassed fun of this nonsports-oriented challenge. *Timothy Wilkey*

HALLOWEEN SCAVENGER HUNT

If you can locate an old, out-of-the-way (deserted) cemetery, here's a spooky Halloween party idea. Get permission from the cemetery custodians or director to have a scavenger hunt. Make a list of names found on tombstones and have the kids try to locate them and write in the dates found on the tombstone on the list. The most complete list of names and dates wins. Do it at night and provide flashlights. Be sure to let the police and neighbors know what's going on. *Tom Galovich*

PIN THE NOSE ON JACK

This is a Halloween version of Pin the Tail on the Donkey. The rules are the same as for that game, but instead of a donkey picture, use a drawing of a jack-o'-lantern minus the nose. Then, instead of a tail, have blindfolded players pin or tape on individual noses created from pictures of noses which have been cut out of magazines and glued onto yellow construction paper triangles. Each person's nose should be unique and can be taken from any person or animal: an elephant's trunk, pig's snout, bird's beak, or whatever. *Warren and Linda Waddell*

PUMPKIN OLYMPICS

Hold a "Pumpkin Olympics" the week after Halloween, when supermarkets and nurseries are practically giving away leftover pumpkins. Plan to use three pumpkins for each person.

Divide into at least four teams. Since these games are messy, hold the Olympics outdoors. Here are events to use.

• **Dodge Pumpkin.** Everyone sits in a large circle with one person in the middle. Choose a large pumpkin and roll it at the person in the middle, trying to hit the person. To make it interesting, increase the number of pumpkins. If a pumpkin splats, replace it.

• **Pumpkin Bowling.** Set up empty 2-liter bottles,

cans, or bowling pins. Each person rolls a pumpkin once and tallies the total number of pins knocked down. A leader can be constantly resetting the pins.

• **Pumpkin Toss.** Similar to an egg toss, two people from a team toss a pumpkin back and forth, stepping farther apart each time, until someone drops it.

• **Pumpkin Put.** Put (as in *putting* the shot) a pumpkin through the air and measure how far it goes. Competition may be based on using the largest person from each team, the smallest person, the largest pumpkin, or the smallest pumpkin.

• **Pumpkin Catapult.** Using a cinderblock with a board over it and the pumpkin on one end of the board, jump on the other end and measure how far the pumpkin goes.

• **The Great Pumpkin Relay.** Set up an obstacle course. Players carry a large pumpkin as they negotiate the course, then hand the pumpkin to the next player.

• **Pumpkin Soccer.** Dribble the pumpkin around a cone or other marker and back to the starting point, where the next person takes a turn.

• **Potentially Popular Pumpkin Pick-up Contest.** By the end of the Olympics, the grounds are a mess, so have a clean-up contest. Provide plastic trash bags and award megapoints to the team that collects the most pumpkin debris. Have a scale on hand to weigh the bags if possible.

After the Olympics, award the "World's Largest Banana Split" to the winning team. This will be much more appealing than a piece of pumpkin (squish) pie. *Allen L. Pickett*

GAME
PUMPKIN PUSH

Here's a good game for your next Halloween party. Divide the group into several teams. Give each team a pumpkin of the same approximate size. Place a chair (one for each team) about 20 feet away from the team. If you have four teams, use four chairs. The object is for each person on the team to push the pumpkin around his team's chair and back to the next player. The first team to have all of its players finish is the winner. The catch is this: the players may only use their pelvises to push the pumpkins while doing a sideways crab walk. Or you might have them push the pumpkin with their heads. For

added excitement and chaos, have two or three teams go around the same chair. *Mark W. Kaat*

GAME
PUMPKIN PUZZLE

Before this relay can begin, you'll need to carve several jack-o'-lanterns (one for each group of four young people). Clean the pumpkins out thoroughly; then carve out two eyes and a mouth. But keep this in mind as you carve: you will pile up the eyes and mouths and lids of all the cut-out jack-o'-lantern parts, and the kids will have to match their teams' parts with their teams' pumpkins.

Line up all the four-member teams at one end of a room with a jack-o'-lantern opposite each team. In between, pile the jumble of pumpkin parts. At the

signal, one member from each team dashes to the pile, grabs what she hopes is a pumpkin part that fits somewhere in her team's pumpkin, races on to her team pumpkin, and tries to plug the eye hole or mouth hole or top with the piece. When a player has made as many trips to the part pile as necessary and finally inserts a part that fits, she races back to her team and tags the next player. The first team to completely plug up its pumpkin wins. *Bill Barnes*

GAME
WITCH'S BROOM RELAY

This game moves kids right into the Halloween mood quickly—and with a lot of laughs.

Provide each of two teams with a big witch hat, a pair of ugly boots, a house broom, a long black skirt, a long black blouse, and a belt. The object is simple:

Each member of both relay teams must run the length of the course and back.

The twist is the getup they must wear during their run. The first players to run must put on the entire witch costumes and ride the broom the whole length of the relay. Upon returning to their teams, they must transfer the outfits to the next players in line, who mount their brooms and take off. The first team to finish successfully wins—the broom, that is. They can either mount it in the youth room as a trophy, or bequeath it to the losing team to use for the after-party cleanup. *Timothy Wilkey*

PARTY GAME

MONSTER MAD LIB

Here's a Mad Lib that would be great for your next Halloween Party (see page 76). It's simply a story with key words left out. Without letting the kids in on the story, have them (orally) supply the missing words as you tell them the type of word needed (noun, part of body, adjective, etc.). Tell them to be as creative and wild as possible while thinking up words. Write the words in the blanks, then read back the story after all the missing words are filled in. *Jim Berkley*

PRACTICAL JOKE

COFFIN TRICK

Here's a fun special effect for a Halloween event. Put a teen in a coffin (a pine box will do) with his head at the foot and his feet at the head. You then put a shirt around his calves and knees and stuff it with rags to look like his chest. The collar of the shirt is around the guy's ankles. Lay a pillow over his feet and just above the shirt collar. Then put a Styrofoam head on the pillow with a mask and a wig on it. Cover the teen's thighs, waist, trunk, and head with a blanket. Tell the kids a scary story, which doesn't really scare them because they think the body is just a dummy. But as they bend over to look at the dummy's face, the guy sits up from the other end and screams in their ears. This works best in a dimly lit room. *Robert Vogel*

PRACTICAL JOKE

SHRUNKEN HEADS

Here's a good special effect for your next Halloween event. Hang a sheet in a dark room (like a closet). Cut two holes in the sheet and have two girls stick their heads through. Tie their hair to the ceiling to give the effect of shrunken heads. Put a little red food coloring under their heads on the sheet for effect. A light turned on and off quickly is the best way to show it. That way the kids don't have time to analyze what it really is. *Robert Vogel*

VIDEO

COSTUME VIDEO

Want to spice up your next costume party? Have two video cameras on hand and divide your group into two teams. Tell both teams that they have 20 minutes to create and rehearse a skit that uses the character of each person's costume.

Send the teams to separate rooms for planning and rehearsing. Have each of their performances videotaped about 20 minutes later—but still keep the teams separate. Then bring both groups together, show the videos, and award prizes to the team that gave the best performance. *Greg Golden*

CRAFT

BALLOON-O'LANTERNS

If you'd like to have a pumpkin-carving contest, but a roomful of the real thing would cost too much, use orange balloons and felt tip markers instead. Have the kids inflate the balloons (save your breath) and be as creative as they like in drawing faces. Give prizes for the ugliest, the scariest, the funniest, or whatever. *Russ Porter*

CRAFT

PUMPKIN CARVING

Next Halloween have your youth group carve messages in jack-o'-lanterns, rather than the traditional pumpkin face. A few suggestions: "Peace," "Love," "God is love," "Smile," etc. *Kim Huffman*

MONSTER MAD LIB

"Once upon a time, _____(number) years ago, in that fiendish place Transylvania—which is now known as _____(local high school), the _____(adjective) Count Dracula _____-ed (verb). Our story finds him just after he has finished his dinner, which tonight included _____(person in group). Since he was still a little hungry and a full moon was out, he decided to catch the next _____(means of transportation) to _____'s (girl in group) house and peek into her _____(room of the house) to see if she was_____-ing (verb). By chance she was, which brought a _____(adjective) smile to his _____(adjective) face. Without wasting a second, he _____-ed (verb) into her _____(noun), startling her so much that she broke her _____(toy). "_____(greeting)" spoke Count Dracula. "I have come to drink your blood!" "_____(exclamation)" she replied, whereupon she kicked Dracula in the _____(part of the body) and fled. Not to be deterred, Dracula chased her as far as _____(place) where he finally tackled her. It looked like the end for _____(same girl), but just before Dracula could sink his _____(adjective) fangs into her _____(adjective) neck, _____(boy in group) arrived on the scene. Quickly sizing up the situation, he grabbed the nearest _____ (noun) and smote Dracula so hard it was heard in _____ (place). "_____ (mushy line)", sighed _____ (same girl). "Aw, it was nothing," replied _____ (same boy) as he flexed his _____ (part of body) for her. "By the way," he asked. "What's a nice girl like you doing in the _____ (your church) high school group?"

HALLOWEEN GIVE-AWAY

This idea not only benefits the community and the church, but will really leave an impression on your young people. This Halloween have each young person bring a costume and a pound of Halloween candy. Provide a number of empty paper bags. After the kids arrive in costume, instruct them to open their candy and divide it equally among the empty bags. Then add to the bags several good pieces of literature which could include things like an introductory brochure about the church, a letter from the youths themselves (see page 78), and a modern translation of the New Testament. *Brad C. Brail*

HALLOWEEN TUNNEL

This year, try a tunnel instead of a spook house. You can construct it out of boxes from refrigerators or other large appliances. Use masking tape or a staple gun to fasten them together end to end. Then run the tunnel like a maze throughout the church building. Include trap doors and dead ends to make the trip more confusing. Decorate throughout with the scary items usually found in a spook house. You can even have them crawl through cooked noodles and wet bread! For some great thrills, cut a few holes in the tunnel wall in several locations so that masked faces and rubber-gloved hands can thrust through to clutch at victims as they pass by. End the tunnel with a slide by rigging up carpeted plywood over some stairs. Then have someone on hand to issue a cardboard toboggan for the final ride. Station another person at the bottom to assist in landings, where the fall can be broken by a few old mattresses. It's a journey they'll long remember! *June Becker*

TOMBSTONE OVERNIGHTER

If your youth group is planning a Halloween overnighter, have your kids bring their sleeping bags to the dungeon (a basement or other potentially spooky place) or to the graveyard (outside). Once there, they create tombstones from poster board or cardboard that read, "Here lies _____. R.I.P." and position them at the heads of their sleeping bags. Or you can make the tombstones for them ahead of time and assign sleeping spaces with them. *Tia Booth*

HALLOWEEN RETREAT

Arrange a retreat weekend on or near October 31. Tell your group to dress up in costumes for the bus ride to the retreat site. On the way, stop at all the towns (usually small ones, since retreat facilities are usually out in the country) and go trick-or-treating. Most of the people you'll meet will get a kick out of a busload of itinerant Halloweeners—not to mention the mountains of candy you'll amass to snack on during the weekend. *Phil Thompson*

HOLY HALLOWEEN

Try offering your kids an alternative celebration on Halloween night this year. You can preserve the pleasure of dressing up by having the kids put together elaborate and authentic costumes. But limit them to characters related to Scripture or the Church: biblical heroes like Esther or Paul; famous figures from church history like Luther or Wesley; evangelists, preachers, or missionaries; and maybe even a couple of seraphim and cherubim!

Party decorations should reflect the same themes, with Bible scenes and characters. Tell Bible stories instead of ghost stories, and hold a contest for the prettiest (rather than scariest) jack-o-lantern face. If you normally have a haunted mansion, try a Bible mansion with live Bible scenes instead.

Take the kids out as a group and travel through the neighborhood singing hymns or praise songs. Instead of asking for treats, leave a small gift at each home you visit—perhaps some fruit or a pocket New Testament—and give them a tract or a packet of information about your church. *Doug Newhouse, Mark Reed, Richard R. Everett, and Ron Camblin*

PUMPKIN PARTY

Have an entire evening of activities centered on that most familiar of autumn symbols: the pumpkin.

HAPPY HALLOWEEN!

The scary-looking bunch who just rang your doorbell shouting "Trick or treat!" are members of the local _____ Church's youth group.

We wanted to take this rather unique opportunity to celebrate Halloween with your family in ways other than soaping your windows, T-P-ing your trees, or asking you for candy. We wanted to be able to share with you this Halloween.

So we put together these little goodie bags with candy for the children and some interesting little booklets for everyone. It is our hope that this little goodie bag will be enjoyed by everyone in your family.

We hope that as you eat the candy, you will take time to look through some of the booklets. They contain some "goodies" too.

Have a Happy Halloween. We have enjoyed this opportunity to talk with you and want you to know that our church is especially interested in your family. If you don't already attend a church regularly, we would love to have you attend our services. If there is ever any way we can be of assistance to you and your loved ones, please feel free to call us.

God bless you all!

HAPPY HALLOWEEN!

The scary-looking bunch who just rang your doorbell shouting "Trick or treat!" are members of the local _____ Church's youth group.

We wanted to take this rather unique opportunity to celebrate Halloween with your family in ways other than soaping your windows, T-P-ing your trees, or asking you for candy. We wanted to be able to share with you this Halloween.

So we put together these little goodie bags with candy for the children and some interesting little booklets for everyone. It is our hope that this little goodie bag will be enjoyed by everyone in your family.

We hope that as you eat the candy, you will take time to look through some of the booklets. They contain some "goodies" too.

Have a Happy Halloween. We have enjoyed this opportunity to talk with you and want you to know that our church is especially interested in your family. If you don't already attend a church regularly, we would love to have you attend our services. If there is ever any way we can be of assistance to you and your loved ones, please feel free to call us.

God bless you all!

Try these games and invent some of your own:

- **Pumpkin Patch Pick.** Like an Easter egg hunt, only you search for hidden pumpkins (which are admittedly a little more difficult to hide than eggs).
- **Pumpkin Pushovers.** Teams or individuals go bowling with pumpkins instead of balls. Mark off alleys with masking tape and use plastic two-liter soft drink bottles as pins. Pumpkins should all be similar in size.
- **Pumpkin Puzzle.** Have teams choose, from a large selection of pumpkins, the one they think comes closest to weighing 40 pounds without going over that amount.
- **Pumpkin Pie Pig-Out.** Each team chooses an eater and a feeder to be seated across from each other at a table. The eaters must keep their hands behind their backs, and the feeders must keep one hand under the table. Feeders are given a pumpkin pie and a spoon and are blindfolded. On the signal, feeders begin stuffing the eaters with pie using the spoon or their fingers. The first team to have its eater finish eating the entire pie wins.

This evening is cheaper if you have your group plant some pumpkins ahead of time so that you'll have your own patch in the fall. *Elizabeth Power*

BANQUET

Halloween Dinner

This is a variation on the Mystery Dinner, in which people order items from a menu without knowing exactly what it is that they are ordering. All the food items and the eating utensils have disguised names. A person orders food in three courses, four items per course, from a menu. A waitress (dressed as a witch) fills the orders and brings the food to the table. The person must consume each course (all of it) before the next course can be ordered and received. It's a lot of fun and full of surprises. Here's the menu (don't include the words in parentheses):

Witches' Brew (punch)
Lapover (napkin)
Jack's Ripper (knife)
Devil's Right Arm (fork)
Grave Diggers Delight (spoon)
Autumn Nectar (milk)
Pig in a Poke (hot dog)
Tombstone (bun)
Irish Eyes (fried potatoes)
Bones (beans)
Slimy Shivers (Jell-o)
Frosted Pumpkin (pie) Malcolm McQueen

Pumpkin Object Lesson

Here's an October object lesson that can be used with all ages—from elementary school through high school—as part of a youth worship service, youth talk, or children's sermon. The lesson is a vivid reminder to young people of what Christ has done for them whenever they see a Halloween jack-o'-lantern.

Before the service, get a very large pumpkin, clean it out, and carve a suitable face (see illustration). Save a handful of the slimy "yuk" from cleaning the pumpkin and put it back inside, though in a dish.

To begin, have the jack-o'-lantern turned away from the audience so its face can't be seen. Ask some leading questions about what kids think sin is,

how they feel when they sin against others as well as when others sin against them. Then remove the dish of muck—the sin—from inside the jack-o'-lantern and quiz the kids about getting rid of sin. (Chances are that, although their answers will vary, the bottom line will still be Jesus Christ.) Lead them in discussing the necessity of asking forgiveness of both God and each other and of how, once Jesus forgives sin, they are free to love as they were created to do.

At this point turn the jack-o'-lantern around so all can see its face. Talk about how something's still missing: the power of the Holy Spirit in our lives, a light that shines in darkness. As you're explaining this, have the room lights turned off and a candle lit and placed in the jack-o'-lantern. After the lesson the jack-o'-lantern can be given to one of the kids to take home. *Dave Washburn*

SERVICE

HALLOWEEN HOSPITAL VISITS

Turn things around and have your youths hand out treats instead of receive them. At the beginning of October, contact your local hospital to see if it will allow your group to visit the pediatric unit on Halloween. Find out what time is best for your visit.

Once your trip is confirmed, contact a local restaurant or store to get some trick-or-treat bags (many are happy to provide them at no cost). Then

have your kids start collecting items to fill trick-or-treat bags: coloring books, crayons, stickers, games, and helium balloons work well. Be sure to check with nurses before putting candy into a child's bag. Include in each bag a note on your youth group's letterhead explaining who you are and the reason for your visit and gifts.

A few days before your visit, call the hospital to confirm how many children are in the ward and how old they are. This will ensure that you make up enough bags and that they are age-appropriate.

On the day of your visit, have everyone come dressed up in costumes. Let the kids know that they should not wear scary costumes or medical garb.

After you hand out the bags and talk for a while with the children, have a special party at someone's home or a nearby restaurant. You might even want to make it a surprise! *Jennifer Carpenter and Tommy Baker*

SERVICE

TRAVELING HALLOWEEN COSTUME PARTY

Start with a traditional Halloween party, complete with costumes, games, and treats. Then take it on the road. Go to a hospital or a residential facility for the physically and mentally challenged. Take a supply of extra items to costume the residents, including hats, streamers, and balloons. You might also have a gentle, artistic youth do face painting on willing residents.

My group had the best time thinking up and developing fantastic costumes to impress each other and the residents. Being in costume and collaborating to design costumes for the residents helped put teens at ease. Helping them play games and enjoying refreshments with them offered additional levels of interaction. One of our students was designated to give a brief devotional so we could keep our focus in the midst of the festivity. *Wyndee E. Holbrook*

SERVICE

TRICK-OR-TREAT FOR THE ELDERLY

Here's a great service project for Halloween. Have your teenagers put together personalized trick-or-treat bags for residents of a convalescent home or elderly-care facility. Obtain from the nurses or administrators names of the residents and their dietary restrictions (sugar, sodium, etc.). Trick-or-treat bags should be colorful, should contain several candy or fruit treats, and should include a note that says something like "Dear _____: Here's a treat since you're so sweet! From the youth group at First Church." The bags can be delivered on Halloween night to the folks. *Tia Booth*

DRAMA

GHOST STORY

Obviously this activity is for Halloween, but it can be used anytime. Divide your group into several smaller units as specified later. As a narrator with a deep clear voice reads the story (found on page 81), the young people provide the sound effects as their key words (in italics) are spoken. It helps to have someone else give hand motions and silent directions. For added fun, rehearse it with the group, then videotape it and watch it together.

Here are the sound effects:
- **Footsteps:** three or four kids say slowly, "Shlop...Shlop...Shlop."

Ghost Story

It was a dark, cold night. The moon was full and bright, its light shining through deep gray, menacing clouds. The light cast strange shadows through the woods and across narrow, grassy fields. *Night sounds* echoed through the darkness. (Pause)

Wind whispered through the pines, singing its song so softly. Suddenly, the *wind* increased in intensity, shaking the leaves and branches back and forth, back and forth. A great clap of *thunder* broke through the night as a jagged lightning bolt lighted up the sky. It began to *rain*. (Pause) The *rain* beat down on the dried leaves and began to fall harder and harder. Soon the ground became slippery and wet as dry, packed earth soaked up the fallen *rain*, turning it into damp, gooey mud. In the distance the *howling* of dogs could be heard through the *wind* and the *rain*. The sound of *footsteps* could be heard moving slowly through the thick mud. All at once another *thunder* clap broke through the night and a piercing *scream* rose above the trees. As the *rain* began to soften and the *wind* died down, a low *moan*ing could be heard through the forest. Suddenly, all became silent. (Pause) And nothing could be heard, (pause) except the *wind*.

- **Wind:** kids make a soft whistling sound
- **Howling:** three or four kids howl like hounds
- **Scream:** group of kids scream like crazy
- **Thunder:** the entire group claps hands once. Begin on the right side of the room and flow to the left across the crowd.
- **Moan:** group gives a long, low moan
- **Rain:** the entire group snaps their fingers as fast as they can; then rub their palms together rapidly; then slap their thighs; and finally clap their hands rapidly. Soften the rain by following the above procedure in reverse.
- **Night sounds:** the adult staff can do this one. Everyone picks a vegetable (carrot, pickle, broccoli, lettuce, peas) and repeats its name over and over softly. It sounds like the noises you might hear deep in the woods.

Ben Sharpton

THANKSGIVING

If you think your mom found a lot of different uses for a Thanksgiving turkey (turkey hash, turkey stew, turkey sandwiches, cream of turkey soup), wait until you see the games youth workers from Cape Cod to all points west have cooked up for you. You'll never look at a turkey again the same way. In addition to games, you'll also find ideas for Thanksgiving craft projects, skits, outings, parties, service projects, and Bible lessons.

GAME

DECORATE THE TURKEY

In commemoration of Thanksgiving, you can have a little competition to see which group can do the best job of making a student look like a turkey. Divide into three or four groups. Give each group a paper sack full of goodies: an old pair of nylons, a roll of toilet paper, scissors, scotch tape, crepe or tissue paper, newspaper, or anything else you might be able to think of that will contribute to making a person look like a turkey. Set a time limit. You explain to the kids what they are to do, then divide the room up. Have the group select one person to be the turkey. Give them three or four minutes to do the decorating and then have the whole group judge the winner by applause. *Ron Wilburn*

GAME

TURKEY GOBBLE-OFF

Use this relay by itself next November, or include it in a Thanksgiving party. This isn't your typical up-and-back relay—teams travel from station to station.

• **Station 1—Turkey Dressing.** First, correctly answer the question, What part of a turkey is like a story? (*Answer: The tail.*) Then, as in Decorate the Turkey (above), prepare sufficient supplies to dress a human turkey with (nylons, orange trash bags, beaks, rubber gloves, etc.). Teams choose one member to be the turkey, then dress it up. Each turkey then struts (with its team following behind) to the next station.

• **Station 2—Turkey Feed.** Discuss the question, "Why is a glutton like a turkey?" (*Answer: It gobbles.*) The turkey must deliver the answer. If the answer is wrong, the turkey must flap its wings and gobble, then try again until it answers correctly. Teams must then measure out a given amount of corn (on the cob or in kernels) onto a plate, and the turkey must eat all the corn—and must gobble loudly between bites.

• **Station 3—Wounded Turkey.** Answer the question "What part of a turkey is like part of a sentence?" (*Answer: The claws.*) The team builds a pyramid, and the turkey hops around it on one foot.

• **Station 4—Turkey Eggs.** Answer the question

"What part of a turkey does the farmer watch most anxiously?" (*Answer: The crop.*) Each team inflates six balloons. The turkey must pop each balloon by sitting on it.

• **Station 5—Flying Turkey.** Answer the question, What part of a turkey do you keep on the dressing table? (*Answer: The comb.*) Each team hoists its turkey into the air, at which time the gobbler spreads its wings while its team flies it around a predetermined course within the building.

• **Station 6—Turkey Music.** Answer the question, What part of a turkey makes the most noise? (*Answer: The drumstick.*) Teams each compose a song that describes the turkey dressing. The turkeys then sing their teams' songs.

• **Station 7—Turkey Shoot.** Answer the question, What are a turkey's last clothes? (*Answer: His dressing.*) A team member shoots its turkey with a Polaroid camera. The team picks up the turkey, carries it to the finish line, and prepares it for Thanksgiving dinner—that is, undresses it. *Stephen May*

SCAVENGER HUNT

THANKSGIVING FEAST SCAVENGER HUNT

Create a youth group Thanksgiving dinner from the neighborhood's leftovers. Give your teams the following list and an empty plate, and tell them that they can receive only one item per house and that they will be judged on neatness of the full plate as well as on completion of the list.

1 slice turkey (white meat)
1 slice turkey (dark meat)
1 tablespoon stuffing
1 tablespoon cranberry sauce
1 tablespoon mashed potatoes
1 tablespoon gravy
1 serving of a vegetable
1 serving of yams
1 thin slice of pumpkin pie
1 serving of whipped cream (for pie)
1 thin slice of mincemeat pie
1 teaspoon salt
1 teaspoon pepper
1 Rolaid tablet
1 Thanksgiving napkin

1 Thanksgiving table decoration

If you want to give this scavenger hunt a charitable twist, take the collected food to needy families. *Randy Hausler*

MUSIC

TURKEY CAROLS

Who says carols are only for Christmas? Warble up some fun singing—try the Turkey Carols on page 87. *Fritz Moga*

LESSON APPLICATION

THANKSGIVING GRAFFITI

Have some young people hang up (and stand by) a large blank sheet of paper in a very well traveled area in your church. The pastor should announce that after the service people are invited to write, print, or draw something that represents what they are thankful for. The young people are ready with felt-tip pens, crayons, watercolors, etc., for people to use. If this is done early in November, the resulting graffiti can be displayed in a prominent place to remind people of how much we do have to be thankful for. *Keith Wise*

BANQUET

LEFTOVER LARK

Is there a retreat or party or progressive dinner scheduled for Thanksgiving weekend? Require that everyone bring two leftover dishes from their Thanksgiving dinners to share. Decorate the setting Pilgrim-fashion, and finish with a hayride or dance. *Valerie Stoop* .

DISCUSSION STARTER

GIVING THANKS

The Thanksgiving holiday weekend is a natural time for teaching kids to be thankful for the spiritual blessings that God gives us. The worksheet on page 88 can open up good discussion on being thankful for the items or experiences suggested by the answers:

Turkey Carols

MICHAEL, COOK THE TURKEY MORE
(to the tune of "Michael, Row the Boat Ashore")

1. Michael, cook the turkey more, alleluia.
I'm drooling knowing what's in store, alleluia.

2. Sister, help to trim the bird, alleluia.
Michael does it like a nerd, alleluia.

3. This glass of milk is chilly and cold, alleluia.
But it's sour—I think it's old, alleluia.

4. The table is deep and the table is wide, alleluia.
Biscuits and honey on the other side, alleluia.

5. Brother, lend a doggie bag, alleluia.
I ate too much—ooh, what a drag! Alleluia.

ON THANKSGIVING DAY
(to the tune of "Blowin' in the Wind")

1. When can you eat four meals in a day,
And lots and lots of pumpkin pie?
When do we eat a big, giant bird
That hardly knew how to fly?
When does he give up his life for us all,
And when, oh when must he die?

   Chorus: The answer, I'll say, is on Thanksgiving Day,
   The answer is on Thanksgiving Day.

2. When did the Pilgrims put on a feast,
And invite all the friends that they had?
When do people on diets give up,
But later on feel really bad?
When do we say, "Lord, thanks for all that we've got,"
And look around, and it makes us feel glad?

TOM TURKEY
(to the tune of "Tom Dooley")

Chorus: Hang down your head, Tom Turkey,
Hang down your head and cry.
Hang down your head, Tom Turkey,
Poor boy, you're bound to die.

1. Met him on a mountain, there I took his life.
Now he's on my china, and I'll cut him with my knife.

2. At this time tomorrow reckon where I'll be—
Eatin' a turkey sandwich with dressing and cranberries.

Thanksgiving in the Bible

"...always giving thanks to God the Father for everything..." (Ephesians 5:20)

What should I be thankful for?

T
H
A
N
K
S
G
I
V
I
N
G

_____ James 1:2-4

_____John 14:26, 16:13; Romans 8:26, 27

_____ Ephesians 5:20; 1 Thessalonians 5:18

_____Mark 1:15

_____Hebrews 12:28

_____ Hebrews 2:3

_____1 Corinthians 1:4; 2 Corinthians 12:9

_____ Ephesians 6:4

_____ 1 Corinthians 15:57; 2 Corinthians 2:14

_____ Colossians 1:12; Ephesians 1:18

_____ Psalm 75:1, 100:4; Philippians 2:9-11

_____ 2 Corinthians 9:15

Psalm 105:1
Give thanks to the Lord.

Colossians 3:15
And be thankful.

Philippians 4:6
Do not be anxious about anything, but in everything, by prayer and petition, with thanksgiving, present your requests to God.

Psalm 30:12
My heart may sing to you and not be silent.
O Lord my God, I will give you thanks forever.

Trials

Holy Spirit,

All things

News (Good News)

Kingdom

Son

Grace

Instruction of the Lord

Victory

Inheritance

Name of Jesus

Gift

Bert Jones

DISCUSSION STARTER

THANKSGIVING WORD ASSOCIATION

Here's a simple, fun word association game to get your kids thinking creatively about all the things they have to be thankful for. Write a word—any word—on a chalkboard, then have the kids make a list of things associated with that word for which they feel thankful.

If you wrote *ring*, for example, your group might suggest class ring, earring, ring of friends, and clothes (ring around the collar). You could make a game out of it—have the kids individually write their own lists of things they're thankful for, then read them to each other. Award prizes for the longest, most creative, etc. *Jerry Meadows*

SERVICE

CANTASTIC CAN CIRCUS

To raise canned goods for distribution to needy families at Thanksgiving, hold a Can Circus one evening in mid-November. Kids bring canned goods with them for admission to the circus, then compete in teams for "cantastic" prizes in several events:

• **Can Collection.** Each team is awarded a point for every can its members brought with them.

• **Can Castle.** Each team vies to construct the best castle (or tallest tower) using only the cans they brought in.

• **Can Quiz.** See which team can identify the most items from the following list (all the items begin with *can*). Use the dictionary to add some of your own as well.

America's northern neighbor *(Canada)*

A Native American water craft *(canoe)*

A heavy cloth *(canvas).*

A mid-Western state *(Kansas)*

A yellow bird *(canary)*

A long, narrow valley *(canyon)*

Someone who would love to have you for dinner *(cannibal)*

• **Bowling Cans.** For each team, set up 10 empty cans like bowling pins. Roll softballs to see which team can rack up the highest total score (each team member gets one roll).

• **Can Crash.** Set up a pyramid of five empty cans for each team, and let them throw Wiffle balls to see how many cans they can knock down (each team member gets one throw).

• **Can Soccer.** This is a relay race with players "dribbling" a can as they would a soccer ball—down around a chair and back.

• **Can the Penny.** Another relay race, where players put a penny between their knees, waddle across the room to an empty can, drop the penny in the can using only their knees, and return to their team.

• **One-Hand Can Wrap.** One contestant from each team must gift wrap a can using only one hand (the other hand remains behind the back). Award points for the best job.

• **Can Rolling.** Each member of a team gets one chance to roll a can toward a target, which is simply a small square of masking tape on the floor. The team wins a point for each can that rolls in the square and remains there.

• **Fetch the Can.** Put all the cans at one end of the room. Have players line up relay style and race down one at a time to bring a can back to their team. The team that has fetched the most in two minutes is the winner (only one can must be carried at a time).

Any number of games can be adapted to utilize the cans your group brings in. It's a great way to turn food collection into fun! *Terry O. Martinson*

SERVICE

THANKSGIVING OUTREACH

Share this holiday with the elderly, solitary shut-ins—the ones who rarely get out of their homes or apartments.

Design a script like the one on page 91X to steer your teenagers through introductory telephone conversations with the shut-ins. Make sure all orders are in before the meal day. The meal preparation itself can be a meaningful happening—just have plenty of hydrogen peroxide and bandages handy. While some kids cook, others can organize delivery routes. Send them out in pairs.

At the homes use the Thanksgiving survey (at the end of the script), more as a conversation starter than to get specific answers. Leave at each home your own version of the "Happy Thanksgiving!" sheet (see page 92), as well as a Thanksgiving card made by your church's elementary children.

After all your youths have returned, dine on the leftovers for your own Thanksgiving feast, then have a quiet time for reflection on the day's experiences. Follow up with a phone call, a card, and another visit at Christmas with teen-made gifts! *David Washburn*

THANKSGIVING OUTREACH

Telephone Order Form and Script
Return to youth director by next Wednesday

Name _____

Address _____

Phone _____

Directions to house (if needed):

1. Identify yourself and the purpose of this phone call:

    Hello. My name is _____. I'm calling you on behalf of First Church Youth Group in Brockport. We are planning a Thanksgiving meal for Saturday, Nov. 20. We would like to bring you a part of our Thanksgiving meal to share with you. It is our way of reaching out in the name of Jesus. Would you be willing to have us bring a Thanksgiving meal to you next Saturday?

2. Explain the meal and choices:
    • Light or dark meat?
    • Gravy or margarine on whipped potatoes?
    • Stuffing?
    • Cranberry slice?
    • Corn or peas?
    • Roll? With margarine?
    • Milk, coffee, or tea?
    • Dessert: cookies made by our King's Kids (3rd to 5th graders)
    Recite their order to be certain you have their correct choices.

3. Specify time for delivery (circle their choice).
    Which time will be best for you, 5:00-5:30 or 5:30-6:00?

4. Directions to house (if needed, write them at top of sheet)
    We are starting from First Church. Can you give me directions to your house?

5. Summary:
    Wow! This is great! Thank you! Let me just verify some information:
    The date is Saturday, Nov. 20.
    The time is—(whatever you arranged).
    The purpose of this is to share our Thanksgiving meal with you on behalf of our youth group.
        How does this sound to you? (Check to be sure date and time are correct.)
        Super! Thank you. It's been nice talking with you. God bless.

First Church Youth Ministry

November 20

Happy Thanksgiving!

We are thankful that we live in a country where we are free. We are thankful for you and that you allowed us to share our meal with you. We are thankful for the Lord Jesus Christ, who continues to teach us that we are loved and forgiven and, therefore, lovable. May Jesus in us reach out and touch you tonight.

If we teens can be of assistance to you in any way, please call on us through our youth minister (below).

Be well, be at peace in Jesus, and have a blessed Thanksgiving.

Love in Christ,

Reality Group (grades 11-12)
Youth Group (grades 9-10)
King's Kids (grades 3-5)

First Church Youth Ministry

November 20

Happy Thanksgiving!

We are thankful that we live in a country where we are free. We are thankful for you and that you allowed us to share our meal with you. We are thankful for the Lord Jesus Christ, who continues to teach us that we are loved and forgiven and, therefore, lovable. May Jesus in us reach out and touch you tonight.

If we teens can be of assistance to you in any way, please call on us through our youth minister (below).

Be well, be at peace in Jesus, and have a blessed Thanksgiving.

Love in Christ,

Reality Group (grades 11-12)
Youth Group (grades 9-10)
King's Kids (grades 3-5)

CHRISTMAS &
ADVENT

Consider these pages your one-stop Christmas programming center. You'll find everything you need for the merriest season ever— goofy games, crazy carols, outrageous outings, and silly skits to fill even the biggest Christmas stocking. And, of course, Christmasy meetings, Bible lessons, and service projects to help your kids focus on the real reason for the season.

MIXER

SANTA'S HELPERS

This is an easy game requiring little advance preparation and only paper and pencil. Announce to your group: "There has been a computer breakdown at the North Pole. Santa has lost everybody's Christmas list. He called wanting your help."

Distribute paper and pencils. On a signal, each person is to seat another person on his or her lap and ask what that person wants for Christmas. Their names and requests are written down for Santa's computers. This continues as each one scrambles to get another person to sit on the lap and make a request.

The one with the longest list at the end of five minutes is declared the winner.

To make the game more difficult, do not allow a person to make the same request twice. Encourage them to ask for crazy things, too. Another variation is to require name, address, and phone numbers on the gift lists. This is a sneaky way to build your mailing list. *Dave Schultz*

MIXER

CHRISTMAS MANIA

Use the ice breaker on page 96 at a Christmas season meeting. You may want to limit the number of times an individual can be used to fill in a space. *Rick Cornfield*

MIXER

CHRISTMAS CONFUSION

This is a great crowd breaker for parties or socials. Simply give everyone in your group a copy of the instructions on page 97, then read them aloud to make sure the group understands them. The object is to finish all the instructions correctly before anyone else. The first one finished can receive a prize of some kind. The instructions can be completed in whatever order you want. *Mark and Joanne Parson*

CHRISTMAS MANIA

- Find three people who have kissed someone under the mistletoe.
- Get three people together. Sing one verse or chorus of a Christmas carol.
- Find two people who are finished Christmas shopping.
- Find someone who hasn't started Christmas shopping yet.
- Find someone who can name all of Santa's reindeer.
- Find someone who has a December birthday.
- Find three people you don't know. Write down their names and what they want for Christmas.
- Find someone who has gotten coal in his/her stocking at any point in life.
- Find two people who don't want a white Christmas.
- Find someone who hasn't gotten his/her Christmas tree up yet or is not putting one up.
- Find someone who has a manger scene inside his/her home.
  - Find someone who is finished baking Christmas cookies.
  - Get five people together. Sing "We Wish you a Merry Christmas." Put their names below.

CHRISTMAS CONFUSION

1. Get five autographs on the back of this sheet (first, middle, and last names).

2. Find three other people and sing, "We Wish You a Merry Christmas" together as loudly as you can. Then initial each other's papers here:

   _____ _____ _____

3. Tell someone the names of three of Santa's reindeer. Then have that person initial here: _____

4. Pick out your favorite ornament on the Christmas tree. Give someone else a 15-second speech on why you like that particular ornament. Then have that person initial here: _____

5. You are Ebenezer Scrooge. Find someone and ask them to wish you a Merry Christmas. When they do, say, "Bah! Humbug!" 10 times while jumping up and down. Then have that person initial here: _____

6. Leapfrog over someone wearing red or green. Then have them initial here:

   _____

7. Find someone of the opposite sex and have them whistle one verse of "Away in a Manger" to you. Then have that person initial here: _____

CHRISTMESS JUMBLE

Here's a Christmas party game that can create a lot of enjoyable confusion. Everyone gets a list like the one shown on page 99, and then the race is on to see who can complete all nine items first. *Jay Firebaugh*

GET-ACQUAINTED CHRISTMAS TREE

For this mixer, make copies of a Christmas tree similar to ours (see page 100), with a variety of descriptive statements on each ornament. Kids must find other kids in the room who fit the descriptions and get their signatures on the appropriate ornaments. Distribute pens in various colors so the Christmas trees look more colorful when they are signed.
Tim Smith

CHRISTMAS BALLOON POP

Write the titles of a few Christmas carols on small slips of paper—several slips for each title. Place one slip inside each of a number of red or green balloons and distribute them to the group. Have them blow up the balloons and tie the ends. As you begin playing music, they must hit the balloons up into the air and keep them there. When the music stops, each person grabs a balloon, pops it, and retrieves the slip of paper inside. They must then sing the carol written on their slip of paper while finding everyone else in the room singing the same song. *Jim Holst*

MUSICAL GIFT UNWRAP

Have everyone sit in a circle. Wrap a gift ahead of time with a great deal of paper, tape, string, ribbon, and whatever you can put on it to make it as difficult as possible to unwrap. Then give the gift to someone in the circle and start the music (Christmas music, of course).

As the music plays, the gift is handed around the circle from person to person until the music stops. Whoever has the gift when the music stops tries to unwrap it as fast as possible, until the music starts again, and then the gift must continue on around the circle. Each time the music stops, someone gets to try to unwrap it, so that the gift is being unwrapped a little at a time. (Try to make the time that each person is unwrapping the gift short enough that they don't get very far.) As soon as someone succeeds in totally unwrapping the gift, that person is awarded the gift as a prize.

HUM A CAROL

Here is a creative way to form teams. As each person arrives, whisper the title of one of four Christmas carols to him or her. After everyone has been assigned a carol, everyone starts humming and mingling to find someone humming the same carol. Eventually, you have four groups humming the carol. No words are allowed; only humming. You can choose as many or as few carols as you wish, depending on the size of your group. A great way to break the ice. This can also be used for other holidays. *Judy Madtes*

CHRISTMAS MAD LIB

On page 101 is a mad lib that is great at Christmastime. Simply ask the group to furnish you with appropriate words to fill in the blanks in the story. To do this, don't let the group see the story (or even know what it is about) until all the words are in. Ask for the wildest words they can think of. For example, if you ask for a noun, the group should come up with the funniest things that they can, like: belly button, manhole cover, outhouse, snail bait, belch, etc. Be selective as the words are submitted, and fill in the blanks with the good ones. Then read the entire Mad Lib back to the group for a lot of laughs.

CHRISTMESS JUMBLE

- Find two other people born in your same group of months by making your "group sound:"
  - **Jan., Feb., Mar.** Santa Group: "Ho, ho, ho"
  - **Apr., May, June** Bing Crosby Group: Sing "I'm Dreaming of a White Christmas"
  - **July, Aug., Sept.** Little Kids Group: Yell "I want my Toobers & Zots!"
  - **Oct., Nov., Dec.** Scrooge Group: "Bah, humbug!"

- Once you've formed your group of three, identify 10 fun things to do in the snow. Have someone in the group initial here:_____

- Leave your group, find a partner from somewhere else in the room, and play Down the Chimney. One of you holds your arms out in a circle in front of you while the other one goes through the circle from the top and comes out at the bottom. Have partner initial here:_____

- Locate someone else who doesn't like eggnog and have him or her initial here:_____

- Get together with two other new people and yell three times in unison, "What are those green things they put in fruitcake?" Have someone from your group who thinks he knows initial here:_____

- Find a new partner and go caroling. Sing "Joy to the World" all the way through. Have your partner initial here:_____

- Find three new teammates. Three of your teammates clumps together and pretends to be a tree while the fourth player runs around the tree four times pretending to decorate it. Have one teammate initial here:_____

- Find a partner who knows the names of at least four of Santa's reindeer. Have partner initial here:_____

Get-Acquainted Christmas Tree

Have someone sign the ornament beside the statement that describes him or her.
Complete this as quickly as you can. Each person can sign only two ornaments.

SOMEONE...

Who is wearing blue shoes

Who plays with dolls

Who uses Scope

Who plays the trumpet

Who has more than
two earrings

With curly hair

Who was born in the
same state you were

With an unusual
last name

With green on

With red hair

With a dog that has a
funny name

th freckles

With
blue
eyes

Who uses your brand
of toothpaste

Rudolph, the Red-Nosed Reindeer

(sing this one to the group…)

Rudolph the _____ (adj.)-nosed _____ (noun)

Had a very _____ (adj.) nose.

And if you ever _____ (verb) it

You would really say it glows.

All of the other _____ (noun),

Used to _____ (verb) and call him _____ (noun)

They never let _____ (adj.) games.

Then one _____ (adj.) Christmas Eve,

Santa _____ (verb) to say,

Rudolph, with your _____ (noun) so _____ (adj.)

Won't you _____ (verb) my _____ (noun) tonight?

Then how the reindeer _____ (verb)-ed him

As they _____ (verb)-ed out with

_____ (noun),

Rudolph, the _____ (adj.)-

nosed reindeer,

You'll go down in _____ (noun).

CHRISTMAS POEM MAD LIB

The idea on page 103 can be used with good results at a Christmas party or any event during Christmas season. Announce to the group that you are in the process of writing a Christmas poem but need help coming up with some key words. You then ask the group to contribute the needed words as you call out the parts of speech, etc., as indicated by each blank in the poem. Ask the group to be as creative and as wild as they can be as they think of words, and you write the best ones in the spaces. Don't let the group know the context of the words; in other words, don't read any of the poem until all your words are contributed by the group. When all the spaces are filled, read the entire poem to the group and the results are hilarious. *Bill Chaney*

LETTER-TO-SANTA MAD LIB

Have the group provide a word to fit each category listed next to the blanks in the Mad Lib on page 104, then read the story aloud for a hilarious letter to Santa. *Carol Abell*

'TWAS THE NIGHT BEFORE CHRISTMAS

Here's a good icebreaker for your next Christmas activity. Go around the room with each person taking a turn. Each person must recite the next consecutive couplet of the poem "Twas the Night Before Christmas." For example:
PERSON 1: "Twas the night before Christmas, And all through the house…"
PERSON 2: "Not a creature was stirring, Not even a mouse."

Keep it going until someone makes a mistake. The person who goofs must stand and lead everyone in one verse of a Christmas carol. Then the missed line is read, and you go on to the next person. Go around the group as many times as it takes to complete the poem, but carol verses may not be repeated. Carols may be repeated as long as a different verse is used. *Scott Davis*

CHRISTMAS CAROL MUSICAL CHAIRS

List the title of every well-known Christmas carol you can think of (one per small slip of paper), including ones such as "Jingle Bells" and "Here Comes Santa Claus." For larger groups, use some carols more than once. Fold and place each slip in a balloon, inflate the balloon, and tie it off.

Then start the game. Players sit in a circle and, to the strains of Christmas music, pass a balloon around. When the music stops, the person holding the balloon must burst it, sing the chorus or first verse of the carol title that is printed on the slip, and then move out of the circle. The music starts up again, a new balloon is passed, and players are gradually eliminated. A little Christmas gift is appropriate for the winner. *Tommy Baker*

CHRISTMAS CAROL MUSICAL CHARADES

List Christmas carols on slips of paper and put them in balloons again. Play as Christmas Carol Musical Chairs—except that after the victim bursts the balloon and reads the carol, he must act out the title, charade fashion. After each round, the charader and the one who first guesses the correct name of the carol both sit out, and play continues with two fewer players each round. *Tommy Baker*

CHRISTMAS DAFFYNITIONS

Prepare a written list of Christmas items and provide one copy, along with a pencil, to each player. Explain that players are to create original definitions for each item on the sheet. Beware! Some of the definitions you'll hear will be pretty wacky. We've heard "blizzard buns" (*snowman*), "a toilet decoration you don't want to sit on long" (*wreath*), and "Ivana Trump's lawyer" (*Santa Claus*). Award points or prizes for the most ludicrously appropriate definitions. *Greg Fiebig*

A CHRISTMAS POEM

'Twas the noun_____ before Christmas and all through the *noun*_____,

Not a creature was stirring, not even a *noun*_____.

The *plural noun*_____ were hung by the *noun*_____ with care,

In hopes that *proper name of a person or creature*_____ would soon be *adjective*_____.

The *plural noun*_____ were nestled all snug in their *plural noun*_____,

While visions of *plural noun*_____ danced in their *noun*_____.

And Mom in her *noun*_____ and I in my *noun*_____,

Had just settled down for a *adjective*_____ winter's *noun*_____.

When out on the *noun*_____ there arose such a clatter,

I *verb*_____ from my *noun*_____ to see what was the matter.

Away to the *noun*_____, I *verb*_____ -ed like a flash,

Tore open the *noun*_____ and threw up the *noun*_____.

When what to my wondering *part of the human anatomy*_____ should appear,

But a *adjective*_____ sleigh and a *number*_____ *adjective*_____ reindeer.

With a little old driver, so lively and *adjective*_____,

I knew in a moment it must be *name of a person in the room*_____.

More rapid than *noun*_____, the *noun*_____ they came,

And he *verb*_____-ed and *verb*_____-ed and called them by name:

On *proper name of a person or creature*_____ and *another proper name*_____,

On *another proper name*_____ and *another proper name*_____.

On *another proper name*_____ and *another proper name*_____.

and *another proper name*_____ and *another proper name*_____.

But I heard him *verb*_____ as he drove out of sight,

"*adjective*_____ Christmas to all, and to all a good *noun*_____!"

LETTER TO SANTA

Dear Santa,
My name is _____ (famous person or someone in room) and I am _____ (number) years old. I live in _____ (geographic location). For Christmas, I would like a big, fuzzy, stuffed _____ (noun) and a cute little wind-up _____ (noun). I would also like a baby doll who, when you pull the string, can _____ (verb). I will need a new _____ (color)/(article of clothing) because mine is worn out. Also, could you bring me a _____ (animal) fur coat? My stocking will by hung by the _____ (piece of furniture) in the _____ (room in a house). Please put a _____ (large noun) in it. My brother wants a _____ (noun). He's real _____ (adjective). By the way, don't go to _____ (person in room)'s house because _____ (he/she) broke my _____ (noun) and pinched my _____ (part of body). I left some _____ (type of food) for you to eat, even though you already weigh _____ (number) pounds. I wonder how you and your sleigh can be pulled by just eight tiny _____ (animal). By the way, is it true that Rudolph has a shiny red _____ (part of body) to guide you through the night? Our roof is not too big, so I hope your _____ _____ _____ (adjective)/(color)/(type of vehicle) can land on it. My favorite Christmas carol is _____ (non-Christmas song). I also like "Deck the Halls With Boughs of _____ (type of plant)." Well, Santa, it's been nice sitting on your _____ (part of body), but I have to go now and help my mother wrap the _____ (noun) she bought Dad for Christmas. I'll see you again next _____ (holiday).P.S. I like the way you say "Ho, Ho, Ho" and how your stomach wiggles like a bowl full of _____ (type of fruit).

CHRISTMAS SCATTERGORIES

Using Scattergories rules, have teams work from a homemade game sheet that lists Christmas categories—Christmas goody, Christmas character, Christmas decoration, Christmas tradition, Christmas song, popular toy to give, etc.

Prepare enough sheets for several rounds of play. Give each player one game sheet and a pencil. In accordance with the rules of Scattergories, choose what letters of the alphabet you'll use by using a word—*Christmas, joy, noel*—or by a more random selection (be creative). The object of the game is to see which player or team can come up with the most answers that begin with the letter of the alphabet selected.

For example, if you choose to use the letters in the word *stable*, then the first round of answers can include Santa Claus (a Christmas character), sugar cookies (a Christmas goody), "Silent Night" (a Christmas song), snowflake (a Christmas decoration), stocking (a Christmas tradition), sledding (something to do at Christmas), and so on. For the next round, think of words in those categories that begin with T, etc.

Points are scored for every word that was not chosen by another player or team. In other words, if more than one player writes "Santa Claus," then no one gets any points for it. To earn points players must write down words or phrases that no one else has written down. *Greg Fiebig*

CHRISTMAS FAMILY FEUD

This game is based on the "Family Feud" television show and has a Christmas flavor.

First prepare a short survey, similar to the one below. Give the survey to one of your adult Sunday school classes or to the entire church if you can. Have people write in anything that will correctly answer each question. After this has been done, retrieve all the completed surveys and tally the results. Find out the top five answers for each question.

After you have the results, the game is ready for the youth group. Divide into teams (as on "Family Feud"). Flip a coin to determine which team goes

first. The first question is then read to the team. The team decides on an answer and tells you what it is. If the team chooses the number 1 answer (according to the survey results), it gets 50 points; if it chooses the number 2 answer, it gets 40 points; if it gets the number 3 answer, it gets 30 points; and so on. Each team gets one guess at a time, and then the other team gets a try. In other words, the first team might guess the number 2 answer on its first try, which would then allow the other team to guess the number 1 answer and collect the 50 points. Any guess that isn't one of the top five answers can be a loss of 10 points. If all the points available on one question have not been won by either team after five guesses by each team, then go on to the next question. It's a lot of fun with a lot of tension.

Here are some sample questions for your survey:
• Name something you hang on a Christmas tree.
• Name a Christmas carol.
• Name one of Santa's reindeer.
• A role someone might play in a Christmas pageant.
• The color of a Christmas tree light.
• The number of days you leave your tree up after Christmas.
• A book of the Bible that tells you about Christ's birth.
• How old were you when you found out there was no Santa Claus?
• Name a Christmas decoration other than a tree.
• Name something associated with Santa Claus.
• Name something people usually do on Christmas day.
• Name a food or beverage that is popular at Christmas.
• The shape of a typical Christmas cookie.
• How many weeks before Christmas should Christmas cards be put in the mail? *Tim Spilker*

CHRISTMAS SANTA CONTEST

Select three guys to sit in chairs and three girls to kneel in front of the guys. Blindfold the girls and give each of them a can of shaving cream. The object is for each girl to use the shaving cream to create a beard that resembles Santa's beard. The pair with the best-looking Santa wins. *Earl Burgess*

CHRISTMAS SONGS AND PHRASES

Give your teens the handout on page 107. Let them work in small groups to translate the illustrations into Christmas song titles and phrases. The team with the most right answers wins.

Here are the answers:
1. Away in a Manger
2. Chestnuts Roasting on an Open Fire
3. Let There be Peace (peas) on Earth
4. Happy Holidays (hollandaise)
5. The First Noel (snow L)
6. We Need (knead) a Little Christmas
7. Jingle Bell, Jingle Bell, Jingle Bell, Rock
8. Angels We Have Heard on High
9. Walking (wokking) in a Winter Wonderland
10. The Holly and the Ivy (IV)
11. Deck the Halls (hogs) with Boughs of Holly
12. Silent Night
13. Out of the East (yeast) They Came Riding
14. Santa, Bring My Baby Back to Me
15. I Heard (herd) the Bells on Christmas Day
16. It's Lovely Weather for a Sleigh Ride Together with You (ewe)
17. While Shepherds Watched (washed) Their Flocks (socks) by Night
18. I'm (lime) Dreaming of a White Christmas

John A. Coen

CHRISTMAS TRANSLATION

Add this game to your next Christmas party. The phrases below are unusually worded versions of well-known titles, lines, or descriptions of Christmas-y songs, sayings, or objects. Your teens must give the traditional version (which is provided for you in parentheses). *Maurice Gillard*

1. Three marine vessels on December 25 (I saw three ships on Christmas Day)
2. Tearing rapidly through crystalline precipitation (Dashing through the snow)
3. A bovine sounding-off (The cattle are lowing)
4. Au + an aromatic gum resin + a perfume (Gold, frankincense, myrrh)
5. Bambi's scarlet-snouted relative (Rudolph the red-nosed reindeer)
6. Who dat kid here? (What child is this?)
7. Some royal dudes from the east (We three kings of orient are)
8. Evergreen leaves with bright red berries and a climbing vine at maturity (The holly and the ivy when they are both full grown)
9. Do, re, mi, —, sol, — (x 8), ti, do (Fa-la-la-la-la-la-la-la-la)
10. A sheep's noise + what you do if you don't know the words to a song + an insect (Bah, humbug!)

A PLURALITY OF US — RELAY OUR DESIRES FOR YOUR MIRTH ON THE 25TH!

CHRISTMAS SONGS & PHRASES

11. Hey, you Judean hamlet (O little town of Bethlehem)

12. An ogre who robbed us of a December holiday (The Grinch who stole Christmas)

13. An evergreen with beautiful, protruding limbs (O Christmas tree, O Christmas tree, how lovely are your branches)

14. The drawing up of a written item-by-item document that is evaluated and reevaluated (He's making a list, checking it twice)

15. Ha ha ha! Fred! Jack! Mike! (All of the other reindeer used to laugh and call him names)

16. A glowing celestial object visible after twilight (A star, a star shining in the night)

17. An old crooner's fantasy (I'm dreaming of a white Christmas)

18. A celestial being uttered the original Christmas to ovine tenders (The first noel the angel did say was to certain poor shepherds)

19. A plurality of us relay our desires for your mirth on the twenty-fifth! (We wish you a merry Christmas!)

GAME

FROSTING THE SNOWMAN

Recruit some gung-ho volunteers for this delightfully messy Christmas party contest between teams. Here's what you need for each team: a tarp or plastic sheet to protect the floor (trash bags cut open work fine) and a large plastic trash bag. Then put these items in a paper bag: a tube of white cake icing, an empty cardboard toilet-paper roll, a box of raisins, two cookies, a carrot, and a roll of colored toilet paper.

The contest consists of each team frosting its own snowman. First, the icing is spread over the volunteer's entire face. Use raisins for a smile, the empty cardboard roll for a nose, the cookies for eyes, the carrot for a pipe, the toilet paper for a scarf—or just let the kids use their imagination. Give the teams three minutes or so, then let them vote for a winner.

Michael Capps

GAME

M&M'S CANDY GAME

With only a few bags of M&M's candies (reds and greens only, if available), a spoon for each team, and paper cups, put on a holiday relay.

Put one pound of candies for each six teens in one large bowl. Divide into teams of three to eight and line the teams up single file, seated on the floor. The first person in line should be about five feet away from the bowl of candies. The object is for each team to get the most green candies from the bowl.

The first person in line uses a spoon to scoop up one green candy, runs back to the team line, and dumps the candy in a paper cup. He then sits down where he started and hands the spoon to the second person in line. This continues until time is called.

To add interest, a leader may occasionally change the number of candies to collect, calling out "Three!" or a another number. After a few minutes, she may yell "Back to one!"

The players will be tempted to interfere with each other's spoons, scoop up more than one candy, or cheat in other ways. You can be strict about the rules, or you can allow some fudging, then lead into a lesson on cheating and how easily we become caught up in it.

Afterwards, feast on M&M's candies of any and all colors. *Chard Berndt*

GAME

REINDEER GAMES

Ever wonder what those reindeer games were that Rudolph was excluded from? This might have been one. This activity can be a prelude to an evening of reindeer games of your own making.

Make your reindeer this way: Before the party, get as many queen-sized panty hose as there will be teams; volunteers will wear them over their heads. Cut a hole out of the backside of each panty hose for the volunteer's face, then cut off both feet. Take lots of balloons to the party (they don't have to be large ones).

The volunteers from the teams slip the panty hose over their heads. Their teammates then have two or three minutes to inflate (only partially) as many balloons as they can and stuff them up the legs of the panty hose, thus creating "antlers." When time is called, teams tie off each leg (to secure the balloons inside the "antlers"). The winning reindeer is judged by number of balloons in its antlers as well as by the aesthetic shape of the antlers. Make the reindeer captains of their teams, then continue your own selection of games. *Michael Capps*

WHITE ELEPHANT GIFT AUCTION

Each person is to bring a white elephant gift, nicely wrapped. The gift can be of any value, but something from around the house that is no longer needed. Special gag type gifts can be purchased if a person cares to, but people should be encouraged not to spend a lot of money. All the gifts are then placed under the Christmas tree or displayed at the front of the room so that everyone can examine them. People can feel, shake, or examine the gifts in any way they want prior to the auction. Each person is given a package of assorted money which can be in the form of poker chips, Monopoly game money, etc. Everyone should get a little different amount.

You as the leader act as the auctioneer, and you auction off each gift to the highest bidder. You should make a big deal out of each gift, and make wild speculations as to what the gift might be. Everyone may bid on each gift, except the person who brought the gift (who must not reveal what he brought), and those who have already bought a gift. Whoever wins the bidding on a particular gift, gets the gift and must open it in front of everyone. He may either keep it or sell it to someone else for the price he paid for it or more. If he sells the gift to someone else, then he can bid again on another gift. Once a person has a gift, he cannot bid on another. He may, if he wants to, give his extra money to a friend who doesn't have a gift yet. That makes the value of the gifts keep rising.

SANTA CLAUS STUFF-AND-DRESS

Divide the group into two teams and have each team choose a Santa. The Santas then put on a pair of red long underwear (which can be dyed red if red ones are not available in your stores). The teams then blow up balloons and stuff them inside the longjohns, until they can get no more in. Balloons should also be stuffed in the arms and legs, so don't use balloons that are too big. Next, a beard is added to Santa with shaving cream (or Crazy Foam, whipped cream, etc.), and the team adds all the finishing touches, such as a hat, boots, bag of toys, and so on. Judge the Santas and award a prize for the most convincing, and then give a prize for the Santa with the most balloons stuffed inside his longjohns. Count them by carefully popping them with a pin.

ONE-ARMED GIFT WRAP

Have couples compete in this game. Each couple is given a box (with a gift inside) that they must wrap in the fastest time possible. All the necessary wrapping paper, ribbon, scissors, etc., are provided. The trick is that the boy may only use his left hand, and the girl may only use her right. Their other hands must be kept behind their backs. A time limit is set, and at the end of the given time (or as soon as one couple finishes), the best-wrapped package is given to the couple who wrapped it.

CHRISTMAS GIFT GUESS

By the time that most of us are grown, we have become experts at shaking and feeling Christmas packages to find out what is inside them. So, the object of this game is to test that skill and allow the kids to shake and feel for prizes. Wrap up about 10 packages and line them up in a row. Number them from one to 10, and give each person a piece of paper and pencil. The idea is to shake and feel each package, and then guess what is in each. Whoever comes the closest to guessing all 10 wins their choice of the 10 gifts, and so on down the line (with the tenth most accurate guess getting the last gift in order of preference). You might help the guessing along a bit by giving the kids a list of possible gifts that might be in the packages. If you have 10 gifts, then you might give them 20 answers, with the correct ones included, and they must match them up with the numbers on the packages.

Draw Santa Claus

Give each team a box of crayons and a large sheet of drawing paper. On "Go!" the first player of each team begins drawing good ol' St. Nick—but must stop 10 or 15 seconds later when the whistle blows and pass the paper and crayons to the next player, who must continue the drawing. This continues until all team members have contributed to the drawing. Best picture wins a prize for its team. *Terry O. Martinson*

Stocking Stuffers

In this game each team stuffs its sock with as many different kinds of objects as possible—a coin, comb,

brush, wallet, key chain, etc. The team with the most different objects wins. *Terry O. Martinson*

Christmas List

In five minutes teams think of words or names that are associated with Christmas; one team member writes them down. Sponsors' decisions on questionable words is final. The team with most words wins. (Or, like the word game Boggle, the team with the most unique words wins.) *Terry O. Martinson*

Santa, Reindeer, Christmas Tree

This game is an adaptation of the old Rock, Paper, Scissors game. It's great with larger groups of 20 or more kids. Here's how it works:

Have kids pair off and stand back to back. On a signal (a whistle, horn, or sleigh bells) kids face each other and take one of three positions:

1. Santa—They hold a hand straight out in front of them, as if they were cracking a whip to make their reindeer fly faster.

2. Reindeer—They hold their hands up over their heads like antlers.

3. Christmas tree—They hold their hands out to their side, in the shape of a tree that gets wider at the bottom.

In each case, one partner will win and the other will be sidelined, depending on which position they take. Santa always beats Reindeer (because he can whip the reindeer). Reindeer always beats Tree (since the Reindeer can eat the Tree). Tree always beats Santa (because the tree can fall on Santa and smash him). In the case of a tie, when partners take the same position, they are paired up with other players until there are only two people left for the championship round.

Make sure kids take their positions before they face each other. *Bruce Schlenke*

Santa's Delivery Race

For a simple Christmas game, divide the group into two teams (each team should have at least 10 players). Each group must arrange itself into Santa's delivery team: One person is Santa, two are Santa's seat, one person is the sleigh, four people carry the sleigh, and the rest are reindeer.

The reindeer line up in pairs, bend over forward, and place one arm over a partner's shoulder and the other arm over the head as antlers. One of these reindeer is Rudolph, who opens and closes one hand in front of his nose (a blinking nose). Immediately behind the deer, Santa is carried by the two people forming his seat with a first-aid carry. Behind them is the sleigh, who lies on his or her back, held aloft by four other people. On the sleigh are Santa's gifts, which can be anything you find on the premises: a cup of water, a ball, a tennis shoe, a hymnal. Each team should have the same number of gifts to deliver.

Now the fun begins. When you give the signal, each team must make deliveries to each of several houses spread out as far apart as possible in the play area. There should be as many houses as there are gifts in each sleigh. Someone stands at each house to receive the gift as Santa comes flying by, takes an item from the sleigh, and hands it to the lucky recipient. The first team to finish delivering a gift to every house is the winner. *Lee Strawhun*

GAME

WHEEL OF FORTUNE'S WACKY CHRISTMAS CAROLS

Play this game as you would *Wheel of Fortune* or Hangman. The phrases the players uncover, however, are revised titles of favorite Christmas songs.

Here are some examples:
• Bleached Yuletide (White Christmas)
• Frigid the Flaky Dude (Frosty the Snowman)
• Sterling Dingers (Silver Bells)
• Minuscule Male Percussionist (Little Drummer Boy)
Award a point for the individual or team who first

names the wacky title and two points to the first individual or team who discerns the title of the real song behind the wacky title. *Greg Fiebig*

GAME

REINDEER HUNT

Use this Christmas party game at your local mall or wherever there are lots of people (especially Christmas shoppers). Secure permission from mall management before attempting this activity.

Divide your group into small teams and give each team a list of Santa's nine reindeer: Dasher, Dancer, Prancer, Vixen, Comet, Cupid, Donner, Blitzen, and Rudolph.

Ahead of time, position nine volunteers somewhere in the mall who look like ordinary shoppers. Each of these people has been named as one of the reindeer. The object of this game is for the kids to find all nine reindeer and get their autographs on a sheet that has been given to each group. This means kids will be asking perfect strangers "Are you Dancer? Are you Prancer?" and so on. Rudolph can be disguised and worth extra points, or more difficult to find.

Use people the kids won't recognize right away. Depending on the location, you might want to make the game easier or tougher, adding clues, or somehow identifying your reindeer with a particular color of socks or a hat. *Tim Smith*

GAME

HUMAN CHRISTMAS TREE

Divide the group into teams and give each team plenty of Christmas tree decorations (lights, balls, tinsel, construction paper, garland, and a few unusual tree toppers) Each team decorates one of its members like a Christmas tree. Set a time limit (10 minutes maximum). Award prizes in various categories such as most creative tree or scariest. For safety, don't acutally plug in the lights.

GAME

CHRISTMAS WORD SEARCH

Here's a word search with a Christmas theme (see page 112). It will provide at least a few minutes of Christmas calm for your meeting opener or party. *Cary W. Sharpe*

Christmas Word Search

Instructions: Words may be spelled forwards or backwards, vertically or horizontally or diagonally. A letter may belong to more than one word.

```
Z X W S Y P G N I K C O T S A R I
G Y A D H T R I B Y P P A H P Q H
C V N F T D A W F S P M N S Y O T
H A G H Q E O B J T T A G T U R A
C J E S U S D W I S E M E N B C E
E D I H A B K B I A O J L E G O R
O R J E S T A R V N L L I S N O W
T K Q P E C H Y K T M I H E H R S
E X S H A C D F M A N G E R B N Z
L L A E Y W T L H U A H J P F A P
T G M R E I N D E E R T X N C M T
S S R D B S D F V Y Q S E V L E C
I E C S L O R A C F O A P M O N Z
M E N F W H O L I D A Y H R K T U
```

ANGEL
BOW
CANDY
CAROLS
ELVES
GIFT
HAPPY BIRTHDAY
HOLIDAY
JESUS

KING
LIGHTS
MANGER
MERRY CHRISTMAS
MISTLETOE
ORNAMENT
PRESENTS
REINDEER
SANTA

SHEPHERDS
SNOW
STAR
STOCKING
TOYS
TREE
WISEMEN
WREATH

CHRISTMAS CAROL TRIVIA

How well do the teens in your group know the details in Christmas carols? Divide your group into two teams, and award a point for each correct answer to the trivia questions found on page 114. If one team misses, the other can the steal the point with a correct answer. Set a time limit—10 to 20 seconds is probably enough.

After the game, *sing* them—the kids have probably hummed through them already trying to come up with the answers. *Greg Thompson*

CHRISTMAS QUIZZES

Your teenagers can show themselves how the peripherals push aside the real meaning of Christmas by taking two quizzes—the Cheater's Christmas Quiz and the Bible Christmas Quiz —and comparing their scores.

Here's how the object lesson works. Give everyone a copy of the Cheater's Christmas Quiz (on page 115) with instructions to trade answers with each other (only one trade with the same person, however, in order to keep things lively).

After laughing your way through the group grading of the quiz, award the highest scorer with something like a Christmas CD or cassette for children.

Then hand out copies of the Bible Christmas Quiz (page 116), this time instructing them to work individually. As you grade this quiz, list Bible references frequently on a chalkboard or overhead projector to support the answers.

Most students, of course, will score much lower on the Bible quiz than on the Cheater's quiz, demonstrating to themselves what you can remind them of in a discussion afterward about how easily Christ can get swallowed up by Christmas trivia. Follow the quizzes with a synoptic reading of the Nativity from Scripture and group prayer.

Here are the answers to Cheater's Christmas Quiz:
1. Dasher, Dancer, Prancer, Vixen, Comet, Cupid, Donner, Blitzen, Rudolph
2. The traffic cop
3. The North Pole

4. Elves
5. Foggy
6. Holly
7. "That old silk hat"
8. Poker
9. "To hear sleigh bells in the snow"
10. Bobtail (as in "bells on Bobtail ring...")

Here are the answers to Bible Christmas Quiz:
1. a
2. d (The Bible never says.)
3. c
4. d ("Wise men" did, the Bible says.)
5. d (The Bible says nothing about the angels *singing* anything—though they *said*, "Glory to God in the highest...")
6. d (They came to Jesus' house, not his manger.)
7. c
8. c
9. b
10. a

Randy D. Nichols

CHRISTMAS I.Q. TEST

Next Christmas give the quiz beginning on page 117 to your youths to determine how much they really know about the Bible's most popular story. The results may be a little embarrassing but should lead to a better understanding of the events surrounding Christ's birth. *Gregg Selander*

Answers
1. False. Not until the 4th century did it settle on the 25th. Other dates were accepted before then.
2. a. See Luke 2:3, 4.
3. f. The Bible doesn't say.
4. False. See Matthew 1:18.
5. False. See Luke 2:5.
6. True. See Matthew 1:25.
7. e. No word about the innkeeper. See Luke 2:7.
8. e. No word about it. See Luke 2:7.
9. c.
10. f. The Bible doesn't specify.
11. e. The wise men did (they were not kings). See Matthew 2:2.
12. a. See Luke 2:9.
13. f. See Luke 2:12.

Christmas Carol Trivia

1. In the carol "The Twelve Days of Christmas," what is given on the eighth day? (eight maids-a-milking)

2. In "Jingle Bells," where are the bells? (bells on bobtail ring)

3. When we "Deck the Halls," who is to hail the new year? (ye lads and lasses)

4. What is given on the 11th day of Christmas? (11 pipers piping)

5. When the Lord comes in "Joy to the World," who repeats the sounding joy? (fields and floods, rocks, hills, and plains)

6. At what time of day was Jesus born, according to "O Come, All Ye Faithful"? (this happy morning)

7. What kind of sleep did the people of "O Little Town of Bethlehem" experience? (deep and dreamless)

8. According to "Away in a Manger," who is lowing? (cattle)

9. Who is blessed in the third verse of "Away in a Manger"? (all the dear children)

10. Who kept time for the "Little Drummer Boy"? (the ox and lamb)

11. What are we going to tell on the mountain? (that Jesus Christ is born)

12. Name three songs with the word "Christmas" in the title. ("The Twelve Days of Christmas," "Have Yourself a Merry Little Christmas," "Christmas Is the Best Time of the Year," "The Christmas Song," "We Wish You a Merry Christmas," etc.)

13. Name two songs with the word bell in the title. ("Jingle Bells," "Silver Bells," "I Heard the Bells on Christmas Day," etc.)

14. How many times do you "fa la la la la" in one verse of "Deck the Halls"? (four)

15. In the song "Up on the Housetop," who came down the chimney? (good St. Nick)

16. What sound does the drum make in "Little Drummer Boy"? (pa rum pa pum pum)

17. What is the last line in the first verse of "Silent Night"? (sleep in heavenly peace)

18. Why should you watch out, not cry, and not pout? (Santa Claus is coming to town)

19. What was the weather like one Christmas Eve when Santa asked Rudolph to guide his sleigh? (foggy)

20. Who said the "First Noel"? (the angel)

21. Silver bells, silver bells, it's Christmas time in the _____. (city)

22. "I'm Dreaming of a _____ Christmas." (white)

23. All I want for Christmas is _____. (my two front teeth)

24. How many ships were seen on Christmas Day? (three)

25. In "Have Yourself a Merry Little Christmas," what is "out of sight"? (your troubles)

CHEATER'S CHRISTMAS QUIZ

(You may trade answers with others—but no more than one trade with the same person.)

1. Name Santa's nine reindeer.
2. To whom did the kids lead Frosty the Snowman down the streets of town?
3. Where does Santa Claus live?
4. What kind of people help Santa make toys?
5. What was the weather like on the night Rudolph the Red-Nosed Reindeer made his first Christmas flight?
6. With what kind of boughs do we deck the halls?
7. What article of clothing had the magic to enable Frosty the Snowman to begin dancing around?
8. From what kind of games did cowboys exclude Randolph the Bow-Legged Cowboy?
9. In the song "White Christmas," what do the children listen for?
10. What is the horse's name that pulls the sleigh in the song "Jingle Bells"?

BIBLE CHRISTMAS QUIZ

Do you know what the Bible actually says about Christmas? Check your Nativity I.Q. by taking this quiz individually. Circle the letter of the correct response.

1. Joseph was from
   a. Bethlehem
   b. Nazareth
   c. Jerusalem
   d. Egypt

2. How did Mary and Joseph travel to Bethlehem?
   a. camel
   b. donkey
   c. Chevy truck
   d. don't know

3. A manger is a
   a. barn
   b. stable
   c. feed trough
   d. disease dogs catch

4. Who saw the "star in the East"?
   a. shepherds
   b. three kings
   c. Brad Pitt
   d. none of these

5. What did the angels sing?
   a. "Glory to God in the highest..."
   b. "For unto us a child is born..."
   c. "Glory to the newborn King..."
   d. none of these

6. How many wise men came to see Jesus in the manger?
   a. 3
   b. 2
   c. 1
   d. 0

7. Who told Mary and Joseph to go to Bethlehem?
   a. the angel
   b. God
   c. Caesar Augustus
   d. King Herod

8. Why did Joseph take Jesus to Egypt?
   a. To show him the pyramids
   b. To be taxed
   c. Because he dreamed about it
   d. He never took Jesus there

9. What is frankincense?
   a. an oriental monster
   b. a precious perfume
   c. a precious fabric
   d. a precious metal

10. What is myrrh?
   a. a spice used in burials
   b. a soft metal
   c. an aftershave lotion
   d. a drink

CHRISTMAS I.Q. TEST

Read and answer each question in the order it appears. Circle the letter of the correct answer (or the word True or False). Guessing is permitted, cheating is not.

1. As long as Christmas has been celebrated, it has been on December 25th. (True or False)

2. Joseph was from...
a. Bethlehem.
b. Jerusalem.
c. Nazareth.
d. Egypt.
e. Minnesota.
f. None of the above.

3. How did Mary and Joseph travel to Bethlehem?
a. Camel
b. Donkey
c. Walked
d. Volkswagen
e. Joseph walked, Mary rode a donkey
f. Who knows?

4. Mary and Joseph were married when Mary become pregnant. (True or False)

5. Mary and Joseph were married when Jesus was born. (True or False)

6. Mary was a virgin when she delivered Jesus. (True or False)

7. What did the innkeeper tell Mary and Joseph?
a. "There is no room at the inn."
b. "I have a stable you can use."
c. "Come back after the Christmas rush and I should have some vacancies."
d. Both A and B.
e. None of the above.

8. Jesus was delivered in a...
a. Stable.
b. Manger.
c. Cave.
d. Barn.
e. Unknown.

9. A manger is a...
a. Stable for domestic animals.
b. Wooden hay storage bin.
c. Feeding trough.
d. Barn.

10. Which animals does the Bible say were present at Jesus' birth?
a. Cows, sheep, goats
b. Cows, donkeys, sheep
c. Sheep and goats only
d. Miscellaneous barnyard animals
e. Lions, tigers, elephants
f. None of the above

11. Who saw the "star in the east"?
a. Shepherds
b. Mary and Joseph
c. Three kings
d. Both A and C
e. None of the above

12. How many angels spoke to the shepherds?
a. One
b. Three
c. A "multitude"
d. None of the above

13. What "sign" did the angels tell the shepherds to look for?
a. "This way to baby Jesus."
b. A star over Bethlehem
c. A baby that doesn't cry
d. A house with a Christmas tree
e. A baby in a stable
f. None of the above

14. What did the angels say?
a. "Joy to the World, the Lord is Come"
b. "Alleluia"
c. "Unto us a child is born, unto us a son is given"
d. "Glory to God in the highest, etc."
e. "Glory to the Newborn King"
f. "My Sweet Lord"

15. What is a "heavenly host"?
a. The angel at the gate of heaven
b. The angel who invites people to heaven
c. The angel who serves drinks in heaven
d. An angel choir
e. An angel army
f. None of the above

16. There was snow that first Christmas...
a. Only in Bethlehem.
b. All over Israel.
c. Nowhere in Israel.
d. Somewhere in Israel.
e. Mary and Joseph only "dreamed" of a white Christmas.

17. The baby Jesus cried...
a. When the doctor slapped him on his behind.
b. When the little drummer boy started banging on his drum.
c. Just like other babies cry.
d. He never cried.

18. What is frankincense?
a. A precious metal
b. A precious fabric
c. A precious perfume
d. An eastern monster story
e. None of the above

19. What is myrrh?
a. An easily shaped metal
b. A spice used for burying people
c. A drink
d. After-shave lotion
e. None of the above

20. How many wise men came to see Jesus? (Write in the correct number.)_____

21. What does "wise men" refer to?
a. Men of the educated class
b. They were eastern kings
c. They were astrologers
d. They were smart enough to follow the star
e. They were "sages"

22. The wise men found Jesus in a...
a. Manger.
b. Stable.
c. House.
d. Holiday Inn.
e. Good mood.

23. The wise men stopped in Jerusalem...
a. To inform Herod about Jesus.
b. To find out where Jesus was.
c. To ask about the star that they saw.
d. For gas.
e. To buy presents for Jesus.

24. Where do we find the Christmas story in order to check up on all these ridiculous questions?
a. Matthew
b. Mark
c. Luke
d. John
e. All of the above
f. Only A and B
g. Only A and C
h. Only A, B, and C
i. Only X, Y, and Z
j. Aesops Fables

25. When Joseph and Mary found out that Mary was pregnant with Jesus, what happened?
a. They got married.
b. Joseph wanted to break the engagement.
c. Mary left town for three months.
d. An angel told them to go to Bethlehem.
e. Both A and D
f. Both B and C

26. Who told Mary and Joseph to go to Bethlehem?
a. The angel
b. Mary's mother
c. Herod
d. Caesar Augustus
e. Alexander the Great
f. No one told them to

27. Joseph took the baby Jesus to Egypt...
a. To show him the pyramids.
b. To teach him the wisdom of the pharaohs.
c. To put him in a basket in the reeds by the river.
d. Because he dreamed about it.
e. To be taxed.
f. Joseph did not take Jesus to Egypt.
g. None of the above.

28. I think this test was...
a. Super.
b. Great.
c. Fantastic.
d. All of the above.

14. d. See Luke 2:14.
15. e. Definition is an "army." See Living Bible also.
16. d. Mt. Hermon is snow covered.
17. c. We have no reason to believe he wouldn't.
18. c. By definition.
19. b. See John 19:39 or a dictionary.
20. No one knows. See Matthew 2:1.
21. c. See most any commentary. They were astrologers or "star gazers."
22. c. See Matthew 2:11.
23. b. See Matthew 2:1-2.
24. g. Mark begins with John the Baptist, John with "the Word."
25. f. See Matthew 1:19, Luke 1:39, 56.
26. d. See Luke 2:1, 4.
27. d. See Matthew 2:13.
28. d, of course.

CHRISTMAS CAMCORDER SCAVENGER HUNT

Divide your teens into small groups and send them out with camcorders (or Polaroids) cameras on a scavenger hunt at a local mall. Set a one-hour limit on the hunt, with a forfeiture of 1,000 points for every minute a team is late returning. Highest score wins. Here is the list of clips to take and the points they're worth.

• **Sending Pictures Home.** Take a picture of your whole group in a photo booth. *10,000 pts.*

• **All I Want for Christmas Is...** Take a group picture of everyone holding their favorite toys in the toy store. *15,000 pts.*

• **All Dressed Up for Christmas and No Place To Go.** Take a picture of your entire group at a gift-wrapping department. All group members must wear bows in their hair. *20,000 pts.*

• **Santa's Little Elves.** Take a picture of your entire group wearing either elves' stocking caps or Santa caps. *30,000 pts.*

• **Bundled Up for Christmas.** Take a picture of two of your group's members bundled up as much as possible. Get a sales clerk's verification of the number of items being worn. *2,500 pts. per item of clothing.*

• **O Tannenbaum.** Take a picture of your group in front of the tallest Christmas tree you can find in the mall. Pose your group as though you were caroling. (*1500 extra points for each additional person not from your group in the picture.*) *40,000 pts.*

• **Will You...?** Take this picture in a jewelry store or jewelry department: a young man proposing to a young lady, offering her a ring. (On his knees, *1000 extra points;* also *1000 points for each sales clerk* looking on in delight.) *45,000 pts.*

• **The Waiting?** Take this picture near a fitting room for women in a women's clothing store or department: Show all guys in your group sitting near the door to the fitting room. They should be buried under a huge mound of packages. The girls in the group should be enthusiastically posing with them in new outfits. Any additional men actually waiting for their spouses or girlfriends are worth *5000 points* each. *50,000 pts.*

119

Truly Tasteless Decoration Hunt

Take the first 45 minutes of your next Christmas party to conduct a scavenger hunt for the most tacky, gaudy, or tawdry Christmas decoration. You'll be amazed at the garish Christmas junk people are glad to get rid of. Then decorate the youth room and the group's Christmas tree with the riffraff for the duration of the party. *Michael Frisbee*

Scavenger Caroling

First, the rules of this Christmas combination:
• Upon arriving at a house, students must sing one Christmas carol before asking people for an item from their scavenger list.
• Carolers cannot stop at the home of a team member.
• Carolers should clearly identify themselves.
• A resident of each house needs to fill out the simple team sheet (a three-columned form: name of householder, song that was sung to him, and scavenger-hunt item handed over to the team).
• Teams must obey all laws and be back at church at a designated time. (Deduct points for each minute a team is late.)
• No more than one scavenger item can be obtained at any one house.
  And here are the items the teams must find:
• A one-square-foot piece of Christmas wrap with Santa Claus on it.
• A Christmas gift tag that has written on it, "From Santa."
• A youth group member who did not originally come to the meeting or party.
• A Santa's hat.
• A piece of Christmas candy.
• One foot each of green and red crepe paper.
• A Christmas bow.
• A box of McDonald's cookies, as evidence of having caroled there.
• An old Christmas card with a sleigh on it.
• A banner that says "Merry Christmas!"
• A red Christmas bulb.
• A cutting of mistletoe with white berries.
• Six Christmas cookies.
• A cutting of holly.
• A tinsel icicle. *John Wortinger*

Crazy Christmas Scavenger Hunt

This Christmas activity (see page 121) is a guaranteed hit for both small and large groups. Here are a few hints to make it more successful.
• Keep the details of the hunt secret.
• Send someone along to videotape the various groups out hunting. (Show the videos at a post-hunt social.)
• Send the groups to separate neighborhoods with well-defined boundaries.
• Depending upon the size of the group hunting, consider 30 to 45 minutes for the time limit.
Michael McKnight

Advent Treasure Hunt

This is a treasure hunt in which the goal is to find words that complete a sentence related to Advent. For example, the mystery sentence might be "The lion will lie down with the lamb." Any sentence will do. The clues are hidden in local merchants' shops. Since there are eight words in the sentence, eight stores are used. At each store, a new word in the sentence plus a new clue is found. There can be a different set of stores per team, though the sentence is the same for all. The clues and the sentence should be difficult enough to cause considerable brain-work. For example, the clue for the post office might be HELP STAMP OUT HARD CLUES. A clue for the plant store might be THIS GAME WILL GROW ON YOU. When the kids find the right store, the teams find a card which the obliging merchant places in plain sight. The word in the sentence and the next clue are on the card.

  The first team to complete the sentence by obtaining all the words and arranging them in the correct order is the winner. They phone in to hunt headquarters, and their time is recorded. The phone number to call can be on the last card (eliminating cheating by guessing the sentence).

  This can be used any time of the year, obviously, by simply changing the content of the sentence. It

CRAZY CHRISTMAS SCAVENGER HUNT

INSTRUCTIONS
- The object is to attempt to collect the items below in the given time limit.
- As you divide up to hunt, you must stay in groups of at least three.
- You cannot get more than one item at any house.
- Be careful out there—it's a crazy world.

GOT IT?

ITEMS TO BE COLLECTED

pine needle off a live Christmas tree

mail-order Christmas catalog

piece of fudge

candy cane

Christmas bow

Christmas card (used or new)

picture of a Christmas tree from a magazine

name tag (used on a present)

piece of mistletoe

hair off a Santa's beard

piece of green candle

Christmas sales ad from a newspaper

pine cone

ornament

recipe for egg nog

scrap piece of wrapping paper

Christmas-related postage stamp

recipe for fruitcake OR a piece of fruitcake

sprig of holly

pecan (in the shell)

poinsettia leaf

piece of white tissue paper

piece of red candle

spare Christmas tree bulb (could be burned out)

piece of peppermint stick candy

picture of Santa

Christmas sticker

paper cup of water from a Christmas tree

Christmas cookie

Ask someone under five years of age what Santa is bringing them—

Child's name: _____ Age: _____

_____   _____

_____   _____

should be done during the day (so stores will be open) and can be done on bikes or in a shopping mall. The benefits are many: cooperation and contact with the merchants, free advertising for them, the teamwork, the thoughts on Advent, plus a lot of fun. *Father David Baumann*

OUTING

CANDY CANE LANE

Choose a neighborhood in your area that is known for extravagant Christmas decorations. Take your group on a tour of the area, giving each person a judging sheet. Have judging categories for Most Creative," "Simple Beauty," "Best Use of a Theme," etc.

Meet back at church or a designated home for hot chocolate and Christmas goodies. Collect the judging sheets, tally the results and announce the winners.

You may want to return to the area to award the winners a small prize from your youth group—and maybe invite them to your church! *Theo Olson*

OUTING

HIGH-RISE HAYRIDE

Hayrides still can be done even if you live in the city! Use trucks and fill them with hay and kids. A flatbed tractor-trailer can hold 50 to 100 kids. Plan a route on not-so-busy streets and keep the speed down to 20 m.p.h. or less for safety. At Christmas, you can go caroling at high-rise apartments or condominiums, and people will come out on their bal-

conies to hear. It's a great way to spread a little Christmas cheer. *Bill Serjak*

TREASURE HUNT

LAST STAND CHRISTMAS TREE HUNT

Toward the end of the shopping season, but before Christmas day itself, when Christmas tree lots are pretty well picked over and the proprietors are desperate to get rid of the last few trees—then it's time for this Christmas party game.

Divide your group into teams of four or five and supply each team with a responsible driver and a few dollars. Give teams an hour time limit and these instructions: The winning teams are the ones with the saddest-looking tree and the cheapest tree. So each team must tour the local tree lots and find the most bedraggled tree possible—and then barter with the salesperson down to the lowest possible price.

Finally, the kids should keep their eyes open for "ornaments" they find along the way—pine cones, soda cans, paper cups, and other junk—that they'll use to decorate their trees when they arrive back at the party. Remember to bring several tree stands to the party. *David Shaw*

OUTING

SHOP 'TIL YOU DROP

Give each team a 10-dollar bill, then let them loose for a specified time to buy objects that are
• Green (like mistletoe)
• Smelly (like frankincense or myrrh)
• Wet (like melted snow)

- Red (like Santa's suit)
- Sticky (like a candy cane)
- Bright (like the star in the east)
- White (like Santa's long underwear)
- Wooden (like the Christ's manger)
- Hard (like Herod's heart)
- Soft (like Santa's belly)

   The rules are few:
- One item counts for only one category.
- Each item must be different (for example, no green bow and red bow).
- Only four of the objects may be food.
- Packaging doesn't count (for example, a green and red box doesn't count for something green and something red).
- Kids must bring receipts back for every item—in other words, they should shop in stores, not rummage through garbage cans.
- They should stay within street or mall boundaries that you announce at the beginning of the game.
- Players must shop in at least five different stores.

   Be creative in awarding prizes to teams that collected every item—a prize for the team that spent the least money, that purchased the most creative objects, the largest item, the smallest, etc. *Mark Taylor*

OUTING

SIGHTS AND SOUNDS OF CHRISTMAS

If most of your kids are city kids, the following Christmas activity could be very meaningful. Take the youth group to a farm or ranch where there is a barn or stable, perhaps similar to the nativity setting, and allow kids to imagine how Joseph and Mary must have felt, having to give birth to Jesus in such an environment. Perhaps the manger scene could be set up there and each young person could symbolically offer a gift to Jesus as the wise men did. Christmas carols and Scripture are appropriate for an effective worship experience.

OUTING

WORLD'S EARLIEST CHRISTMAS EVENT

Be the first next year to throw a Christmas event. While some would call it an "after-Christmas" affair,

bill it as the earliest—after all, you can claim, "Only 359 days 'til Christmas." Try these activities, for example—then add some of your own.

- **A Christmas Shopping Trip.** To catch those after-Christmas sales, visit a large mall. Buy cards, calendars, decorations, etc., that your group can use in the coming year.
- **Service Projects.** Many people take food and gifts to shut-ins at nursing homes and rest homes during the weeks preceding Christmas, but there's just as great a need to help these folks dispel the post-Christmas blues. Or you can conduct a Christmas cleanup project to help neighbors clear out all their holiday debris—boxes, wrappings, trees, etc.
- **Christmas Sights.** Since most decorations and lights remain up at least a week or two after Christmas, plan a half-day bus trip—meals included—to visit a building or park or community known for its extravagant ornamentation. Or stretch the day more and take in a holiday production at a little theater.

   Why an early Christmas event? Kids love to be the first to do something, and they'll enjoy the novelty of the idea. Also, crowds decrease dramatically after December 26. Finally, young people have calendars as crowded as adults' during the pre-Christmas rush but hardly anything to do between Christmas and the resumption of school. *Randy D. Nichols*

PARTY

BIRTHDAY PARTY FOR JESUS

During December have a birthday party for Jesus, complete with potluck meal, birthday cake, and wrapped presents. The gifts should be those that can be used around the church—Sunday school craft items, kitchen supplies, garbage bags, nursery games—as well as more expensive items. You may want to schedule the party so that elementary children can unwrap the gifts and take them to their proper places around church. *Cheryl Ehlers*

PARTY

GRINCH PARTY

Plan this year's Christmas party around the showing of the video version of "How the Grinch Stole Christmas," the modern classic by Dr. Seuss. Remind your group to come to the party costumed as characters from the story. Following is a game, refreshments, and even a devotional that relate to the Grinch theme.

• **Grinch Video.**
• **Grinch Refreshments.** Who Pudding, Who Hash, and Roast Beast.
• **The Grinch Quiz.** See page 125. Conduct this either orally or in writing; kids may team up or answer individually. Here are the answers to the Grinch Quiz:

1. *How the Grinch Stole Christmas*
2. Boris Karloff
3. Welcome to Who-ville
4. "Just north of Who-ville"
5. His heart was two sizes too small
6. Noise
7. Jing tinglers
8. Zoo Zitter Carzay
9. Lacrosse and croquet
10. Who pudding and roast beast
11. The people stand hand in hand and sing
12. 53 years
13. A curtain
14. Max
15. Bags and sacks
16. Stockings
17. Candy canes
18. Who Hash
19. Cindy Lou Who
20. No older than two
21. Because of a light on the tree that won't light on one side, he is taking it to his workshop to fix it and then return it
22. A quarter of dawn
23. Mount Crumpit
24. 10,000 feet
25. His heart grew three sizes
26. He found the strength of ten Grinches plus two, and he saved the stuff
27. Who Who
28. The Grinch

•**The Grinch Song.** Instruct the teams to write out all three verses to the Grinch Song from memory. (You should write down the lyrics for yourself against which to check the teams' efforts to recall them.)
•**Grinch Virtuosity.** Students now test their talent by composing a fourth verse to the Grinch Song—then by singing all four verses. Judge them for creativity of composition and vocal enthusiasm.
•**Grinch Tableau.** Team members choose a scene from the show that they recreate in a "freeze frame." They are judged (best to worst), and a Polaroid is taken of each entry.
•**Grinch Devotional.** Give a brief talk along the lines of The Grinch story. For example, Christmas is more than noise; the power of the true meaning of Christmas; community is made possible and meaningful through Christmas; Christmas makes a change in heart possible.

Jim Liebelt

SANTA'S BIRTHDAY PARTY

Around Christmastime plan a birthday party for someone in the youth group. (Depending on the person, it might be best to clue them about what you are doing.) Use a lot of publicity and include the fact that Santa will be appearing at the party with gifts for everyone. Each person who attends the party should bring a gift for the birthday person and one other gift.

Although the party is supposed to be a birthday party, do everything you can to emphasize Santa's appearance. Hang signs that say WELCOME SANTA, put the Christmas tree with gifts in a central location. The HAPPY BIRTHDAY signs and the cake should be small and off to the side.

At the party play some games and sing. While you are singing "Happy Birthday" to the birthday person, have Santa appear with surprises and gifts for everyone. Make a big deal out of Santa's appearance with picture taking and kids sitting on Santa's lap.

After Santa leaves and there is a pause, *then* remember whose party it is and have the birthday person open their gifts.

At the end of the get-together, discuss what took place. What happened to the birthday person? How did they feel when Santa got all the attention? Would you want to be the one for whom the party was given? *Dave Gilliam*

The Grinch Quiz

1. What is the title of the Grinch Christmas special?

2. What famous actor narrated the special and whose voice played the part of the Grinch?

3. When you come into the town, you pass under an arch, on which are inscribed what words?

4. According to the narrator, where did the Grinch live?

5. Why did the Grinch hate Christmas?

6. What was it about Christmas that the Grinch especially disliked?

7. In their Christmas celebration, the Whos dance with what tied onto their heels?

8. Name a noisy Who game.

9. This game is said to be a "roller skate type" of what other games?

10. What do the Whos eat at their Christmas feast?

11. What did the Grinch hate most about Christmas?

12. How long did the Grinch put up with the Whos' Christmas celebrations?

13. From what did the Grinch make his "Santy Claus" hat and coat?

14. What is the name of the Grinch's dog?

15. Before the Grinch and his dog headed for town, what did the Grinch load his sleigh with?

16. What was the first item the Grinch stole from the Whos' houses?

17. What did the Grinch steal from the hands of the sleeping Who children?

18. The Grinch took the last can of what out of the Who's refrigerator?

19. What's the name of the little Who girl who surprised the Grinch?

20. How old is she?

21. Give the Grinch's excuse for taking the Who's Christmas tree.

22. What time was the Grinch finished with packing up all of the town's Christmas stuff?

23. Name the mountain the Grinch ascended to dump all the stuff.

24. How tall is the mountain?

25. What happened to the Grinch while he was trying to save the stuff from falling off the mountain?

26. When the Grinch finally understood the true meaning of Christmas, what happened to him?

27. The Grinch announced his return to the town by playing what on his trumpet?

28. Who carved the Roast Beast at the Whos' feast?

CHRISTMAS COSTUME PARTY

A unique touch for a Christmas party or program would be to have everyone come dressed as a character or thing that is associated with Christmas or the Christmas story. Possibilities might include any of the biblical characters like Mary and Joseph, the wise men, the innkeeper, the shepherds, Herod, and so forth. Or someone could dress like one of the animals, the star of Bethlehem, an angel—the list could go on and on. It could also be expanded to include Christmas characters such as Santa, Mrs. Santa, Rudolph, Frosty the Snowman, a Christmas package, a toy soldier, a doll, or even a Christmas tree.

Discuss what Christmas means to each person from the perspective of the person or thing kids are portraying. *Susan Norman*

CHRISTMAS IN JULY

This really goes over because it's so crazy. Hold a full-fledged Christmas party in July or August (anytime during the summer) complete with Christmas decorations, singing Christmas carols, and all the rest. If it's done properly, a real Christmastime spirit can be created. Have everyone bring a gift to exchange. Surprisingly enough, the Christmas story makes a deeper impact at this time of the year when it is separated from all the hustle and bustle of the usual holiday season. *Andy Stimer*

CHRISTMAS MISSIONARY DINNER

Have your youth group select some missionaries abroad whom the church supports for this special Christmas activity. The group should get to know the missionaries they have chosen by corresponding with them and by reading their newsletters. Then begin making plans for a Missionary Dinner sometime in November or early December. There should be Christmas decorations and pictures or letters from the missionaries posted so that people can see them.

The youth group cooks and serves the meal, which might include dishes from the country where the missionaries are serving. Adults of the church are invited to the dinner. Following a talent show by the youth and a presentation on the work being done by the missionaries, the people are asked to give a free-will offering. The offering can then be sent to the missionaries as a 'Christmas bonus,' something they might not ordinarily get. It's a good idea to hold this event as early as possible (even early November) so the money will reach them before Christmas. *Cherie Friend*

CHRISTMAS PIZZA

Your teenagers can relish Christmas pizza during one of your December meetings or parties. A week or so ahead of time, ask your local pizza parlor to add green food coloring to the dough (or add it yourself if you make your own pizza), and voilà—green and red pizza!

Your kids may take the celebration home with them, however, for the green dough sometimes turns their teeth green, too—temporarily, that is. *Dave Mahoney*

CAROL PIX

Spruce up your Christmas caroling by equipping each team of carolers with a video camcorder (or a Polaroid) and a church directory. Their instructions: to photograph themselves singing several Christmas carols, each in an especially appropriate part of a church member's house.

Here's a list to spur your creativity:
• "Deck the Halls" (hallway)
• "Silent Night" (bedroom)
• "Away in a Manger" (kitchen—i.e., a manger is a feeding trough)
"Christmas Tree" (living room—or wherever the tree is)
• "I Saw Three Ships" (bathtub)
• "Angels We Have Heard on High" (attic)
• "Silver Bells" (doorbell)
• "What Child Is This?" (nursery)
• "We Three Kings" (driveway— "...travel afar...")
• "Jingle Bells" (garage, family car—"...it is to ride...")
• "The Twelve Days of Christmas" (porch swing,

love seat— "...my true love sent to me...")
- "Frosty the Snowman" (deep freeze)
- "Rudolph the Red-Nosed Reindeer" (den, family room— "...join in any reindeer games...")
- "It Came upon the Midnight Clear" (clock, with hands at midnight)

Award bonus points for including family members in the videos or photos, too. Serve hot apple cider and gingerbread cookies to everyone afterward. *Michael Capps*

CAROLING

THE 12 DAYS OF CHRISTMAS

Divide the entire group into 12 small teams. Each team thinks of something that their true love gave to me that will fit into the song The 12 Days of Christmas. Each group is assigned one of the 12 days. The items that they come up with can be anything: six sticky sewers, 12 green burritos, etc.

Encourage the groups to be as creative and as wild as they can be. After each team has had time to think of their item, then sing the song. At the appropriate time in the song, each team inserts their item, and the song continues as usual.

CAROLING

CRAZY CAROLING CONTEST

Here's another creative way to go Christmas caroling this year—if your group likes a little excitement. Divide into caroling teams and print up the instruction sheet on page 128 so that each group has one. Provide song sheets too. All teams start and end at the same place. Set a time limit. The first team to follow all 10 instructions and return wins. Have a party afterwards. *Charlie Cornett*

CAROLING

CAROLING SCAVENGER HUNT

Here's a new way to go Christmas caroling this year. Divide up into caroling groups and give each group a list similar to this one:
- Sheriff's station—300 points
- Convalescent hospital—250 points
- Shopping center—200 points
- Airport (arrivals)—500 points
- McDonald's restaurant (inside)—100 points

This list can include as many locations as you want. Some can be easy to reach and some can be hard. The object is for the group to go Christmas caroling at as many locations on the list as they can within a given time limit. At each location, they must sing three Christmas carols all the way through, and then have someone in authority at each location sign their list to verify that they were actually there.

All groups may then return to a meeting place at the end of the time limit to determine the winners, talk about their experiences, and to enjoy refreshments. *Gerry Blundell*

CAROLING

CAROLING TREASURE HUNT

Create teams of carolers and hold a treasure hunt. Each team gets its own set of envelopes with clues. Each team takes out its first clue (from envelope 1) that will lead it to the first location where it is to carol (a home, nursing home, mall, outside movie theaters). Send each team to a different location. Once a team reaches its first location, it must sing three preselected Christmas carols, followed by "We Wish You a Merry Christmas." Then each team opens its envelope 2 and heads for the next location, and so on. All teams' final destinations should be your Christmas party with refreshments and games.

CAROLING

MARSHMALLOW HAYRIDE

If you live in a warm climate and are tired of celebrating Christmas without snow, try marshmallow snow instead! Rent a truck you can fill with hay and go Christmas caroling around some neighborhoods. (Check first with your local police about any laws there might be against riding in the back of a truck).Have each person bring a bag of marshmallows for mock snowball fights. Keep the tosses inside the truck and make sure you pick up the snowballs afterward; they don't melt. End at someone's home with refreshments. *Mike Roberts, Tyler Becker, and Kerri Davis*

CRAZY CAROLING CONTEST

INSTRUCTIONS

Go to houses in the neighborhood and at each house sing a carol according to the directions. After you have completed the carol, get the signature of a resident of the house in the space provided. Do a different number at each house; only one per house. You have a thirty-minute time limit. Do all you can in that time. Have fun and spread some Christmas cheer!

1. Sing all verses of a carol (in the book) backwards. _____

2. Sing a carol over the phone to _____ (_____). _____
Phone #

3. Sing a carol sitting cross legged on the porch. _____

4. Sing a carol opera style. _____

5. Form a human pyramid and sing a carol. _____

6. Sing a carol to someone under five years old. _____

7. Sing a carol in a kitchen. _____

8. Sing a carol around a Christmas tree. _____

9. Sing a carol to someone over 60 years old. _____

10. Sing all three verses of Deck the Hall and act it out. Ham it up.

Everyone must participate. _____

THE CHRISTMAS SONG— CAMP VERSION

For less-than-serious Christmas caroling or for wacky events anytime during the year—try our version found on page 130. Make up your own endings, too!

George Wright

JINGLE BELLS

This is a great way to put new life into an old song next Christmas. Divide into six groups and assign each group a phrase of the first verse of "Jingle Bells":

1. Dashing through the snow...
2. In a one-horse open sleigh...
3. O'er the fields we go...
4. Laughing all the way...
5. Bells on bobsled ring...
6. Making spirits bright...

Each group is instructed to decide on words, actions, or both to be done by the group when its phrase is sung. For example, the group that has "Laughing all the way" might hold their stomachs and say "Ho, Ho, Ho." The entire group sings the chorus ("Jingle Bells, Jingle Bells," etc.) together, followed by the first verse. As each phrase in the verse is sung, the assigned group stands, does its thing, and sits down. Do it several times, getting a little faster each time through. *Dallas Elder*

THE TWELVE DAYS OF YOUTH GROUP

Here's a way to relive the youth group's memorable moments of the past year—have the adult sponsors make up verses to the tune of "The Twelve Days of Christmas." Begin each verse with "On the ____ day of Christmas, the youth group gave to me..." Here are some examples.

• First day—"Another pizza party." (*Sponsor holds an old pizza box with leftover pizza in it.*)
• Second day—"Junior high romances." (*Sponsor unrolls toilet paper with a girl's name on it and the crossed off names of several boys; while singing, the sponsor cries and wipes tears with the toilet paper.*)
• Third day—"Another all night lock-in." (*Sponsor holds basketball, No-Doz, and videos.*)
• Fourth day—"Head banger music." (*Sponsor wears long-haired wig and a Walkman and "bangs" his head while singing.*)
• Fifth day—"A losing softball team." (*Sponsor wears jersey and cap and breaks a plastic bat over his knee.*)

Tom Lytle

CRAZY CAROLS

Tired of singing the same old Christmas songs year after year? Try turning those old songs into new ones by playing Mad Libs with this sample game (see page 131). Kids will love it. *Richard Starcher*

CHRISTMAS STOCKINGS

Spare the Christmas party host's home some of the dirt and mud of the season by asking the teens to decorate and wear their own Christmas stockings. Award prizes for categories such as brightest, most colorful, most original, etc. Who knows? Battery-operated Christmas light footwear may be the hottest new fad. *Carolyn Peters*

B.Y.O.S.

For our Christmas party, we ask each youth to bring a sock—no traditional hung-by-the-chimney-with-care-types allowed. Anything else is okay. Hang the socks around the room and have the advisors fill them with candy, goofy or inexpensive gifts, and a note of blessing to each teen.

The socks can be judged for prizes in categories like dirtiest, cleanest, most bizarre, and most worn. *Mark Simone*

CHRISTMAS DISCUSSION

Here are some questions on the birth of Christ that are effective for stimulating thought and discussion

The Christmas Song
(camp version)
(with apologies to Mel Tormé and Robert Wells)

Chipmunks roasting on an open fire;

Jack Frost picking at his nose;

A mule named Carol, being flung in a fire,

And folks dressed up like twinkletoes;

Everybody knows some turkey stole the mistletoe,

And now there's gonna be a fight.

Tiny tots, with their eyes filled with coal,

Will find it hard to sleep tonight.

They know that Santa's made of clay,

He's going to run some people over with his
sleigh,

And every mother's child is gonna cry—

To know that Rudolph was served for Christmas
pie.

And so I'm offering this simple phrase, for kids
from one to 92:

Although it's been said many times, many
ways—

Don't count your chickens before they're
hatched.

A bird in the hand is worth two in the bush.

The early bird gets the worm.

I'M DREAMING

I'm dreaming of a _____ (*adjective*) _____ (*noun*), just like the ones I used to _____ (*verb*). Where the _____ (*plural noun*) _____ (*verb*), and _____ (*plural noun*)_____ (*verb*), to hear _____ (*plural noun*) in the _____ (*noun*). I'm dreaming of a _____ (*adjective*) _____ (*noun*), with every _____ (*noun*) I _____ (*verb*). May your _____(*plural noun*) be _____ (*adjective*) and _____ (*adjective*); and may all your _____ (*plural noun*) be _____ (*adjective*).

WHO'S COMING TO WHERE?

Oh! You'd better not _____ (*verb*); you'd better not _____ (*verb*); you'd better not _____ (*verb*); I'm telling you why:_____ (*person in group*) is coming to _____ (*name of a place*)! He knows when you've been _____ -ing (*verb*). He knows when you're _____ (*adjective*). He knows if you've been _____ (*adjective*) or _____ (*adjective*); so be _____ (*adjective*) for goodness' sake. Oh! You'd better not _____ (*verb*); you'd better not _____ (*verb*); you'd better not _____ (*verb*); I'm telling you why: _____ (*same name as above*) is coming to _____ (*same place as above*)!

(see page 133). Have the kids write their answers on their own and then discuss them as a group. *Paul Young*

CHRISTMAS GIVING

At Christmas the emphasis is often on getting. To focus on Christ and his ultimate gift of love to us, and to emphasize giving and placing others ahead of ourselves, distribute the handout on page 134 and use the following discussion guide.

• Which list was easier to fill in? Why?

• Of the items listed, star the six items you want the most, from either list, then share them with the group.

• You've heard the statement, "It's more blessed to give than to receive." Is it true or false? Why?

• Why is giving so important at Christmastime?

• Look up John 3:16. What did God give? Why?

• Look up Matthew 6:19-21. What are earthly treasures? What are heavenly treasures?

We often emphasize getting, yet the Bible places emphasis on giving and placing others' needs ahead of our own. Getting Christmas presents is great, and we enjoy Christmas Day, but let's think of how we can give to others who are less fortunate. *Scott R. Fairchild*

CHRISTMAS TREE GIFTS

This strategy is designed to help young people examine the values expressed in giving and receiving gifts and is obviously most appropriate during the Christmas season. Print up copies of the Christmas Tree drawing, page 135, on 8½x11-inch sheets of paper, one for each group member.

Each person should then "trim" his or her tree with symbolic drawings or words according to the instructions.

After the exercise you may want to divide into small groups and allow teens to share what they drew and wrote on their Christmas trees.

John Boller, Jr.

CHRISTMAS WORDS

Make up a list of words associated with Christmas and assign each word a value in points. For example:

Nativity—10 points
Santa Claus—3 points
Yule—12 points
Gift—5 points
Angel—9 points
Shepherds—10 points

Your list should be as complete as you can make it, but it doesn't need to be exhaustive. Assign point values to the words randomly, according to how common they are, according to the number of letters in each word, or some other criterion.

Then ask each person in your group to make a list of the first 20 Christmas words that come to mind. When they're finished, distribute your prepared list of Christmas words with their assigned points. Each person should determine the point value of their own words by locating them on the master list. Any words not on the master list can receive extra bonus points.

Award a prize to the person with the most points; award a booby prize to the person with the fewest points.

Finally, have kids number their word lists in order of importance to them, with 1 being most important and 20 being least important. Or give them another list of Christmas words containing a variety of both religious and secular words and ask them to do the same thing. This way all the kids are working on the same list, and they can share their results with each other and compare the points assigned to each word. It's a good way to begin a discussion on what Christmas means to each person. *Jim Olia*

EXMAS IN ACREMA

Here's a great idea for Christmas (see pages 136–137) that can be read as a sermon, duplicated and discussed after everyone has read it, or even narrated while being acted out. Here are some questions for discussion that might be used:

1. If you could control Christmas, what would you change?

2. What would you consider a good way to keep Exmas and Crissmas from getting confused?

3. Do you think it would be best for the church just to cancel Christmas and celebrate Christ's birth

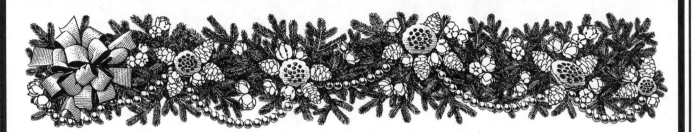

Christmas Discussion

1. Why did Jesus become a man? (Look up Heb. 9:22, Isa. 53:5-6, Jn. 1:29, Luke 19:10)

2. Do you really think that Jesus was born of a virgin? State your reasons with evidence. (Look up Matt. 1:18-25; Luke 3:23, 1:34-37; Gal 4:4)

3. Put yourself in Joseph's place. What would you do if your fiancée showed up pregnant and you knew you weren't responsible? Would you:

   a. Have her stoned? (Which was permissible by law at that time.)

   b. Beat her until she told you who was responsible?

   c. Not let it bother you?

   d. Give her the cold shoulder?

   e. Tell everyone that you are the true father and marry her (fake it)?

   f. Ask God to give you wisdom?

   g. Something not listed above. (Explain.)

4. Why do you think God chose Joseph and Mary to be Jesus' earthly parents? (See Matt. 1:19, Luke 1:17, 28)

5. If God ever wanted to do it all over again, would you be a good candidate to be one of Jesus' earthly parents?

6. Share what the birth of Jesus means to you.

CHRISTMAS GIVING

Fill in the lists below with an item that starts with each letter. When everyone is done, share with the group what you want and what you will give away.

WANT LIST	GIVEAWAY LIST

C
H
R
I
S
T
M
A
S

CHRISTMAS TREE GIFTS

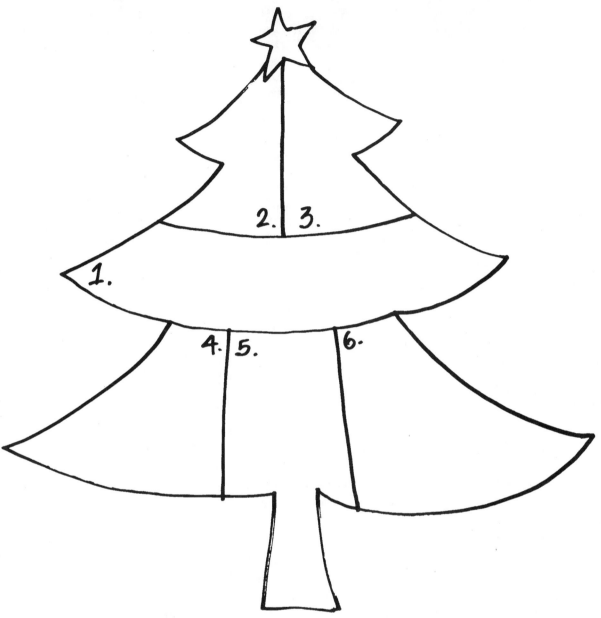

1. On the space labled "1", write a Christmas message that you would like to give to the world.
2. In space two, draw the best gift you ever got at Christmas—something so special that it is a high point in your Christmas memories.
3. Next draw the gift that you would like to receive this Christmas more than anything else. You don't have to be realistic here—it can be anything.
4. Draw a gift that you gave to someone else that was especially appropriate and appreciated.
5. Draw the gift you would bring to the manger.

(Remember the wise men?) Let your gift say something about how you see Christ and your relationship to him.

6. In the sixth space symbolize some of the gifts God has given you.
7. At the base of the tree, write out some of the feelings that this exercise may have stirred up. What is the purpose of giving? Why do we give at Christmas? Do you feel uncomfortable about some of the drawings you have made? Do you feel pride? Thanksgiving?

EXMAS IN ACREMA
(A Letter Home)

My travels have taken me to a strange and wonderful country called Acrema. It is a land of many contradictions. It has high mountains, yet It has flat plains. It has vast open spaces, yet it has cities crammed with people. It even has a holiday filled with contradictions—a holiday called Exmas.

Preparations for this festival last for over 50 days, and yet on the one day of what is supposed to be celebration, there is more quiet than merriment. It is difficult to determine whether the holiday itself or the preparation for it is the reason for the season. The preparations are very strange. They begin when people purchase tremendous quantities of cardboard cards with pictures and messages upon them. The pictures are of various subjects. Some portray snow scenes, some depict fireplaces; some have quite a modern tone; some are pictures of the way Acremans believe their ancestors lived. The pictures convey no central theme. The messages inside the cards are equally nebulous. Most often they say, "Seasons Greetings," which could be said at any time of the year. It is very difficult to say what the whole Exmas Season is supposed to represent. Some have proposed that its name be changed to "Great Religious Leader's Day" and that it be celebrated the fourth Monday of December. Although the cards are seemingly innocuous and vague, they cause untold suffering. The Acreman keeps long lists, which are called Exmas Card Lists. A card is sent to everyone on the list. Great care is taken that no one on the list is missed. Apparently some curse is associated with neglecting someone. When the task is finally finished and the cards are mailed, the Acreman sighs with relief and gives thanks to the gods that the task is over for one more year. All is peaceful then, as the Acreman receives cards his friends have mailed him, unless he receives one from someone to whom he did not send an Exmas Card. Then there is much wailing and cursing of the gods as the Acreman pulls on his overcoat and boots, drives through unspeakably crowded streets to the equally crowded marketplace and mail the Exmas card that was forgotten.

An equally strange custom is the purchase of Exmas Gifts. This is a very difficult procedure. Another list is made after which an elaborate guessing game begins. Every citizen has to guess the value of the gift which every friend will send him so that he may send one of equal value, whether he can afford it or not. And they buy as gifts for one another such things as no man ever bought for himself. For the sellers, understanding the custom, put forth all kinds of trumpery, and whatever, being useless and ridiculous, they have been unable to sell throughout the year, they now sell as an Exmas Gift. And although the Acremans profess to lack sufficient necessary things, such as metal, leather, wood, and paper, yet an incredible quantity of these things is being wasted every year, being made into gifts. When the gifts are exchanged, gratitude must be profusely expressed. Though the gifts are often useless and the gratitude is largely insincere, the Acreman must manufacture a show of delight. He even has to grind out written notes to express his unfelt gratitude. The sellers of the gifts, as well as the buyers, become exceedingly exhausted from the strain of the crowds and traffic. They are frantic in their attempts to finish everything on time and yet are in constant need of stopping and resting. This frenzied state, in their barbaric language, is known as the Exmas Rush. The people become pale and weary so that any stranger visiting Acrema at this time of the year would suppose that some great calamity had befallen the land. When the day of the festival arrives, the Acremans, except those with young children, sleep until noon, being worn out from the Exmas Rush and the excesses of the Exmas Parties. In the evening on Exmas Day, they eat five times what they usually eat. The next day heads and stomachs are greatly distressed from the food and spirits consumed in excess.

The motivation for this strange behavior is most confusing to our best scholars. The motivation could not possibly be merriment, for most Acremans seem more weary than joyful. Our best explanation is that their motivation must have its source in their pagan worship. Two deities seem particularly popular at this time. One is a weak, comical deity, represented by a man in a red suit and a long white beard. He seems to be a harmless totem of a worship of materialism. Only small children take him seriously. Adults usually greet this totem with a condescending smile.

The other object of worship centers around a very interesting contest of deities called bowls. Constant reference is made wherever Acremans gather to Super Bowls, Orange Bowls, Rose Bowls, Sugar Bowls, etc. It is probably named after the Bowl-shaped headgear worn by the participants. Each deity is represented by some fierce animal, e.g., Bears, Lions, Rams, Falcons, etc. At the exact time coinciding with the Exmas Rush, these deities have annual contests to determine supremacy. At least weekly, the spiritual leaders of the households gather in large numbers at the actual site of the contest. Those unable to make the pilgrimage to the contest worship in front of the family altars or receiving sets in their homes, urging their favorite deity on to victory. Hecataeus, a second-rate scholar, believes that these are not worship services, but only games that the people are playing. But no real scholar agrees with him. These contests are taken much too seriously to be mere games. Their statistics are chronicled far too thoroughly and remembered far too long.

My opinion, which is shared by many scholars, is that perhaps there is a connection between the worship of these deities and the annual ritual called the Exmas Rush. Perhaps the Exmas Rush is a type of self-flagellation the Acremans believe their deities require of them. Why else would the people punish themselves so? If it is

not to help their deities, the Exmas Rush just doesn't make sense.

There is another group in Acrema, almost too small to be mentioned at all, that celebrate a completely different festival at this time of the year. They call their celebration Crissmas.

The celebration centers around an ancient story about a baby who was born of very special birth many, many years ago. The story has it that there were signs in the heavens proclaiming this baby's birth. This unusual baby grew into an extraordinary man. The story has it that this man could walk on water. He could heal the sick. He could open the eyes of the blind and raise the dead. His life was absolutely perfect. Many said he was the son of some god which they claimed was the only god. His life was cut short by execution. He was pronounced dead and buried. Those who believe in this person say that he came back from the dead and that he was reborn and went into the heavens. The believers in this occurrence say that this person will come back again to judge the world. His followers claim that only those who believe in him will be forgiven.

So every Crissmas they remember again the birth of this one who is their "savior." They continue to retell the story of his birth. They use figures of his mother, of a baby born in a stable, and other helps in remembering his birth. They gather together on the eve of his birthdate to sing and praise him. They light candles and say that he is the truth that came into the world as a small light and that he now illuminates the whole world with his truth. These people call themselves Crisstians, I assume after this beautiful holiday.

I talked to the priest of one of these groups and asked him why they

celebrate Crissmas on the same day as Exmas. It seemed terribly confusing to me. He said the date of Crissmas had long ago been established and had hoped that more Acremans would celebrate it as his group did, or that God would put it in their minds to celebrate Exmas on some other day or not at all. For Exmas and the Rush distracts the minds of even the few from sacred things. He was glad that men make merry at Crissmas, but in Exmas there is no merriment left. And when I asked why Acremans endured the rush, he replied, "It is, O Stranger, a racket." Using the words (I suppose) of some ancient oracle and speaking unintelligibly to me (for the racket is an instrument which the barbarians use in a game called tennis).

Hecataeus, in his usual way of oversimplifying the facts, has formulated a hypothesis that Crissmas and Exmas are the same. This is utterly impossible. First of all, the pictures stamped on the Exmas Cards have nothing to do with the sacred story which the priests tell. Second, although most Acremans don't believe the religion of the few, they still send gifts and cards and participate in the Rush. It is unlikely that anyone would suffer so greatly for a God they did not know. Hecataeus's hypothesis also fails to account for the central event of the Exmas season—the Bowls—the contests of the deities for supremacy. Something as important as the Bowls would not be allowed to continue if the people were trying to remember their God. No, my theory ties it all together, except for those who celebrate Crissmas. They are the strange ones. I have no idea where their story could have originated—unless it actually did happen. ◆

some other time?

4. What is the best way to get people to understand the real meaning of Christmas? Advertising, church pageants, what?

Bill Serjak

DISCUSSION STARTER
First-Century Dear Abby

Read the letter on pages 139–140 to give students an up-to-date scenario for discussing the emotions and choices of Mary and Joseph as they faced Mary's unusual pregnancy. *Greg Asimakoupoulos*

DISCUSSION STARTER
Letter from Mary and Joseph

Here is a great idea that can be used as a discussion starter for the topic of Christmas, marriage, or you can even select some letters for use in a worship service, or introduction to a talk on Christmas. First, have all the girls follow these instructions: Pretend you are Mary. Write a personal letter to a close friend telling them about your pregnancy and all the events surrounding the birth of your son, Jesus.

Then, have all the guys follow these instructions: Pretend that you are Joseph. Write a personal letter to a close friend telling them about your engagement to Mary, her pregnancy, and all the events surrounding the birth of your foster child, Jesus. *Joyce Crider*

DISCUSSION STARTER
The Spirit of Christmas

This discussion starter on giving is best suited for camps and retreats around the holiday season, although it could be used at any time of the year. Display Christmas decorations and decorate a tree. Sing Christmas carols and play a few Christmas games. After that, begin the main activity using predetermined groups that have already brought unwrapped Christmas gifts (useful or gag gifts; one gift from each group). Give groups plenty of wrapping paper and tape and have them wrap their gifts in private.

Place all the wrapped gifts under the tree and have groups exchange gifts. Some groups will be pleased with their gifts and some won't. Some groups

will have given a thoughtful gift only to receive a worthless gift.

Use the following questions to spark discussion:
• How did you decide what to give?
• How does it feel to give a useful or thoughtful gift?
• How does it feel to give a worthless gift?
• How do you feel about the gift you received?
• How did it feel to receive a gag gift if you gave a nice gift?
• How did it feel to receive a nice gift if you gave a gag gift?
• What does Christmas mean to you?
• What do you think is the true meaning of Christmas?
• God has given us the greatest gift, his only Son. How do you think God feels about the gifts we give to him in return?

Tommy Baker

CRAFT
Christ Tree

This Christmas try this simple suggestion for decorating your Christmas tree. After a short discussion about the symbols Christ used for himself and the symbols others have used, have each young person make several tree ornaments representing Jesus Christ. Be sure to have available plenty of construction paper, marking pens, scissors, tape, etc. You will be amazed how many different ornaments your kids can come up with. *Linda Storey*

CRAFT
Christmas Cards for Jesus

Have kids create a Christmas card for Jesus using construction paper, scenes from magazines and old cards, plus sayings or verses that they make up. Have them think in terms of what they would say on a card if it were going to be sent to Jesus on his birthday. Stress creativity and originality, and allow the group plenty of time to complete them. You might also ask the kids to present a gift to Jesus along with the card. Display and/or discuss the results.

David R. Oakes

CRAFT
Do-It-Yourself Christmas Cards

Why not have your youths make their own Christmas cards this year? Use a simple block-printing technique or collage on construction paper, or

Dear Abby

Dear Abby,

I don't know where to begin. Only a few weeks ago everything seemed perfect. My life was fulfilling and full. I graduated from school with honors, my father made me a partner in his woodworking business, and after weeks of getting up enough courage I asked my steady girlfriend to marry me. The day after my father made me a partner, she said yes. I was so elated and so in love. Life seemed complete. I was healthy, free from stress, and without a worry about the future responsibilities that my job and marriage would bring. Even my faith was at an all-time high. I have been a religious person all my life (I'm Jewish), but only recently has my personal awareness of God's love and power been so much a part of my consciousness. My rabbi often comments about my depth of belief, my moral convictions, my unswerving values. My reputation as a successful businessman who does not believe in sex before marriage has earned me many opportunities to speak to our Sabbath school students.

But Abby, my dream has become an unending nightmare. I feel like ending my life.

Last Friday my fiancée met me after work—our weekly routine. Her face told me something was on her mind. No matter how I pried at dinner, I couldn't get her to talk about it. Leaving the restaurant, we went to the synagogue. I couldn't concentrate on the service. My imagination ran wild with fantasies...she didn't love me any more...she wanted to call off the wedding...maybe she's dying...does she have cancer?...had her father abused her?...had she rejected her Jewish faith at the hands of some proselytizing gentile group?...

On the other hand, maybe it wasn't bad news at all. Maybe the year-long engagement we set was too long for her, and she simply wanted to shorten it, but was afraid of what I might say. But that didn't explain why she didn't talk to me over dinner.

The questions kept coming. I was a nervous wreck. As we left the service, I was so preoccupied I didn't hear the Rabbi ask me if I was free to speak to the youth group the coming week. He had to grab my shoulder to get my attention. I told him I'd have to think about it.

I was determined to not take Mary Beth home until I succeeded in discovering her secret. We went out for dessert to one of our favorite spots. I took my time ordering, hoping she would volunteer the information. She didn't speak. Finally, looking down into her coffee, she started to cry. "I'm pregnant," she whispered.

Abby, I was numb with shock. I didn't speak the rest of the night. I paid the bill, walked her to the car, drove her home, and left. I cried myself to sleep that night. I woke up early the next morning, drained of tears but filled with angry questions. How could she do this to me? Didn't she love me? Hadn't we promised to save ourselves for each other? Who was he? How long had they been sleeping together? Who initiated it? Did she? How could this person exist and I not even know about him? I was the only man in her life—or so I had thought. How could Mary Beth share such intimacy with someone else when things were so good between us? Didn't she believe in God's standards for successful relationships? Was she thumbing her nose at my faith?

I avoided her for a whole week, Abby. Didn't see her, didn't even call her. I just couldn't bring myself to talk to her. My heart ached. My stomach burned. I called in sick the first three days of work. Then today she showed up just as I was closing up shop. "We need to talk," she said. "I can't stand this. I love you."

"If you loved me, you wouldn't be in the condition you're in." But I couldn't help seeing love in her eyes (for me) and that face I cherish. I knew I still loved her with all my heart. That's why I hurt so much. But Abby, how can I keep loving someone who sleeps around?

I finally forced myself to ask

The Question, though even as I asked it I wondered if I really wanted to know the answer. "Who is he?"

She looked down. "I can't tell you. You wouldn't understand. I'm not sure I understand myself. Actually, I don't know who it is."

"You don't know who it is?" I nearly lost it right there. How many guys had she been with that she didn't know who the father was? "You mean you don't know who the father is because...because..." But the thought was too painful to say out loud. The words wouldn't come.

"No, Love," she said. "It's not that at all. I just can't explain it to you now. But I want you to know I still love you and want to be your wife." As she spoke I could see the innocence in her face...the look that had first attracted me to her.

"I've made arrangements to leave town for a while," she continued. "I think it's best for you and me and our families. I'll be staying at cousin Beth's home upstate. She's a special lady. I've always been close to her. In fact, I was named after her. I'll be in good hands.

"By the way, she's expecting a child, too." She reached into her pocket. "Here's where I'll be," she said, handing me a piece of paper with a phone number penciled on it. Then she turned and walked away.

What should I do? I love Mary Beth so very much in spite of my anger and anxiety. Yet I can't go ahead with the engagement. She's destroyed my trust in her. Still, the thought of walking away from that girl leaves me empty inside. But the shame and embarrassment of being pregnant and not married in our small town is unbearable. She'd be the target of countless harassments. Her reputation would be ruined forever.

All the same, for me to stand by her and pretend that the child was mine would destroy my reputation. All my advice to young people about chastity and commitment... what a joke. And the integrity and credibility I've established in my shop with the guys would take years to rebuild.

Abby, is this the time to terminate a pregnancy? It would make everything more manageable. She doesn't show yet—Mary Beth would be spared the shame, I'd be spared my reputation...perhaps even our relationship could be spared.

Everything would be spared, that is, except that tiny life. What a sad joke...here I pride myself in morality and virtue, but I'm ready to justify abortion when it can benefit me. Besides, who knows who that baby will become someday?

I don't know, Abby. My gut feeling is to break off the engagement and try to forget what happened. I care too much for Mary Beth to make an ugly scene, though she deserves an ugly scene. I could tell everyone we called off the wedding...that it was my idea to break up, that she felt she had to get out of town to escape the pain of an unexpected jilting. Then everyone will think she got pregnant by some guy upstate. That would at least remove some of the stigma from her. I'd be the bad guy for calling off the wedding, but I wouldn't lose my reputation.

So what do I do, Abby? Stay with Mary Beth regardless of what others think? Urge her to an abortion? (I mean, she doesn't even know the father.) Break off the engagement and get on with my life?

—Devastated Boyfriend

Dear Devastated Boyfriend,
Your last idea is the best—drop her now and get on with your life. Your Mary Beth is a pathological liar, has a very vivid imagination, or is unbelievably naive. You deserve better. I know it's painful for you to think of life apart from her, but face it—there's more fish in the sea. She may seem special, but she's not the one for you.
For what Devastated Boyfriend finally decided to do, read Matthew 1:20-25.

use graphics software on a PC. Here are some ways to use the cards you make.

• If you can make enough, package them in bundles of five or 10 and sell them to members of your congregation as a fundraiser to buy presents for needy children.

• Ask your pastor for a list of the shut-ins in your congregation and assign each young person one or two names to send a card to.

• Send cards to patients in a nearby nursing home or in the pediatric ward of your local hospital.

Marja Coons

CRAFT

POLAROID CHRISTMAS TREE

If your youth group has a Christmas tree, you might try this very rewarding idea. Take a picture of each person in your youth group. (If you don't have a Polaroid camera, have the kids bring pictures of themselves.) Have them glue their pictures on small paper plates. Punch a hole in the top of each and put in a piece of yarn to hang the ornament. Then have the kids decorate the plate with crayons, magic markers, and whatever else you can provide. On the back of the plate have the kids write a Christmas wish. Hang the ornaments on the tree and encourage the kids to read the wishes written on each other's ornaments. *Charles Wiltrout*

MEANING OF CHRISTMAS

MIND TRIP TO BETHLEHEM

Young people have vivid imaginations. This short meditation gives them the opportunity to use those imaginations to gain a new appreciation for the Christmas story. Simply read the script on page 142 while kids sit comfortably with their eyes closed. Read slowly, allowing time for kids to picture the scenes in their minds. Feel free to change the script as you see fit. You might want to adapt the references to mountains, snow, and the like, to fit wherever you live (the plains, the coast, the mountains, wherever). *Sandy Peterson*

MEANING OF CHRISTMAS

GIFTS FOR JESUS

This year invite your kids to a Christmas gift exchange in which they actually purchase gifts and give them to Christ. Set a price limit on the gifts or have the kids make them by hand. They should be wrapped as any Christmas gift would be and placed in a manger at the party or meeting. Allow each kid to open a gift. Let the giver explain why it was chosen and how Christ can use it. For example, someone might give a pair of child's athletic shoes and tell about an orphanage that needs new shoes for its children. By giving to "one of the least of these," the youth actually gives to Christ. This can be a meaningful way for kids to understand the true meaning of Christmas. *Randy Pierce*

MEANING OF CHRISTMAS

THE PRAYER TREE

Have someone in your group cut down a small hardwood tree, spray paint it white, and set it in a Christmas tree stand in the sanctuary. Decorate it with a purple construction paper chain made of links stapled together. Then cut a number of four-inch lengths of ribbon in various colors.

Each Sunday during Advent, explain that the links of the chain represent our individual burdens. Invite members of the congregation to come forward, take a link off the chain, and replace it with a ribbon tied in a bow on one of the tree's branches. The ribbons symbolize hope in prayer that God will lift the specific burden the person has in mind.

If any chain links are left after the last Sunday in Advent, they should be taken off and replaced with ribbons for the Christmas service. The tree will be blossoming with symbols of hope that Emmanuel has come to free his people and to be among them. *David Washburn*

MEANING OF CHRISTMAS

NEW YEAR'S RESOLUTIONS AT CHRISTMAS

Use this activity to help students and their families establish a unique Christmas tradition of making, discussing, and reviewing New Year's resolutions. Provide all youths with one of each of the following items:

• Ring-size cardboard jewelry box
• 6-by-12-inch Christmas foil wrapping paper

MIND TRIP TO BETHLEHEM

Imagine that you are leaving your comfortable position and that you are getting up now to leave the room. Put on your coat and go out the door. As you open the door, a blast of cold air hits you. You go out the door and walk toward the mountains. It is early afternoon, and as you walk through the snow, the warmth of the sun on your back feels good. As you walk along, you notice the beautiful winter scenery around you. The snow is melting, patches of green grass peek through the snow here and there, and the mountains become rolling hills.

It is late afternoon now. You see a group of people at the top of a hill and you walk up the hill to join them. They have built a campfire. The heat of the fire feels good in the chilly air. Evening is closing in on you. You smell the food cooking on the fire and it makes you hungry. The people invite you to eat with them and to spend the night. The food is good—warm bread, hot beef stew, warm apple pie, hot tea.

As the stars come out you begin to feel tired from your long walk. You lie down and pull a blanket over you. The sky is clear, and a million stars are twinkling. You fall asleep.

Suddenly the night is as bright as day. Your heart pounds. You are terrified. Then you hear a voice: "Don't be afraid. A child has been born in the nearby town. This very special baby is God's Son. You can find this baby in a manger."

Then the night is filled with what sounds like a million voices singing the most beautiful song you've ever heard. They sing, "Glory to God and peace on earth," over and over and over. "Glory to God and peace on earth." Your fear drains away. The light recedes, and the sound fades away. You look at the people around you. You all know you have to find this baby.

You run down the hill to the edge of town where the caves are, where all the animals are kept at night. Lights shine from several of them. You run from one cave to the next until you find what you have been searching for—a tiny baby. You tiptoe in to see this baby. A cow softly moos at your intrusion. The baby's startled parents look up at you. You gaze at the sleeping child; then you tell this baby's parents what has happened this night. You slowly turn and leave. You return to the hill and the others quietly join you there. Each of you thinks his own thoughts about this baby.

When the morning light comes, you say farewell to your friends and begin walking back home. The green grass gives way to brown and small patches of snow begin to appear. By noon you are walking through deep snow and are close to home. You enter the front door, take off your coat, return to our room and sit down. You slowly open your eyes...

• Gift tag/Bow/Pencil

Also have several rolls of adhesive tape available.

Instruct everyone to place the piece of foil wrap so the undecorated side is facing up. Direct students to write a letter to their families expressing thanks and appreciation for such things as being wonderful relatives, being supportive or encouraging, etc. Finally everyone should write one resolution to work on throughout the upcoming year to improve the quality of the family, to make life more special at home, or to help others. For instance, someone may write, "I want to be more patient this year," "I hope to budget my allowance better," or "I want to spend more time with my family at home."

After students have finished their letters, they should sign their names and wrap the jewelry boxes with the foil paper (decorated side out). Use the gift tags to write the names of the family members to whom gifts will be given. You may want to ask everyone to write both first and last names on the gift tags, so packages do not get mixed up during the party. Finish by attaching the bow.

Explain to the students how to finish this activity with their families. They should place the gifts underneath the family Christmas tree. If possible, this gift should be opened last when the family exchanges gifts on Christmas Eve or Christmas Day. After the teen's resolution has been read, family members are to write resolutions of their own on the same piece of foil wrap. Read and discuss them, then rewrap the gift box, and place it back under the tree. When the family gets around to taking down the Christmas decorations, store the wrapped gift box with them. When Christmas rolls around again,

unwrap the gift box to see how well the family has kept the resolutions.

This activity can turn into a family tradition. Even though memories of the actual resolutions may fade, a special bond can be established among family members as they recall the time the whole family thought of ways they could grow closer, be a little more patient, and otherwise strengthen the family unit. *Michael W. Capps*

MEANING OF CHRISTMAS

THE REAL MEANING OF CHRISTMAS

This Bible study (page 144) gets kids searching the Scriptures for the real meaning of Christmas. It lets the kids see the Christmas message in other places besides the traditional Christmas story.

GIVING

ALTERNATIVE CHRISTMAS GIVING

Reinforce a noncommercial Christmas among your group! Design a Christmas card with the message at the bottom of this page to give to members of your youth group. *Randy Nichols*

GIVING

CHRISTMAS COUPONS

Here's a December youth activity that generates creativity in your kids and should endear you to their parents as well. During a youth meeting a few weeks before Christmas, supply each student with 12 colored three-by-five-inch index cards, a collection of

Dear Friend—
The annual rite of gift-giving is lots of fun for kids—but it can be just another stress for grownups.
So if you were gonna spend dough on me this year, instead remember me by just dropping me a note—you can even wait until after the holidays. And then spend the money that you were gonna lavish on a gift for me on something for the poor, the needy, or the lonely. (Matthew 25:35-40 makes this seem appropriate for Jesus' birthday.)
Who knows? Maybe we'll start a new stress-free tradition!
Pastor Randy

THE REAL MEANING OF CHRISTMAS

Fill in the blanks by looking up the Scripture passages (from the NIV).

C _____ came into the world to save sinners. (1 Timothy 1:15)

H The Word became flesh and made _____ dwelling among us. We have seen _____ glory, the glory of the One and Only, who came from the Father, full of grace and truth. (John 1:14)

R But when the time had fully come, God sent his Son, born of a woman, born under the law, to _____ those under law, that we might _____ the full _____ of sons. (Galatians 4:4)

I "The virgin will be with child and will give birth to a son, and they will call him _____"—which means, "God with us." (Matthew 1:23)

S For the grace of God that brings _____ has appeared to all men. (Titus 2:11)

T _____ be to God for his indescribable gift! (2 Corinthians 9:15)

M And he will be called Wonderful Counselor, _____ God, Everlasting Father, Prince of Peace. (Isaiah 9:6)

A But the _____ said to them, "Do not be _____. I bring you good news of great joy that will be for all the people. Today in the town of David a Savior has been born to you; he is Christ the Lord." (Luke 2:10)

S This is how God showed his love among us: He _____ his one and only Son into the world that we might live through him. This is love: not that we loved God, but that he loved us and sent his Son as an atoning _____ for our _____. (1 John 4:9-10)

stickers, decals, old magazines with pictures they can

cut out, colored pencils, pens and markers, etc.

Instruct them to design a year's worth of service coupons for their parents or other family members to use once a month—one service per card. The coupons should be designed to reflect the sort of service they're good for: washing dishes, 10 minutes of good conversation, vacuuming the house, taking out the garbage for a week, responding to a parent's request without complaining, etc.

The kids can devise their own services, decorate their cards, and seal them in attractive envelopes with explanations of how the coupons are to be redeemed. Family members just present their son or daughter or sibling with a coupon, and the teenager will willingly perform the service. This can be a great tool for encouraging healthy family relationships. *Ed Laremore*

GIVING

CHRISTMAS LIST FOR PARENTS

It happens every Christmas—parents of teenagers wonder what they could possibly give their kids that conveys their interest in them as growing, maturing Christians.

Enter you, their youth worker! During November compile a list of Bibles, devotional books, specific topical books, and Christian tapes—your personal inventory of high school-related reading material and music available at your local Christian bookstores. Give prices, maybe a brief description of each item, and perhaps even your personal number-one choice in each category. Some bookstores may negotiate a discount for families buying from your list. Be sure to update your lists every year.

While you're in the list-writing mood, why not give parents a list of parenting resources just for

them? Your lists will become ways for you to touch your kids and their parents throughout the year. *Michael McKnight*

GIVING

CHRISTMAS POSTCARDS

Recycle old Christmas cards as Christmas postcards for a group service project. Simply have teens collect used cards that don't have writing on the back of the front cover. Cut the cards in half. Give kids the names of elderly and single people in your congregation. Let kids choose a name or two (or more) and write holiday greetings on the instant postcards. Kids can address, stamp, and mail the postcards, distribute them personally after services, or deliver them personally to the people at their homes. (You may want to provide the addresses and stamps.) *David Washburn*

GIVING

LIVING CHRISTMAS GIFT

Here is a clever and meaningful Christmas gift suggestion that will become more valuable as the years go by. Have your young people interview their grandparents on videotape about their experiences in life. Suggest that the young people duplicate the tape and give a copy to each of the relatives for Christmas.

GIVING

CREATIVE CARD WRITING

At the first youth meeting in December, lead your group in an artistic encouragement of others in your local congregation by supplying them with stationery, envelopes, colored construction paper, glue, a variety of pens and markers, scissors, Christmas seals, etc.—and postage stamps.

Have a few church directories spread out to spur the students' thinking about who could use an encouraging, homemade Christmas card. Perhaps they'll want to zero in on graduates from your group who are away at college, or their parents, or the elderly in your congregation who are confined to their homes.

And with the Christmas greeting, of course, throw in some news about what the youth group has been up to recently or what they're planning for the new year. *Michael Bell*

PROMOTION
ADVENT CALENDAR

Inside the windows of this advent calendar are not pictures of four calling birds, magi, and toy soldiers, but info about December's activities. For example, you can provide 31 windows and fill days having no activities with Bible verses, or you can just cut as many windows as there are activities. *Daryl Wright*

PROMOTION
CALENDAR FOR ADVENT

To get your youths in the spirit of Christmas, and to keep them abreast of holiday activities, try a special calendar for Advent. Note the days when youth activities and all-church affairs will be held. On the days still blank, add suggestions for special holiday projects:
- CLEAN UP YOUR ROOM AND DECORATE IT FOR CHRISTMAS
- TAKE SOME CANNED GOODS TO THE LOCAL FOOD BANK
- DECORATE A FRIEND'S LOCKER FOR CHRISTMAS
- PREPARE DINNER FOR YOUR FAMILY AND DO THE DISHES.

Dianne E. Deming

PROMOTION
CHRISTMAS CHURCH AD

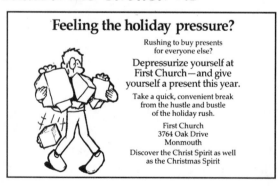

During December suggest to your students that they try their hand at designing and writing a newspaper ad like the one shown here. It's a practical way to provoke discussion among your kids about the suitability and effectiveness of advertising about Christ. The cost is usually reasonable in weekly newspapers or small-town dailies. *Keith Curran*

VIDEO
CHRISTMAS VIDEO

Your kids probably love two things to excess: videos and seeing their youth leaders get trashed. So combine both ideas for what will become a tradition at your Christmas party or banquet.

Have yourself and your adult staff videotaped as you sing custom-written lyrics to the "Twelve Days of Christmas" (see sample lyrics below)—and as a few of your students or interns pour the mentioned food or goop over your heads.

> On the first day of Christmas the interns gave to us—
> A pie for holy _____ (fill in name of youth leader).
> On the second day of Christmas the interns gave to us—
> Two bowls of oatmeal, and a pie...(etc.)
> Three dozen eggs
> Four quarts of chocolate
> Five pounds of whole-wheat flour...

Ron Sylvia

OUTREACH
CHRISTMAS TREE TRACTS

Secure permission to decorate a tree in a shopping mall or other public place. At least six weeks before Christmas, write to the American Bible Society to find out what Scripture leaflets (sold below cost for just a few cents) are available for the Christmas season. They usually have a good selection. Their address is: American Bible Society, Volunteer Activities, Dept. YS, 1865 Broadway, New York, NY 10023. If you live in a Spanish-speaking area, buy some Spanish selections also. Wrap the leaflets Tootsie-Roll style in colored cellophane and dangle them from the tree. Arrange for your youth choir or other musicians (or a good tape recorder when live music is not available) to furnish background music.

Also line up volunteers to man the tree, to invite people to take tracts, and to answer questions. You'll need a supply of extra ornaments to replenish your tree.

Christmas is a special time to communicate God's love. This can be one effective way to do it. *Geri Mitsch*

OUTREACH

Drive-Through Nativity

Here is an idea that really makes the Christmas story come alive. Set up a number of nativity scenes using kids from your group as well as live animals. Make the scenes as authentic as possible. Each scene should have its own 4-by-8-foot sign designed as a scroll with appropriate Scripture verses. Also, the use of colored lights is very effective.

The people view the scenes from their cars. When they drive through they are first met at the welcome point with a program explaining the scenes. Cars proceed through the scenes with lights out. The route is outlined with luminarios. (A luminario is a paper bag filled with two to three inches of sand in the bottom and a six-inch candle placed in the center of the sand. Make sure the side of the bag is taller than the candle.)

After viewing all the scenes, the cars pass the exit point, where they are thanked for coming and reminded to turn on their lights. In addition to the nativity scenes, it is a good idea to show a film about sChristmas in a building about once every 20 minutes. The people come, view the film, then drive through the scenes. The drive-through runs continuously for two hours. Kids work one-hour shifts.

It's important to publicize to the entire community through newspapers, TV, radio, etc. Families really appreciate the scenes, especially if you do them two or three days before Christmas to attract people who are out doing last-minute shopping or looking at Christmas lights and decorations. Any Christmas scenes will work, such as Mary and Joseph on their way to Bethlehem; the traditional manger scene; the wise men following the star; and the appearance of the angels to the shepherds. This event is very effective and can grow from a church event to a community tradition. *Don Hinkle*

SERVICE

Christmas Lock-In

If you are looking for a significant and meaningful activity for your youth group (ninth grade and

above), the Christmas Lock-In is it. The Christmas Lock-in is a 36-hour event that is held one week before Christmas on a Friday and Saturday. The schedule is on page 148. *Douglas Janetzke*

SERVICE

Jesus Birthday Presents

Give the handout on page 149 to your students to make Matthew 25:40 come alive for them. Here are concrete specifics for giving Christ a Christmas present by serving "the least." *Tom Lytle*

SERVICE

Give Some Christmas Warmth

Literally! Instead of leading your group in collecting toys for needy kids in your town next December, ask your students to bring one of their winter jackets or coats to donate to the poor. Give your city's social services department a call—they'll probably know whom to distribute the coats to. *Scott Cunningham*

SERVICE

Christmas Tree Trimming Service Project

Trimming the Christmas tree is always lots of fun— but not necessarily for the elderly, the handicapped,

Christmas Lock-In

FRIDAY

7:00 p.m.   Contemporary Worship Service-run entirely by the kids focusing on the practical meaning of Christmas.

8:00 p.m.   Free time for socializing.

9:00 p.m.   Doors locked and work begins. Begin by making favors for the nursing home that the kids will be visiting Saturday. Then wrap gifts for poor families and the children at local children's hospital (or the children's floor of any hospital). After that, pack food baskets for the poor (get the food from a congregational door collection along with funds raised from the youth themselves). The food that is purchased for the food baskets is bought during a midnight shopping spree.

After midnight: The kids sleep in the church.

SATURDAY

8:00 a.m.   Breakfast.

9:00 a.m.   Deliver baskets to the poor.

11:30 a.m.   Lunch.

1:00 p.m.   Carol singing and favors given out at nursing home.

3:00 p.m.   Carol singing and gifts distributed at the children's hospital.

6:00 p.m.   Dinner.

7:00 p.m.   Caroling to church member's homes.

9:00 p.m.   Gala Christmas party with lots of singing and fellowship. Close with communion.

Give Jesus a Birthday Present

That's right—this year you'll hear all about the gifts he gave us, but why not give him a present, too? "I tell you the truth," Jesus told his followers, "whatever you did for one of the least of these brothers of mine, you did for me" (Matt. 25:40). So here are 12 practical ideas for the 12 days of Christmas!

1. Give the money you earn during one day or shift to the Salvation Army.

2. Volunteer one day or night per month (or per week) for a year at a nursing home or hospital.

3. Volunteer time and service at our church (wash dishes in the kitchen, clean the van or bus, etc.)

4. Organize a small-scale clothing drive with some friends, and donate your earnings to the charity of your choice.

5. Baby-sit free for an evening for a single mother once a month for a year.

6. Shovel an elderly person's walk next time it snows.

7. Visit a shut-in just to chit-chat and play a game.

8. Prepare a meal for a shut-in.

9. Run errands or clean house for an elderly person.

10. Make a "Kind Deeds Coupon Book" and give it to your parents ("This coupon good for one clean room whenever asked," "...good for one free night of babysitting without complaining," or "...good for one week's worth of trash duty").

11. Volunteer to teach in next summer's vacation Bible school.

12. Make paper bag puppets for the children's Sunday school.

"Whatever you did for one of the least of these brothers of mine, you did for me."

maybe not even for some of the single. Just to get the tree to stand straight in its stand is well nigh impossible for just one person to do.

So arrange a day in December when your group can circulate among the homes of folks who need help setting up and trimming their trees. You can haul boxes of ornaments down from the attic, put up outdoor lights and decorations, hang ornaments on high, difficult-to-reach branches. Some folks will need help with only heavy lifting; others may enjoy watching the high schoolers decorate the entire tree.

You may want to plan a party for that night; your group will be in the Christmas spirit much more than if they'd simply sung carols at these homes.

Howard B. Chapman

SERVICE

MEGA MERRY CHRISTMAS CARD

Residents of convalescent homes or hospital patients will especially appreciate this gargantuan holiday greeting—although anyone will get a kick out of it. Lead your kids in cutting, taping, and papering or painting a refrigerator box so it resembles a huge Christmas card. You can write the greeting either to Jesus or to the residents themselves. What the residents like, of course, is to see their names on the card (so you'll have to get a list of the residents from a nursing home or hospital administrator).

A day or two before Christmas, take the card with you as your group carols through the halls, and take the mega-card into the rooms as you visit, pointing out the residents' names to them. Then leave the card with them in the hospital! *Jim Johnson*

RUDOLPH GOES TO THE HOSPITAL

Here's a good way to bring a little Christmas cheer to folks in the hospital during the holidays. Have your youth group go caroling or just visiting at your local hospital and allow the kids to wish each patient a merry Christmas personally by presenting them with a little Rudolph that they make ahead of time.

Rudolph is simple, inexpensive, and fun to make, and people really enjoy receiving them as gifts. To make one, you'll need three wooden clothespins (not the spring type), some red and green felt, a red marker, a cotton ball, little wiggly eyes, scissors, and glue. Cut the ears out of green felt in this pattern:

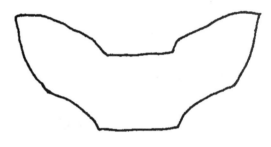

A rectangular piece of red felt is used for the body. Glue two clothespins together at the flat sides for the body; then flip the third clothespin up for the head and antlers. Glue the ears between the body and head. Color the nose, add the tail (cotton) and the eyes, and you have a Rudolph. You may also glue a loop of fishing line between the head and body to make Rudolph a tree ornament.

You can also write a message such as "Get well soon and have a merry Christmas," along with the name of the church, on a small piece of paper or card and place it between the antlers. It's a great way to allow your kids to do something nice for others at Christmas. *David Oakes*

150

CHILDREN'S CHRISTMAS COLORING BOOK

That's right—your teenagers can create homemade coloring books to distribute to children in your city's hospitals.

Ask each student to draw a couple of pictures on a Christmas theme. The drawings should be of bold lines (not too many) with lots of open space in which kids can color. Ask one of your artists to design a cover picture. Assign another youth to write up the Christmas story (Luke 2:8-14) for the back cover. Choose the most suitable drawings, run 200-300 copies of each picture and the covers, then bind the sheets together (give your local quick printer a call for inexpensive binding methods).

Toward the beginning of the Christmas holidays, tour some of your hospitals and give the youngster there a coloring book as well as a new box of crayons.

If you must cover your costs, you might sell the books to your church members to give as Christmas gifts. If you don't need to cover your costs, give the proceeds to a mission project that your group adopts. *Timothy Wilkey*

CHRISTMAS SITTER SERVICE

As a service project at Christmas, members of your youth group can staff the church's nursery each evening the entire first week of December. Parents and children up to age 10 can then drop off their kids between 6:00 and 10:00 P.M. while they go Christmas shopping. This can be done for free, or donations can be accepted for a worthy project. Most adults really appreciate this kind of service. It is important, by the way, to have some adult supervision present each night. *R. Albert Mohler, Jr.*

CHRISTMAS GIFTS AUCTION

This December event is part publicity and part fundraiser—but you'll have to start a few months earlier to pull it off. If you do, it may become a tradition with your group.

The idea is simple:

Determine how the money you'll raise from the auction will be used—Compassion International, World Vision, Habitat for Humanity, or local causes such as nursing homes, adoption agencies, shelters for homeless families or abused women, pro-life organizations, camp scholarships for your own church, etc.

Then solicit new merchandise from area businesses—items like lift tickets to ski areas, gift certificates to restaurants, autographed basketballs (solicit these from professional sports teams in your area), quilts, dolls—anything!

Assign one student to a business so no one is bombarded with multiple requests for merchandise. Carefully draft a letter that your young people can use when introducing themselves, your youth group, and the auction's purpose.

Besides the tax-deductible nature of these donations, sweeten the deal further by offering to run ads for free in the auction program (which will also list the merchandise to be auctioned), which is distributed to not only all auction-goers, but throughout your church congregation.

A week before the auction, send an announcement or a press release of the auction to your local radio and newspaper. Any coverage they give is free publicity.

Be sure to have one or two good auctioneers who can keep things moving for an afternoon.

An early December date for the auction may be ideal for many who want to get a large share of their Christmas shopping done early. *Terry O. Martinson*

CHRISTMAS POST OFFICE

Here's how to raise money at Christmastime for missions. Construct a plywood box with slots or compartments large enough for letters and Christmas cards (at least 25 compartments).

Build it, paint it, label it, and place it in a prominent place in your church. Announce that the Christmas post office is now open. Invite people to mail their cards and letters to each other simply by placing them in the appropriate compartment and by paying ten cents (or whatever) per card. Each week until Christmas, church members can check the compartment with the first letter of their last name, and pick up their Christmas mail.

The money that's raised can then be used for missions or some other Christmas project. One church has done this for three years in a row, and each year it's more successful than the last. *Larry Lawrence*

FUNDRAISER

CHRISTMAS TREE PICKUP SERVICE

Here's a simple fundraiser for your youth group this Christmas. Spend one or two days after Christmas (before school starts up again) driving pickup trucks to retrieve discarded Christmas trees, oversized gift boxes, etc. Advertise in advance, both in the church and neighborhood. Try to place free ads in your local newspaper or try to persuade the editor to send a reporter to interview your group about the project. Try to get radio time too. If you can borrow the trucks, your only expense will be gas and the fee to dump the trees at your local dump.

Charge a flat fee for the service or accept donations. This will work especially well in communities where refuse disposal companies either don't pick up Christmas trees or charge extra for it. *R. Albert Mohler, Jr.*

FUNDRAISER

GIFT WRAP FUNDRAISER

Once your high schoolers start their Christmas vacation, but before Christmas, plan a fundraising gift-wrap service at a local discount store (Wal-Mart or K-Mart, for example). Buy your wrap, boxes, and ribbon from a paper company at wholesale prices. A few nights before the fundraiser, rent a bow machine and pre-make your bows.

Set up shop in the store's layaway department and ask the manager to announce your service over the intercom throughout the day. Last-minute shoppers are usually in a panic and extremely grateful for your services. *Mark Reierson*

FUNDRAISER

HANDMADE CHRISTMAS WRAP

This fundraiser costs you pennies and gives your kids a chance to use their artistic abilities. Purchase a bolt

of brown wrapping paper from a wholesaler, butcher, or newspaper publisher. Cut simple Christmas shapes from clean kitchen sponges (Christmas trees, holly, stars, bells, and wreaths work well).

Have students use the sponge shapes dipped in acrylic paints to create unique repeated designs. Be sure to let each color dry before adding additional colors. Measure the paper and cut it into two-yard lengths. Roll it into tubes and tie it with natural jute.

Publicize your sale in your church newsletters and bulletins. Sell your original wrapping paper in November and December. For display purposes wrap boxes of various sizes, tie them with jute, and place them with the rolls of Christmas wrap on your selling table. *Heather Monkmeyer*

FUNDRAISER

CHRISTMAS TREE OF LOVE

Put a Christmas tree (either real or artificial) in the church foyer. Place a few decorations on the tree, but leave it embarrassingly bare. Leave a package of ornament hangers under the tree, along with a donation box decorated to look like a gift. As an alternative to sending out individual cards to everyone, ask each person, couple or family consider hanging one of their Christmas cards on the tree with greetings to the entire congregation. The cards can be hung on the tree by using one of the ornament hangers provided. Also ask them to donate the money they would have spent on cards and postage to whatever worthy project you happen to have. The money can be deposited in the gift box under the tree. Of course people can give more than the money they save if they choose.

People are generally more responsive to this if you have a specific project in mind, such as a missionary project, providing toys or other gifts for an orphanage, giving to a hunger relief agency, etc. Be sure to stress that this project is optional. If people would rather send personal greeting cards, they should be encouraged to do so. *Larry D. Spicer*

DRAMA

CHRISTMAS GROUP DRAMATICS

Here's an audience participation that can be a lot of fun. Divide the audience into six groups. Each group is given a word and a corresponding response. Then a poem is read (see page 154). Every time their word is mentioned, they respond with the correct phrase.

David Conrad

DRAMA

Christmas Melodrama

Here's a Christmas version of the spontaneous melodrama (page 155). It's a great skit that requires no rehearsal. The characters are selected from the audience and given the props The narrator simply reads the script while the characters spontaneously do what the script indicates. Choose people you think will ham it up and have some fun with their parts.

Tom Lowry

DRAMA

A Christmas Tale

This impromptu melodrama (page 156) has a Christmas theme. Actors, chosen from the audience, act out whatever the narrator describes in the narration. *Lynn H. Pryor*

DRAMA

Away in a Modern Manger

Modernize the traditional Christmas story with the script found on pages 157–159. Fill in the blanks with the appropriate officials' names, youth group members' names, and towns and states near you. Let the kids videotape the action in different locations to produce a modern-day Christmas story. Show it at your Christmas party. Besides the good laughs, the experience can enhance the students' appreciation of the gospel message. *Bert L. Jones*

DRAMA

The Department Store Window

The Christmas pantomime on page 160 is a dramatic way to present the moment when Jesus was in the manger. *Ruth Sowpel*

DRAMA

The Guest

The short Christmas play on pages 161–146 is an adaptation of the poem "How the Great Guest Came" by Edwin Markham. While the original poem's setting was in Europe a few centuries ago, the setting for this version of the story is the present. *Dan Johnson*

DRAMA

He's Going to What?

The dialogue on pages 165–167, makes a great short Christmas play for two people. Use your own creativity to come up with props, costumes, or whatever. Be sure your actors memorize their lines and rehearse. The story is also effective simply as a reading or as a discussion starter during the advent season. Use it however you wish. *Stephen A. Bly*

DRAMA

The Innkeeper's Wife

If someone in your group has the ability to act, the short monologue on page 168 would be effective at Christmas time. The lines should be memorized, and a few props would be helpful. Use your own imagination, and change or add any lines that you feel would improve the impact or delivery of the material. It could be followed up with a discussion about how we are often like the innkeeper's wife, missing opportunities to be of service to Christ. *Mary Kent*

DRAMA

Joe's Story

Unfortunately, Joseph the husband of Mary has been traditionally depicted as a two-dimensional historical figure who seemed (if we don't read the narrative closely) to be at peace in circumstances that would unhinge most men in similar dilemmas today. For the sake of realism, then, the monologue on pages 169–170 attempts to bring the Incarnation into the late twentieth century and Joseph into high schoolers' own realm of feelings. *Jack Hawkins*

CHRISTMAS GROUP DRAMATICS

GROUP RESPONSES

When the audience hears the word...	...it should respond with...
• Santa	• "Ho, Ho, Ho!"
• Reindeer	• "Clippity Clop"
• Rudolph	• "Beep, Beep" (While pinching nose)
• Bells	• "Jingle, Jingle"
• Snow	• "Br-r-r-r-r-r"
• Sleigh	• "Wheeeeee!"

One time long ago in a fake little town
A happening happened and the story's told 'round
How a reindeer named Rudolph was of no help to Santa
Delivering presents in this town near Atlanta.

The sleigh owned by Santa was loaded with presents
By the elves and the reindeer and a large group of peasants.
The reindeer were harnessed with bells on their toes,
But Rudolph must stay home (because of his nose).

Santa, the reindeer, and the sleigh were all ready
To deliver the presents when a problem quite heady
Developed. It stopped them, they just couldn't go.
The problem, you see, was a large storm of snow.

The snow came so hard that Santa couldn't see.
The reindeer wouldn't know where to pull the sleigh (whee).
The reindeer, bells jingling, and Santa made tracks
Through the snow to see Rudolph, a question to ask.

"Rudolph," said Santa and the reindeer in unison,
"If this snow stops us this year our act is for sure done.
We've a sleigh full of presents to deliver tonight,
And the snow is so heavy, we have little sight.

Will you and your nose guide the reindeer to housetops
So that Santa with presents can make all of his stops?"
Rudolph yawned and looked out at the wind-driven snow
And said, "Santa and reindeer, I just cannot go.

The sleigh is too heavy with presents delightful,
But if you ask me, the job seems a might dull.
Besides, all this snow and your bells out of tune,
The cold is too much. Ask again come next June."

CHRISTMAS MELODRAMA

CHARACTERS
Penelope Pureheart
Dirty Dan
Elmer Schmidlap
Faithful Dog Shep
Christmas Tree
Narrator

PROPS
Chair
Tree decorations
Clean toilet brush

Our action takes place in the deep, snow-covered woods. Poor Penelope Pureheart is out with her faithful dog, Shep, trying to find a Christmas tree for their poor, dreary hut. Penelope finds a pretty little tree...but...no...Shep's already found it.

After searching farther, Penelope finds the perfect tree! She chops it down, yells "Timber!" and down it falls. She drags it back to her house with the help of her faithful dog, Shep.

Now we see the poor, dreary hut. It looks so poor and dreary except for the beautiful Christmas tree in the corner. She doesn't have any presents to go under it, but it is pretty anyway. ·

Suddenly, we hear a knock at the door. In bursts Dirty Dan. He demands that poor Penelope Pureheart pay him the $29.65 plus tax for the tree. She pleads with him to let her have it. Doesn't he know it is more blessed to give than to receive?! "Bah, Humbug!! I'll give you six hours or I'll take it back!" he says as he leaves.

Poor Penelope Pureheart doesn't know what to do. She has no money. She sits down on the chair and starts to cry. Her faithful dog, Shep, comes over to comfort her. She pats him on the head. She scratches him under the chin. She rubs his ears. He loves it!

To comfort her, he licks her hand; then licks her arm all the way to the elbow. She loves it! It makes her feel so much better.

"What will we do?" she asks. "I wish Santa Claus would help us."

All of a sudden, there is a knock on the door. She knows it is Dirty Dan coming to get the money or her tree.

"Come in," she says sadly. But instead of Dirty Dan it is Elmer Schmidlap, former Fuller Brush salesman and now Santa Claus' vice president in charge of public relations. With him, he has his magic toilet brush, with which he performs various and sundry deeds of prestidigitation and other magical acts.

"What's wrong poor Penelope?" asks Elmer. She tells him and then breaks down crying. This goes on and on. Then her faithful dog, Shep, starts howling. This goes on and on.

At that moment in bursts Dirty Dan. He demands the money or the tree.

Elmer says, "Can't you be nice, you dirty thing?"

Dan pushes Elmer and he falls into the beautiful Christmas tree.

"Now look what you've done," says Dirty Dan, "You've ruined the Christmas tree."

Elmer says, "We've had enough of your dirtiness, Dirty Dan. From now on you'll bring joy to the hearts of people." Then Elmer touches Dirty Dan with his magic toilet brush, and Dirty Dan turns into the most beautiful Christmas tree there ever was!

Elmer, Penelope and Penelope's faithful dog, Shep, go out for a Christmas walk, celebrating with all of Santa's assistants. Dirty Dan just stands in the hut looking beautiful.

And thus our story ends.

Moral: When you get to the root of it all, all dirty, evil people are really saps.

END

A CHRISTMAS TALE

CHARACTERS

Mother
Clara Belle
Maynard
Cat
Angel
Virginia
Fester
Dog
Santa Claus

PROPS

Christmas tree
Rocking chair
Door

Our story opens with Mother sitting in her rocking chair by the Christmas tree. It's not a particularly pretty tree, but it does have a pretty angel on top.

Mother's younger daughter, Clara Belle—the little brat in our story—rushes into the room.

She asks, "Mommy dearest, can I have some dessert?"

Mother shakes a finger at Clara Belle and says, "Don't touch those desserts! Your sister is having a guest over."

Clara Belle kicks the floor and says, "Jeepers!"

Meanwhile, Fester—Virginia's steady boyfriend—walks up and knocks on the door.

Clara Belle shouts, "I'll get it!" and opens the door. As Fester steps in, Clara Belle slams the door in his face.

"It's that yucky Fester," she says in disgust.

Mother opens the door and lets Fester in. She says, "Hello, Fester. I'll get Virginia." She shouts, "Hey, Virginia! Yucky Fester is here!"

Virginia sweeps into the room, batting her eyes. Virginia says sweetly, "Hello, my dearest Fester." Virginia passionately shakes his hand.

Fester says, "Oh, Sugar Plum, I've brought you a gift." He opens the door and brings in a dog.

Virginia says sweetly, "A dog!"

Mother screams, "Oh, no—a dog!"

Clara Belle exclaims, "Far out! A dog!" Clara Belle tries to ride the dog. The dog bites Clara Belle's leg.

Just then comes another knock on the door. Clara Belle and Virginia both say, "I'll get it!" They race to the door and fight for control of the doorknob.

Virginia gives Clara Belle a karate chop on the neck and opens the door.

Maynard, Fester's rival for Virginia, stands at the door. Maynard says, "Hiya, toots," as he grabs her in a bear hug.

Fester shouts, "Unhand her, you animal!" as he madly separates the two.

Maynard says, "I brought you a gift, my love."

Fester says, "Oh, you shouldn't have!" and hugs Maynard.

Virginia jumps in between the two of them. "Enough!" she shouts. "Where's my gift?"

Maynard opens the door and brings in a cat. Virginia coos, "A cat!"

Mother screams, "Oh, no—a cat!"

Clara Belle shouts, "Far out! A cat!"

Fester sneezes, "Not a cat!"

The dog barks and chases the cat around the Christmas tree.

The tree falls on the dog.

The angel falls on the cat.

The dog and cat begin to fight.

Maynard and Fester begin to fight over Virginia. They repeatedly shout at each other, "She's mine!"

Maynard picks up the rocking chair and throws it at Fester.

Fester shields himself behind Clara Belle.

Mother cries, "My Christmas is ruined!"

Suddenly Santa Claus flings open the door. "Ho, ho, ho!" he exclaims as he grabs his stomach.

Clara Belle runs to him and grabs hold of his leg. She squeals, "Oh, Santa!"

Virginia run and jumps into Santa's arms and squeals, "Oh, Santa!"

Santa says, "Yes, Virginia, there really is a Santa Claus."

Santa shakes Clara Belle off his leg.

Maynard and Fester ask together, "What does he have that I don't have?"

As Santa carries Virginia out the door, Virginia says, "Eight smelly reindeer!"

THE END

AWAY IN A MODERN MANGER

(based on Luke chapter two)

CHARACTERS

Narrator

Mary

Astrophysicist 1

Astrophysicist 3

High Schooler 1

Joseph

Clerk

Astrophysicist 2

Youth Minister

High Schooler 2

SCENE 1

NARRATOR: *(Speaks in a voice-over or on location in Mary's bedroom with a microphone, like a news reporter.)* About this time _____, the president of the United States, decreed that a census should be taken throughout the nation. (This census was taken when _____ was governor of _____.) All citizens were required by the US Census Bureau to return to their permanent residences for the sake of this census. Joseph was working out of state on a long-term project (the Defense Department had subcontracted to him the construction of an office complex in _____, _____), so he had to return to his own town— _____ in _____. He took with him Mary, his fiancée, who was obviously pregnant.

JOSEPH: Everything packed? I'd like to leave before rush hour traffic begins.

MARY: Yes, Joseph. You know, while we're in _____, we need to go shopping for the baby. There is so much we still need to buy.

JOSEPH: All I have to do is check the oil and tires, and we're ready to go. It'll take us ____ hours to get to _____. The baby might come while we're home for the census, so make sure you have everything you need. *(Close-up of MARY closing suitcases. Pull back to follow MARY and JOSEPH walking out the door to their pickup, loading it, getting in, and driving away.)*

SCENE 2

(MARY and JOSEPH have arrived in their own city. Film several landmarks of the city, then catch the car. MARY and JOSEPH ad lib small talk while film rolls: "They've put in a new Burger King there!", "So much has changed in a year," etc.)

NARRATOR: And while they were driving around _____, the time came for Mary's baby to be born.

MARY: *(Move shot to inside the car, where Mary's eyes go wide and she puts a hand quickly to her belly)* Ooohh!

JOSEPH: What's wrong?

MARY: It's time.

NARRATOR: And so Joseph floored it all the way to the hospital.

SCENE 3

(Their pickup squeals up to a hospital's emergency room door. JOSEPH leaps out, runs around to the passenger door, opens it, and helps MARY out and into the hospital. A member of the youth group is at the admissions desk.)

CLERK: May I help you?

JOSEPH: *(frantically)* My wife is going to have a baby any minute.

CLERK: We don't have obstetrics or maternity at this hospital. But the general hospital at the far end of town can—

JOSEPH: She'll never make it that far.

MARY: *(panting heavily)* Joseph...there's a...Motel 6 next door *(here and throughout script, use the name of a budget motel in your area)*...I saw it as we drove in...take me there...

JOSEPH: A Motel 6? Look, Mary, I'm not taking you to a cheap motel, you need a hospi—

MARY: Motel 6 is fine...just—*(another contraction comes)* ooohh—get me there...fast.

CLERK: *(as MARY and JOSEPH hurry from the desk back outside)* I can arrange for an ambulance if you can wait a few minutes...

SCENE 4
(Long shot of the Motel 6. Move in through the door of one of the ground-floor rooms. A pile of clothes lies on the floor; the suitcase has obviously been emptied quickly. Camera moves to bed, on which sits Mary and Joseph, gazing at the opened suitcase on the bed. Close-up on the suitcase, which is found to be lined with blankets, in which is cradled a baby.)

NARRATOR: And she gave birth to her first child, a son. She wrapped him in a blanket and laid him in an empty suitcase because they had no time to get to the general hospital.

MARY: What can we name him?

JOSEPH: We will name him Jesus, for he shall save his people from their sins.

SCENE 5
(A car pulls into a service station. While NAR-

RATOR *reads, an* ATTENDANT *walks toward the car as the driver rolls down his window. There are three* ASTROPHYSICISTS *in the car. It is dusk.)*

NARRATOR: After Jesus was born in _____ in the state of _____, during the time _____ was president of the United States, astrophysicists came to the city of _____.

ATTENDANT: Unleaded, unleaded plus, or unleaded supreme?

ASTROPHYSICIST 1: Where is the one who has been born King of the Jews? We have seen his supernova in Virgo and have come all the way from _____ to worship him.

ATTENDANT: Funny you should mention that. An old geezer came by a few weeks ago, talkin' crazy...said something about a supreme leader being born right here in _____, and mumbled something about a star and Motel 6...or was it Best Western?

ASTROPHYSICIST 2: *(quick to pick up the clue, to ATTENDANT)* You got a Yellow Pages in there? *(cut quickly to next scene)*

SCENE 6
(Back at the motel. As NARRATOR reads, ASTROPHYSICISTS pull up in their car, get out holding objects, check the room number against what's apparently written on a scrap of paper in the hand of one of the ASTROPHYSICISTS, and knock. JOSEPH opens the door and lets them in. Camera follows them in.)

NARRATOR: After they had heard this, they went on their way. As they followed the directions to the motel Joseph gave them over the phone, they could have sworn that the supernova they had first seen from their observatory in _____ went ahead of them until it stopped right above the motel.

ASTROPHYSICIST 1: We have followed the supernova from _____ and have come to worship the child.

ASTROPHYSICIST 2: We have brought our finest gifts for the child—

ASTROPHYSICIST 3: A _____
(popular video game title).

ASTROPHYSICIST 1: A _____
(popular recording artist) Christmas video.

ASTROPHYSICIST 2: And a
_____ *(the nearest college)* sweatshirt to keep the baby warm.

NARRATOR: And with this they left, because they had heard on Traffic Watch that a tomato truck had overturned on the _____ freeway *(expressway, tollway, highway, boulevard, etc.)*. There were five tons of tomatoes spread across every lane, and traffic was backed up all the way to _____
(overpass, exit, a cross street, etc.). So they went back to _____ by a different route.

SCENE 7
(Afternoon of the next day. As NARRATOR reads, YOUTH MINISTER pulls up next to a park, gets out, and approaches a half dozen high schoolers playing an informal game of football.)

NARRATOR: And there were in the same city some guys, playing football in a park after school. And lo, the messenger of the Lord appeared next to them.

YOUTH MINISTER: Hey, guys! Guess what? I've got the greatest news. Today, here in _____, a Savior has been born to you; he is Christ the Lord. Let's go to the Motel 6 down on _____ Street *(Ave.,*

Blvd., etc.) and see him.

NARRATOR: *(Background Christmas music plays as they all pile into the car of the YOUTH MINISTER and pull away from the park into traffic.)* So they all left their game and went to visit the Christ child. As they were leaving, they heard Christmas music playing in the heavens. *(Increase volume of music as they pull away.)*

SCENE 8
(back at motel 6. Inside are MARY, the BABY, YOUTH MINISTER, and HIGH SCHOOLERS.)

NARRATOR: They drove to the motel and found Mary and the child with her lying in a suitcase.

HIGH SCHOOLER 1: Where's the father?

MARY: He ran down to 7-11 for some Pampers. He'll be back any minute...

HIGH SCHOOLER 2: *(to YOUTH MINISTER in a whisper)* She doesn't have a ring on...are they even married?

YOUTH MINISTER: *(also whispered)* Long story. Tell you later.

NARRATOR: Next day at school, the high schoolers spread the word around campus about what they had seen. *(Camera begins to gradually back out of open motel room door. By the time NARRATOR finishes, camera has entire motel in view.)* It even made the newspapers—section B, page 8. Everyone who heard the story was amazed. Mary clipped the article and read it often, treasuring in her heart those things that had happened. The next afternoon the high schoolers returned to the park for another hour of football, praising God for the messenger. Because they had seen the Christ child, their lives would never be the same again.

END

THE DEPARTMENT STORE WINDOW

CHARACTERS

Window dresser
2 Window Washers
Several Mannequins (actors)
Angel
One or two Shepherds
Mary
Joseph
One or two Wise Men
Two sheep (use the pastor or youth pastor—the kids will love it)

PROPS

Manger with baby dolls, hay, other Nativity scene props: shepherds' staffs, gifts for the Wise Men, window washing equipment

HERE'S HOW TO SET UP THE STAGE:

1. Shepherd #1
2. Wise Men
3. Shepherd #2
4. Mary
5. Joseph
6. Sheep #1
7. Sheep #2
8. Angel
9. Manger

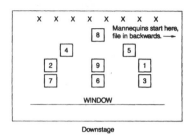

The scene opens with the MANNEQUINS at the back of the stage with their backs to the audience, barefoot and dressed in appropriate costumes (wearing shorts underneath—no pant legs showing). The two WINDOW WASHERS are stage front, complete with sponge, squeegees, buckets, overalls, and caps. Both are washing a huge imaginary window that covers the entire front of the stage. These two characters should be chosen for their ability to be real hams (for example, spitting on the window when they can't get a spot off). The WINDOW DRESSER enters from backstage, pencil behind ear, with clipboard, in business dress. She ignores the WINDOW WASHERS at first, dragging a large box to stage right full of scarves, crowns, gifts, halos, and other Nativity props. Just offstage, out of sight but easily accessible, should be two chairs, the manger and doll, staffs, and the larger props. The DRESSER steps backwards (toward the audience), takes a look at what she has to work with, and goes to the MANNEQUINS to drag one backwards to stage front. All MANNEQUINS must lock their knees, remaining stiff and staying absolutely still. One of the SHEPHERDS is brought out first and positioned to the right of the stage near the front. As the DRESSER tries to adjust him into position—hands, head, legs, and arms—she realizes she could use the help of the WINDOW WASHERS. She mimes talking to the one on the inside, he agrees, and she motions the other one to come inside. Both WASHERS join her, making sure to drop all their equipment backstage before continuing. As the DRESSER has the WASHERS drag MANNEQUINS one by one to the places she indicates (see diagram), she adds a sash here, a headpiece there, a scarf here and there—never dressing one MANNEQUIN completely so the audience will not be aware of the Nativity scene yet. The procedure of positioning the MANNEQUINS takes quite a while, and the key to its success is the ability of the WINDOW WASHERS to ham it up while the DRESSER seeks with

great seriousness to arrange her display. Every time the WINDOW DRESSER'S back is turned or she's involved with a MANNEQUIN, the WASHERS goof around by sticking fingers of MANNEQUINS in their noses, raising their arms, holding their noses, or whatever—the more laughs the better. The WASHERS should be doing this between dragging around the MANNEQUINS as directed by the DRESSER. As the DRESSER keeps discovering their antics, she keeps shooing them to the side, shaking her head, and putting them back in position. The DRESSER should also change her mind a few times and have the WASHERS move MANNEQUINS backward or forward a few inches as if she is really arranging a display. When MARY is brought out, the dresser should have a chair brought out for the mannequin to sit on. The last MANNEQUIN to be brought out should be the ANGEL (in a white robe). The ANGEL should be one of the last to be completely dressed; and when dressed with halo on head, should be lifted up (knees locked) by the two WASHERS onto another chair. A word of caution: As this pantomime can take quite a while, be careful not to have the ANGEL spread his or her arms out too soon, or the actor won't be able to hold that position. The same goes for the other MANNEQUINS. Keep everyone in easy positions until just before the end, when some last-second adjusting can be done.

After all the characters are positioned, the DRESSER places the final headpieces on the MANNEQUINS, then gets the gifts and staffs. The WASHERS bring out the manger and doll. The DRESSER motions her thanks and shoos the WASHERS offstage, having them take the box with them. The DRESSER does any final arranging needed, and when clearly satisfied, she leaves the stage.

The house lights go off. The spotlights come on, and a soloist then sings two verses of "O Holy Night" or "Silent Night." The impact will be dramatic.

THE GUEST

CHARACTERS

Conrad
Barclay
The Old Man
Two Passersby

Ellspith
The Poor Woman
The Kid
Narrator

PROPS

Streetlamp
Bookshelf
Milk
Chairs or sofa
Costumes

Fireplace
Shoes
Honey
Lamp

Table
Bread
Door
Other furnishings

NARRATOR:

Before the cathedral in grandeur rose
At Ingelburg where the Danube goes;
Before its forest of silver spires
Went airily up to the clouds and fires:
Before the oak had ready a beam,
While yet the arch was stone and dream—
There where the altar was later laid,
Conrad, the cobbler, plied his trade.

ELLSPITH

ELLSPITH: *(knocks)*

CONRAD: Bark! Bark!

ELLSPITH: *(knocks)*

CONRAD: *(as he walks to the door)* Bark! Bark! Down, Fang! Bark! Bark! Quiet. Bark! Growl...*(opens door)* Hello, Ellspith! Merry Christmas! Come in, come in.

ELLSPITH: Conrad, old friend. A merry Christmas to you, too. Conrad, what was barking? You don't have a watchdog.

CONRAD: I know. I can't afford one. So when someone comes to the door, I have to bark myself.

ELLSPITH: Oh, Conrad—we are all feeling the financial pinch.

CONRAD: Where's Barclay?

ELLSPITH: He's coming any minute.

BARCLAY: *(knocks)*

ELLSPITH: That's him now.

BARCLAY: *(knocks)*

ELLSPITH: Who's there?

BARCLAY: Snue!

ELLSPITH: Snue? *(opens door)* What's Snue?

BARCLAY: I don't know. What's Snue with you? Say, Conrad old boy—did you fix my sole?

CONRAD: Only the Lord can fix your soul, Barclay. But I did fix your shoe. *(hands him shoe, tapping on the sole)*

BARCLAY: How delightful. Now I have my Christmas shoes to wear with my Christmas stockings. They were knit by my dear, dear aunt. Do you know what they called my aunt, Conrad?

CONRAD: Probably Mamie Farnstock. That was her name.

BARCLAY: *(exasperated)* I mean after she died.

CONRAD: They called her the <u>late</u> Mamie Farnstock.

BARCLAY: They called her Marner the Darner. She used to say, "The hand that darns the sock..."

ELLSPITH: "...is usually the one that socks the husband!" Come, Barclay. We have to get you home into your socks. *(they start to leave)*

CONRAD: Ellspith. Barclay.

ELLSPITH: Yes, Conrad.

CONRAD: Before you leave, I must share my heart with you.

ELLSPITH: Conrad, please do.

BARCLAY: Yes, we are your friends.

CONRAD: *(dramatically, gazing heavenward)*
At dawn today
As night slipped away. . .
The Lord appeared in a dream to me
And said, "I am coming your Guest to be!"
So I've been busy with feet astir,
Strewing the floor with branches of fir.
The wall is washed and the shelf is shined,
And over the rafter the holly twined.
He comes today, and the table is spread
With milk and honey and wheaten bread."

ELLSPITH: *(staring blankly at Conrad)* Why is he talking in poetry?

BARCLAY: Too much Lutefisk, I suspect.

ELLSPITH: Listen, Conrad. It's Christmas, and your thoughts are filled with Christ's coming. No doubt your dreams merely reflected what you have been thinking all day.

BARCLAY: Ellspith's right, Conrad. I mean, Christ's not really going to come to your door.

CONRAD: *(pause)* Perhaps you are right. That is a little unusual. But it seemed so real.

ELLSPITH: We have to go, old friend—have a delightful Christmas.

BARCLAY: And if Jesus does come, send for us. We wise and royal beings will come bearing our gifts of mirth and franken-stein. *(Ellspith pulls Barclay out through door by scarf. They exchange appropriate farewells.)*

THE POOR WOMAN
(Conrad sees woman shivering in the cold, selling coal to passers-by. He invites her into his home to warm herself.)

WOMAN: Thank you kindly, sir. The weather is miserable out there.

CONRAD: It certainly is foggy.

WOMAN: The visibility is so bad even the birds are walking. *(she sneezes in his face)*

CONRAD: *(slightly put off, but polite)* Excuse me ma'am, but could you sneeze the other way?

WOMAN: I don't know no other way.

CONRAD: Here. Sit by the fire and warm yourself. Tell me how you came to such a wretched condition!

WOMAN: I was raised in poverty. We had nothing when I was growing up. And then I met John. He was rich. Sophisticated. He was the only banker unaffected by the crash of '29.

CONRAD: Really?

WOMAN: He went broke in '28. Ever since then we lived in a little dreary apartment in town. Our furniture was meager and shabby. We had one little worn rug on our cold floor. It looked so bad my mother would say, "That rug looks terrible. Sweep it under the dirt!"

CONRAD: What does your husband do now?

WOMAN: Oh, he passed away last year. I told him that if he were to die, starvation would stare me in the face. He said, "Doesn't sound pleasant for either of you!" So now it is just me and my children.

CONRAD: Woman, how can I help you?

WOMAN: You dear man. You can't help. *(gets up to go to the door)* I can see that you are not much better off than I. I am simply trying to sell some coal in order to purchase some fresh milk and bread for my family.

CONRAD: *(turns and picks up bread and milk on table)* Here—take this.

WOMAN: *(awed by this great sacrifice)* God bless you, my friend.

CONRAD: Merry Christmas.

THE OLD MAN

MAN: *(knocks)*

CONRAD: Bark! Bark! Ah! It'll never work! I just don't sound enough like a dog. Coming! *(opens door. Man throws bone in.)* What's that for?

MAN: I thought I heard a dog.

CONRAD: Ah, yes. He passed away. I just laid him to rest. What can I do for you, old man?

MAN: I am receiving Christmas donations for the Buford T. Ellis Memorial Fund.

CONRAD: And who, may I ask, is Buford T. Ellis?

MAN: At your service, sir. *(bows dramatically with top hat)*

CONRAD: *(chuckling)* Come in, old timer. You look like you could use at least a rest.

MAN: Thank you, sir. Usually I am not received in such kindness.

CONRAD: It's the least I can do. Here. Sit down.

MAN: *(sits down. Puts feet up on little table. Pulls out stogie.)*

CONRAD: So you are collecting money?

MAN: I am. I need some extra bucks for my expensive hobby.

CONRAD: And what hobby is that?

MAN: Eating.

CONRAD: You know it would be nice to have a lot of money. But really, money only brings misery.

MAN: But with money you can afford to be miserable. This Thanksgiving I asked myself, "What do I have to be thankful for?" I can't even pay my bills.

CONRAD: Be thankful you're not one of your creditors.

MAN: That's true. You know, I used to get by fairly well with my small business. But I have suffered one financial disaster after another.

CONRAD: It's been a tough life for you, hasn't it?

MAN: It hasn't been easy, but God has helped me.

CONRAD: Listen, old man. I don't have much. But here, take these shoes. You could stand a new pair.

MAN: *(looking very happy)* You are very generous. *(rips off his old shoes. They fall apart. Puts on new ones.)* They fit perfectly! Thank you, sir. *(he leaves. They exchange farewells.)*

THE KID

KID: *(knocks)*

CONRAD: *(opens door)*

KID: *(sings)* While shepherds washed their socks by night, all seated on the ground...

CONRAD: *(interrupts)* Hold it! Hold it! I think you have some of the words mixed up there. It's <u>watched,</u> not <u>washed.</u>

KID: While shepherds watched their socks by night...

CONRAD: Wait! And it's <u>flocks,</u> not <u>socks.</u>

KID: What are flocks?

CONRAD: They're a bunch of sheep. Do you know what sheep are? *(kid shakes head no)* They're little wooly things...kind of like socks! Merry Christmas! What can I do for you on this blessed day?

KID: I'm collecting arms for the poor.

CONRAD: That's <u>alms.</u>

KID: What are alms?

CONRAD: They're gifts, usually money.

KID: Oooh, nooo!

CONRAD: What's the problem?

KID: I've been going through the streets crying, "Arms for the poor; arms for the poor!"

CONRAD: Land o' Goshen! And what did you get?

KID: Strange looks. I'll never get any money.
CONRAD: Who are the poor you're collecting for?

KID: Conor Johnson's *(use the name of a kid in your group)* Home for Wayward Children.

CONRAD: There's no home there.

KID: Well, there's the Agony General Hospital, too.

CONRAD: Never heard of it.

KID: Would you believe the Shuffleboard Retirement Center?

CONRAD: *(shakes head)* Why don't you just tell me where the money is really going?

KID: *(face down, ashamed of his poverty)* It's for me.

CONRAD: That's what I thought. It looks like you need it.

KID: But it's not really for me. It's for my sister. I want to give her a present this Christmas. We don't have very much, and, well...I love my little sister. I thought I might give her something special.

CONRAD: *(looks at table; gives the kid the honey)*

KID: *(looks inside)* Wow! Is this real honey?

CONRAD: Yes. Give it to your sister. And here. Give her these shoes, and here is a pair for you.

KID: Wow! You are something, mister. Thank you. *(excitedly leaves)*

CONRAD: *(as he leaves)* Hey lad! What's your sister going to give you for Christmas?

KID: I don't know. Last year she gave me the measles! Goodbye, mister!

CONRAD: Merry Christmas!
(While the narrator reads, Conrad wanders around his room looking sad; but as he realizes that Christ came to him in those three people, he begins to smile radiantly.)

NARRATOR:
The day went down in the crimson West
And with it the hope of the blessed Guest,
And Conrad sighed as the world turned gray:
"Why is it, Lord, that your feet delay?
Did You forget that this was the day?"
Then soft in the silence a Voice he heard:
"Lift up your heart for I kept my word.
Three times I came to your friendly door;
Three times my shadow was on your floor.
I was the beggar with the bruised feet;
I was the woman you gave food to eat;
I was the child on the homeless street!"

END

HE'S GOING TO WHAT?

CHARACTERS
Angel 1
Angel 2

ANGEL 1: He's going down himself.

ANGEL 2: What?

ANGEL 1: I said, "He's going down!"

ANGEL 2: Who told you?

ANGEL 1: This morning during devotions he called Michael and Gabriel up and began to tell them, in front of us all, about the plan.

ANGEL 2: Why do I always miss the good parts?

ANGEL 1: Where were you?

ANGEL 2: Bythnia. I had to help little Lydia across that icy bridge again. But, do go on. What is The plan?

ANGEL 1: It has to do with the prophets' predictions.

ANGEL 2: So! The Day of the Lord is finally here. I guess I wasted my time helping Lydia. If he's bringing it all to a close now she'll be up here with us soon anyway.

ANGEL 1: It's not that simple. He's planning to straighten out the situation down there.

ANGEL 2: Well, why doesn't he send Moses? Or Elijah? Or Gabriel?

ANGEL 1: He will—each at his appointed time. But they can only take messages. I did hear that Gabriel is arranging the entrance preparations.

ANGEL 2: Oh, wow! I can see it now...all those humans wandering about in their busyness when all of a sudden the sun, stars, and sky roll back. Then, out of the deepness of eternity he steps foot on their planet. I wish I could be there to see their faces. How about old Augustus? He'll fall right off his pedestal.

ANGEL 1: It's not going to be that way. He doesn't even plan to show up at Rome.

ANGEL 2: No Rome? So! He's going to Jerusalem. Imagine, the high priest will look up and suddenly there he is. Won't that wrinkle his robe!

ANGEL 1: I doubt that will happen.

ANGEL 2: Oh? Don't tell me he won't see the high priest.

ANGEL 1: Yes, He will see the high priest and all his council, but I doubt if they will recognize him.

ANGEL 2: Not recognize the Lord of Glory? Does he plan to disguise himself?

ANGEL 1: In a way...

ANGEL 2: Why doesn't he want them to know who he is?

ANGEL 1: The way I understand it, he wants them to recognize him by his life and works, not by his appearance.

ANGEL 2: I'm assuming he'll go as a man, a Jewish man no doubt.

ANGEL 1: I hear he's planning his entry as a baby.

ANGEL 2: A what?

ANGEL 1: A baby, a humanette.

ANGEL 2: Incredible! But, but, isn't he taking a big chance? The security will be fantastic. Why, we'll have to form a couple myriads of bodyguards 24 hours a day.

ANGEL 1: He's going to be on his own.

ANGEL 2: Turn him loose with that pack of crazies?

ANGEL 1: Do you honestly think there's any way they can harm him against his will?

ANGEL 2: Of course you're right: He'll be taking his power with him. Can't you see the little tyke lying there in his mother's arms one minute, then jumping up the next to give a Roman soldier a karate chop?

ANGEL 1: I've heard his power will only be used to help others. He doesn't think it necessary to show all his credentials. And he already has the mother picked out.

ANGEL 2: I hope it's not Lydia's mother.

ANGEL 1: Who?

ANGEL 2: Lydia, the little girl from Bythnia. Imagine letting your four-year-old walk across a slick bridge like that. Anyway, I suppose he's picked out a priest's family or a family of the Pharisees.

ANGEL 1: No, she's a poor, young unknown by the name of Mary. And...now keep this quiet, I wouldn't want every angel in the galaxy to hear this...he's going to be born in a stall, a cattle stable, right in the stench of earthly hay and stubble.

ANGEL 2: But, that's criminal! It can't be! I won't allow it! I protest!

ANGEL 1: To whom?

ANGEL 2: I just don't understand the purpose in all this.

ANGEL 1: You know as well as I do how he loves them. Now, listen, here's where we fit in. He does want us to line up a few witnesses to record the event for future generations.

ANGEL 2: Sure, I've got it. How about 1000 men from each of the 12 tribes of Israel?

ANGEL 1: I said just a few.

ANGEL 2: How about 100 each?

ANGEL 1: No. He wants only a few.

ANGEL 2: Well, how about a couple scribes, a lawyer, a politician, and a news reporter, of course.

ANGEL 1: That definitely won't do. Besides, he has them picked out already. Here's the list... *(hands ANGEL 2 the list)*

ANGEL 2: Let's see...three astrologers from Arbela. Where's that?

ANGEL 1: Over on the east side of the Tigris.

ANGEL 2: But they're foreigners, outsiders.

ANGEL 1: Don't forget the others too.

ANGEL 2: Oh, yes, there's Jason, Demas, and Hakiah. Who are they?

ANGEL 1: Shepherds, I believe.

ANGEL 2: Just common, ordinary hillside shepherds?

ANGEL 1: It's his style, you know. Look at Abraham. What was he? And David? And what was Moses doing out there when the bush caught on fire?

ANGEL 2: I see what you mean.

ANGEL 1: One thing does bother me, though. Who down there will believe the shepherds?

ANGEL 2: Lydia would.

ANGEL 1: Yes, I love those humanettes. They believe whatever we tell them.

ANGEL 2: They do until Satan gets hold of them. By the way, what will Satan be doing all this time?

He won't like this one bit.

ANGEL 1: I figure he'll try to incite the humans to hateful and brutal actions.

ANGEL 2: You don't suppose they'll keep falling for his old lines, do you?

ANGEL 1: They're like putty in his hands most of the time. But, I do hear that our Lord will pull off some pretty big miracles...and then, there's the Final Presentation.

ANGEL 2: What's that?

ANGEL 1: I don't know for sure. It's top secret.

ANGEL 2: I see. Well, now, let me review. All we have to do is go down, talk to the shepherds, and come back here and watch him do the rest. Right?

ANGEL 1: Right. There's the preliminary signal. It's just about time for us to go down.

ANGEL 2: Wow! What a day. I thought I wouldn't have anything to do until the bridge freezes over again.

ANGEL 1: Remember, only a few shepherds. And please don't scare them.

ANGEL 2: I promise, I promise.

ANGEL 1: There's the signal. Let's go.

ANGEL 2: Do you think we could stop by Bythnia on the way back? It's about time for Lydia to say her prayers. I just love the way she prays.

ANGEL 1: Oh, I guess so. Now, hurry.

ANGEL 2: I'm right behind you. But, I was wondering...what if it doesn't work out the way we think? What if there's a lot of resistance to his plan? Down there as a vulnerable human, why, he could get himself killed!

ANGEL 1: Don't be ridiculous!

And in the same region there were some shepherds staying out in the fields, and keeping watch over their flock by night. And an angel of the Lord suddenly stood before them, and the glory of the Lord shone around them; and they were terribly frightened. And the angel said to them, "Do not be afraid; for behold, I bring you good news of a great joy which shall be for all the people; for today in the city of David there has been born for you a Savior, who is Christ the Lord. And this will be a sign for you; you will find a baby wrapped in cloths, and lying in a manger." And suddenly there appeared with the angel a multitude of the heavenly host praising God, and saying, "Glory to God in the highest, and on earth peace among men with whom He is pleased."(Luke 2:8-14, NASB)

END

The Innkeeper's Wife

Woman appears with cleaning rag and apron. She mutters to herself while cleaning.

I'm so tired of all this cleaning! Seems like that's all I ever do! *(phone rings)* I'll never get finished if this phone doesn't stop ringing. *(answers phone)* Hello, Bethlehem Inn, may I help you?...Oh hi, Mabel...terrible, just terrible! Hardly got any sleep last night!...Why?...You mean you haven't heard?...Well, you know Caesar has passed this amendment about taxing! I just don't understand this government—it's such a mess!...That's right...Because of all this, so many folks have been traveling—we've been packed! You should see the parking lot—it's full of camels and donkeys! And you know what a mess they make! Yes, David has been sick, and the girls gave up their room to some travelers. Why, we even had folks sleeping in the hall last night...and you know what a fire hazard that is!...

Well, Joe had to cut some more wood, so I had to get all the kids in bed and check in the guests. Got 'em all to bed, fixed Joe some supper, and finally got to bed myself!...Yeah...Uh-huh...Along about two o'clock there was this loud banging on the door! I nearly flew out of the bed with heart flutters! Oh, goodness me! That was so frightening...Uh-huh...So Joe goes down to the door and I peeped out the window...Couldn't believe what I saw! There was a young couple on a donkey and she was pregnant!...Yes...uh-huh...real far along!...And out in that cold, too! I heard it got down to ten below here in Bethlehem last night...No! We didn't have a choice! Every room was packed! They said every inn for the past two miles was full, too...

Yeah...Well, Joe gave them the key to the barn so they could at least get out of that wind...and she looked like she could have had that baby any minute!...Uh-huh...Uh-huh...By that time the kids were awake and fighting over the pillows—Man, did I need an Alka-Seltzer!...Uh-huh...

Just barely got back to sleep, and heard some more noise outside. Looked out the window and saw more camels! People looked kinda like shepherds—I figured they could just find their way back to the barn, too...Yeah...*(looks at watch)*...Uh-huh...Uh-huh...Who?...Oh, yeah, she had the baby all right...I found out this morning...A king after Caesar?...Sure, Mabel, you've really lost it this time! I'm sure a king is going to be born in a barn...Well, I don't care who it is! I'm not going down there to help after all the trouble they've caused me!...I'll just be glad when they're gone!...What?...Mabel, I'm sorry!...We just didn't have room! *(looks at watch again)* I just don't have time! I've got lots to do here. I'll probably be the one who has to clean up all this camel mess! Yuk! Yeah...Uh-huh...I gotta go! Bye! *(hangs up and mutters)* Some people just don't understand! I've got work to do! *(exits)*

END

Joe's Story

Some vacation this turned out to be. And it started out with such great promise. I'm a computer programmer at a company that rewards its employees over the holidays by shutting down for two weeks. So my fiancée Marie and I had planned to go up the coast to see my folks in Seattle. We had planned to get married in about a year, but I didn't want to make any definite plans without my parents' approval. My folks had never met Marie, so I was a bit nervous—but I was sure they'd like her. After all, my mom would always say, "Ah, my boy Joey, as long as she's Jewish, she can't be all bad." I knew my folks would be proud. Especially after they tasted Marie's cooking.

I can't explain how much I loved that woman. I had done a lot of dating, but no one came near to Marie. She is the most beautiful woman I've ever seen. At first that made me a bit cautious. All the other women I had known who were exceptionally beautiful knew they were exceptionally beautiful. And it wasn't just the arrogance and conceit that turned me off. It was the selfishness, the vibes they gave as if the world revolved around them. But Marie was different. She was the most loving and kind woman I had met. I realized that she was something special when I went with her to her synagogue one Saturday. We sat through the service and then I followed her to her classroom. Expecting to see a roomful of singles or college students, I found instead a large group of mentally and physically handicapped students. And it made me uncomfortable. Some students were confined to wheelchairs, others could talk only with grunts and groans; I deduced from the odor in the room that others were incontinent.

I was repulsed. But this was Marie's mission field. She started with only a few students in her class, but the news of this ministry traveled fast. People from other synagogues began to bring their students to her to be ministered to. The minute Marie walked in the door, she was mobbed with students who wanted to talk with her, hug her, kiss her. Anything just to be near her. As I watched her love and care for those students over that next hour, I made up my mind that I would do all I could to make sure that I spent the rest of my life with that woman.

Everything was set for our departure. The plane tickets bought, our bags packed, all our gifts for the family from sunny California had been wrapped. I was really getting excited about going.

Then my world collapsed. I'll always remember that Friday as the worst day of my life.

I got off work early Friday night and went straight to Marie's apartment. I bolted up the steps to the second floor where she lived, hiding behind my back the flowers that I had bought from a kid on the corner. I rang the doorbell, she opened the door, I whirled the flowers from behind me, and braced myself for the squeal and hug I always got when I did something special for Marie.

They never came. Something was missing from her eyes, which usually glowed but now only looked hollow and red around the corners. "What's wrong?" I asked, but she deflected my question with a question about my last day at Rockwell before vacation. We sat down for dinner, but our conversation was strained and uncharacteristically trivial. When we finished clearing the table, Marie immediately turned on the TV.

"What's going on?" I demanded, and she at once began crying. "Marie, is it something I've said, something I've done? Are you worried about the trip? I need to know so I can change or apologize or whatever. But I can't go on not knowing!" I put my arm around her, waiting for a hint of what her problem was.

"Joe," she said between sobs, "I'm pregnant." I took a deep breath—and when I exhaled, I felt all energy leave my body. This can't be happening, I thought. All I hoped for was shattered in two words. I unconsciously pulled my arm off her shoulder. The woman I loved only minutes before seemed now as distant as a stranger.

I wasn't the father—I knew that much. Sure, we'd kiss and hug like any other engaged couple, but we had made a deal that we would save making love for marriage. We were both convinced that it'd be best in the long run. So how could she do this after all that talking we had done?

"I know you're hurting now." After a long pause, Marie broke the silence. She was always good at understatement. "But please, Joe—please believe what I'm going to tell you, though it sounds crazy and impossible." She paused and looked at me deeply before she spoke again. "God gave me my pregnancy."

I almost walked out. Of all the excuses. At least she could have told me the truth: Who was it? What happened? And why? Why did she betray me?

"An angel came to me and told me that God had chosen me to carry his son and give him birth—Joe, don't look at me like that. You know—you've read the words from the Scriptures—about the Messiah. This child—our child—is the Messiah. No, I wouldn't have believed either, if it hadn't been for the angel who told me."

Nothing was making sense—Marie's pregnancy (how could she?), God's Son inside her, an angel. I wanted to believe her story, but it was too far-fetched. I moved toward the door without a word.

"Joe, I love you. Only you. No one else. I will always love you. But if you want to leave me, I understand. I don't want to disgrace you. If you don't believe me, I can't expect anyone at church or in our families to." I mumbled something about thinking things over and needing to rest, then left her. I drove the long way home, replaying in my mind what she had told me. I cried and felt hopeless, despairing, empty, angry tears. I couldn't imagine seeing Marie again, and I couldn't imagine not seeing her again. I hit the sack when I got home and fell asleep no earlier than one in the morning or so.

I'm typically a heavy sleeper. Remember that big earthquake we had a few years back? Slept right through it. As drained as I was that night, you'd think I could sleep through World War III. But sometime early that morning I was awakened by a piercing light in my bedroom. It took a few seconds for me to wake up enough to discern the shape of a man sitting on the foot of my bed. The 200-watt glow wasn't all—he seemed seven or eight feet tall, yet didn't even crease the mattress.

What a dream! was my first thought. Then I remembered what happened earlier that night; the stress must be making me delirious. Though my self-diagnoses were unspoken, a voice coming from this being boomed in my head in answer. "You're not dreaming, Joe, neither are you out of your mind. I know you've had a hard night, a terrible night, and that's why I'm here. What Marie told you is true. She's carrying a child of whom you are not the biological father. And though this is difficult for you to believe, she is still true to you. She is still a virgin."

I didn't understand at all. But who's gonna argue with a eight-foot flashlight?

"Go ahead with your plans to marry each other," the humanoid alien continued. "Your families and friends will understand in time that it is the right decision. Name the boy Joshua, and raise him as if he were your biological son."

Before I could argue with him, he was gone, leaving me with a whirlwind of emotions. Marie still a virgin! Marie chosen by God! Me a father to the Messiah! Yet what would people say? No one would believe what was told to Marie and me. And if I married Marie without making a big fuss about the miracle of her pregnancy, everyone would assume—I would, too—that we had slept together before the wedding.

Let them think what they will. It won't be easy, but I'm marrying Marie—and I'll be a father to Josh. I just hope you know what you're doing, Lord. ◆

A Little Girl Looks at the Christmas Story

Here's a short one-act play (pages 172–174) for Christmas that can be done with only two people (a lady and a little girl). The father is just a man's voice offstage. The girl can be someone just dressed like a little girl and acting like one. For best results, the lines should be memorized. The set doesn't have to be too elaborate—just a makeshift living room with a front door and perhaps a couch and some other simple furnishings.

Mary's Story

The play on pages 175–177 is based on the Christmas story, and is excellent for use during the holiday season. But it is perhaps even more effective when presented at a time other than Christmas, to heighten the element of surprise at the ending. The names of the characters are not given during the play itself. The setting is modern times. Each of the scenes can be set up any way you choose, and the dialogue has been written in such a way as to allow you the freedom to change or add to it as you see fit. This play was written by Beverly Snedden and the youth group of Calvary Baptist Church in Kansas City, Missouri. *Larry Bradford*

TV Christmas Story

Here is a dramatic presentation (pages 178–179) centered around a television newscast, that can be given at Christmastime. The newscast occurs on the first Christmas day but is done with a modern set. Simply reproduce a large TV News set complete with monitor, station call letters in the back, etc. You could even go so far as to construct phony cameras, etc. All the news commentators should be dressed in modern clothes. Feel free to adapt, add to or subtract any part of the script you want.
Fred Davis

Whose Birthday Is It?

This discussion-starter (page 180) is related to Christmas. You can add as many characters as you wish. After the skit, discuss what happened with the family. See how long it takes for the group to make the connection that Jesus' birthday is often ignored as people celebrate Christmas. *Jim Ruberg*

A Little Girl Looks at the Christmas Story

CHARACTERS
Father (voice offstage)
Mrs. Hansen
Laney Joy

LANEY: *(singing)* Away in a manger, no crib for a bed,
The little Lord Jesus laid down his sweet head.
The stars in the sky looked down where he lay,
The little Lord Jesus, asleep on the hay.
The cattle are blowing, the baby awakes,
But little Lord Jesus, no crying he makes...
(doorbell rings)

FATHER: Laney...Laney Joy! Will you get the door?

LANEY: I would, Dad...but what if it's not a friendly person?

FATHER: It's probably Mrs. Hansen. Just tell her to wait downstairs until I'm finished with this appointment.

LANEY: *(opens door)* Hello, lady.

LADY: *(very cheerfully)* Well, hello. You must be the preacher's little girl...I'm Mrs. Hansen...from church. I have an appointment with your Dad. May I come in?

LANEY: He's already got one 'pointment upstairs. I don't think he needs another one.

LADY: I don't think you understand, dear...You see—

LANEY: In fact, I am certain that he does not need any. My mama always says that Papa has too many 'pointments.

LADY: *(mildly amused)* No, dear, you don't under-stand. I want to talk to your Daddy...about marrying my daughter.

LANEY: Oh, lady, you're too late. My Papa is already married. He married my Mama a couple of years ago.

LADY: A couple of years?

LANEY: Yes, lady. I think it was even before I was born...and I'm five years old.

LADY: Yes...I'm sure it was—

FATHER: Laney, Is that Mrs. Hansen?

LANEY: Yes, sir. I'm trying to tell her that you aren't innerested in marrying...

FATHER: Laney, just invite her in. I'll be with her in a few minutes.

LANEY: Well...it's against my better judgment. But I guess I have to do what my Papa says. Come in. While we're waiting I'll entertain you.

LADY: Oh, that's not necessary, dear.

LANEY: Oh, yes, lady. It's part of my role as the preacher's daughter. First I will tell you about myself. My name is Laney Joy, and I'm five years old...and I'm a very precarious child.

LADY: *(whispered)* I'm beginning to see that. *(aloud)* Precarious?

LANEY: Yes. That means I'm ahead of other kids my same age. I can sing...and I can read the Bible all by myself.

LADY: Read the Bible? And you're only five?

LANEY: Aren't you impressed, lady? Would you like to hear me read something?

LADY: Well, I...uh...

LANEY: I know. Since it's nearly Christmas, I'll read the Christmas story to you. Have you heard that one?

LADY: Yes, a few times.

LANEY: But I bet you've never heard it the way I read it.

LADY: Somehow I can believe that!

LANEY: Okay. This is how it goes: Once upon a time, a long time ago, an angel came to Mary and said, "Mary, would you like to have the baby Jesus?" Mary said she guessed she would someday, after she married Joseph. But she didn't know if she would name her first son Jesus. But the angel said that was not what he had in mind. He wanted to know if she would have the Son of God. Well, Mary didn't know about that. She said she would have to think about it.

LADY: Wait. Are you sure that's the way the story goes?

LANEY: Certainly. You don't think she would agree to something like that without thinking about it first, do you?

LADY: I guess I never thought of it quite that way.

LANEY: You have to think about these things, lady... Anyway, Mary finally said she guessed it would be okay, as long as she could wait until she married Joseph. They would want to wait until they had enough money to support a baby. But the angel said, "No way. Don't you ever read your Bible, Mary? 'Cause in the Bible it says that Jesus was born at just the right time. And that right time is right now." So Mary had to make up her mind quick. It was one of those now-or-never deals. You know about them, don't you, lady?

LADY: Well, yes. But not quite in that way...So Mary decided to have the baby Jesus?

LANEY: I was just coming to that next part. Mary said it would be okay with her if it was okay with Joseph. You can kinda see how he might not like it, can't you, lady?

LADY: I never thought about it before, but yes, I can.

LANEY: Well, the angel said if she was really worried about it, he would appear to Joseph in a dream and tell him all about it. But would she please make up her mind because he had to go on and do other things for God. So then Mary said okay, she'd do it if the angel would promise her that everything would be all right. But you know what the angel said to that?

LADY: No, I don't.

LANEY: The angel said he didn't know what would happen. He only knew what God said to do. But he reckoned if Mary did what God wanted her to do, chances were things would turn out okay in the end. Then he quoted Hebrews 11:1 to her and left...So that's how it all began. Then you know what happened?

LADY: I used to think I did, but I'm not so sure now.

LANEY: Well, next, Mary and Joseph had to go to Bethlehem to pay up their back taxes. You see, God had to get them to Bethlehem so what Micah had said would come true—about Jesus being born in Bethlehem—and God figured taxes were as good an excuse as any...My Papa's been to the Holy Land—that's where Bethlehem is—and he says that's a hard trip even in a Jeep. So you can imagine what is was like on a donkey. I bet by the time they got to Bethlehem Mary was sorry she ever got involved in the whole business. But that's not the kind of thing you can change your mind about, so she had to go through with it. But by the time they got to Bethlehem, I bet she wasn't singing that same song.

LADY: Song? What song is that?

LANEY: 'Bout how her soul doth magnify the Lord. She was probably saying she'd just as soon somebody else had all that honor and let her just be a plain housewife—which was all she ever wanted anyway. You know, in one way it would have been nice if God could have waited 'til today and let some fem'nist lady have baby Jesus. But that was not God's style. He wanted Mary to do it. So they got to Bethlehem, but all the hotels were full 'cause Joseph hadn't phoned ahead for reservations. Then you know what happened?

LADY: They had to stay in a stable?

LANEY: That's very good, lady. They had to stay in a stable 'cause there wasn't room for them in the Holiday Inn. Well, the angel was looking down at them, and you know what he did?...He told God he didn't think it was fair, making them have it so rough. And he offered to go down with a whole squad of other angels and sort of clean up the place, and make it a little better looking since it would be the first place baby Jesus would see on earth. And if it was too bad, it might make him change his mind and decide not to live on earth, after all. Well, God said that would be a shame, 'cause the world was counting on Jesus. But he wouldn't let the angels come and fix things up. He said he'd already taken care of that.

LADY: Oh? How had he done that?

LANEY: He made baby Jesus be just like any other human baby, so he wouldn't notice if he was born in a stable or a house or a palace. The angels said they guessed that was all right—they hadn't thought of it that way. Which is why God is God—'cause he had a better idea... Then the exciting part happened.
LADY: And what was that?

LANEY: That was when the angels started singing "Glory to God in the Highest." The shepherds heard it, and they started singing "Do You Hear What I Hear?" Then the—

LADY: Now, wait a minute. I think you're confusing your stories.

LANEY: I just elaborated a little, that's all. It could have happened. Anyway, the little drummer boy heard it, and he started playing his drum. And that was the first Christmas concert. All these people went to the stable and...Oh, lady, it was so exciting! *(excitement builds, growing into awe)* They saw baby Jesus...and they knew he was the Son of God...and they—Lady, can you imagine what it was like? The Son of God on earth! So God would know what it was like to be a man...'cause that was the only way he could ever save people from their sins. Oh, lady, it must have been wonderful!

LADY: *(getting caught up in it, too)* Yes, it must have been!

LANEY: I guess it was 'bout as wonderful as it is today.

LADY: Huh? As what is today?

LANEY: As finding out that God came to earth.

LADY: *(slightly puzzled)* Finding out that God came—...? *(she understands)* Oh. Yes. I guess it was almost as exciting as that. And that's mighty exciting!

LANEY: Yes, lady. That's the truth! I can't think of anything—

FATHER: Good-bye, Mr. Petersen. Hope I was able to help...*(louder)* Mrs. Hansen, I can see you now.

LADY: Yes, pastor, I'll be right in... Laney Joy, thanks for the story.

LANEY: Oh, that's all right, lady. Any time. *(resumes song)* "Away in a manger, no crib for a bed..." *(fade)*

END

Mary's Story

CHARACTERS

Mary
Joseph
Mother
Dad
Carpenters (1 and 2)

Teachers (1 and 2)
Neighbors
Elizabeth
The Doctor
The Psychiatrist

The Rabbi
Joe's Parents
Mary's Friends (1 and 2)

SCENE ONE

Girls are sitting around a table discussing the upcoming dance.

GIRL 1: What are you going to wear?

MARY: I don't know if I'm going.

GIRL 2: Everybody's going. It'll be a good dance.

MARY: I can't even dance. Anyway, I wouldn't know how to ask a guy for a date.

GIRL 1: This is your chance to get around.

GIRL 2: What about that guy your parents like? Do they still want you to marry him when you get out of school?

GIRL 1: I hear he's got his own business and a sharp car.

GIRL 2: The guy I'm going with has a new Corvette.

SCENE TWO

Mary kneels beside her bed.

MARY: *(this can be ad-libbed somewhat)* Why me? What am I going to tell Mom and Dad?...What will my friends think?...What is he going to do?...They're never going to believe me...

SCENE THREE

The living room. Mary's parents are sitting on the couch.

MOM: Well, I asked her what was wrong, but I wasn't able to get much out of her. She claims there's a lot of pressure from her teacher giving her a big assignment.

DAD: Well, that doesn't sound like our little girl. She doesn't usually let something like that bother her so much. I've heard a lot about the drug problem at her school. I'm sure our daughter has been raised well enough not to do anything like that, but that doesn't mean the pressure isn't hurting her. Maybe I could talk to her.

MOM: Well, I guess it couldn't hurt but be careful not to hurt her more. She's been awfully touchy lately.

SCENE FOUR

Two girls are talking on the phone.

GIRL 1: I'm worried about her. She's been acting strange lately. Crying about silly things.

GIRL 2: Yeah, I've noticed.

GIRL 1: Have you noticed she's gained weight?

GIRL 2: Yeah, maybe it's from all that broccoli and other health food she's been eating.

GIRL 1: She won't go out with us—not even to the dance we all went to. She says she's too tired.

GIRL 2: She's had the flu a lot lately. Maybe I'll call her and see how she's feeling.

SCENE FIVE
The teachers' lounge at school.

TEACHER 1: She's been acting differently lately.

TEACHER 2: Her grades have dropped and she's been missing my class a lot.

TEACHER 1: She seems lonely. She isn't with her old crowd anymore.

TEACHER 2: She's also been putting on weight and wearing those loose tops.

TEACHER 1: She's in my first hour English class, and she's asked to see the nurse a lot. Do you think she's in trouble? She's so sweet.

SCENE SIX
Two neighbors are talking over the back fence.

NEIGHBOR 1: I just know she is! And with those wonderful parents; they've tried so hard to bring her up right.

NEIGHBOR 2: I bet I know who the father is...that older boy her father knows. He's the only one I've seen at the house.

NEIGHBOR 2: You never know, do you? She just didn't seem the type...so well-behaved and respectful.

NEIGHBOR 2: She goes to Synagogue every week. What is the world coming to?

SCENE SEVEN
Two carpenters are sawing boards.

CARPENTER 1: Poor guy...that's too bad.

CARPENTER 2: He's got to be crazy to marry her.

CARPENTER 1: I'd hate to be in his place.

CARPENTER 2: Be quiet! He's coming.

SCENE EIGHT
The living room. Mom and Dad are talking to Mary and Joseph when three men enter.

MOM: Where did I go wrong? (*doorbell rings. Father gets up to answer it and escorts in the Doctor, Psychiatrist And Rabbi*)

FATHER: Gentlemen, we have discovered our daughter is pregnant and we don't know what to do. We need your expert opinions about what we should do. We don't want her life and future ruined.

DOCTOR: As a physician, the only option I can see for a girl her age is to terminate the pregnancy. If you choose abortion, we'll have to act quickly. Then no one else will have to know.

PSYCHIATRIST: From the viewpoint of a psychiatrist, her emotional stability would probably stand an abortion better than adoption. If you choose for her to give birth to the child, she might want to keep it and I believe that would be a grave mistake.

RABBI: They must get married. I know they're young, but with prayer the marriage can work.

FATHER: *(to Joseph)* You got her into this—what do you have to say?

MARY: I'm going to have my baby and keep it. With the Lord's help, I can handle it.

JOSEPH: I had considered breaking it off, but I've prayed about the situation and have decided it's God's will that we should be married. I'll do my best to be a good father to the baby.

SCENE NINE
The living room. Mary and Elizabeth are talking.

MARY: He wonders whether or not our marriage will work. I want it to work.

ELIZABETH: He's a quiet person who loves his work. I'm sure he's worried about the gossip you've told me about.

MARY: Yes, I feel it's affecting our relationship. He's so practical that he can't believe how I got pregnant. No one believes him when he says he isn't the father.

ELIZABETH: I understand what you are going through, but we know it will be worth it. When the baby is born everything will be okay, you'll see.

MARY: You're only my cousin, but you're more like a sister to me.

SCENE TEN
Mary and Joseph meet privately.

MARY: I'm really frightened about your leaving on this trip. The doctor says that the baby could come anytime now.

JOSEPH: Yeah, I know but I have to go! The only solution is having you go with me.

MARY: Well, I'd rather be with you when the time comes. You know, I am really excited about the baby. God has given me peace that we have done the right thing.

JOSEPH: I really feel that way, now. We have a big job ahead of us. We first of all must be sure that we are completely dedicated to God so we can guide our little son.

SCENE ELEVEN
Mary and Joseph are with the new baby. The Doctor, the Psychiatrist, and the Rabbi enter, bringing gifts for the baby. They kneel and worship Him.

DOCTOR: *(to Mary and Joseph)* Forgive us, for our prejudice and judgments. We are here to give you and your son our love.

PSYCHIATRIST: Through prayer we were able to understand your situation.

RABBI: Mary, what will you name Him?

MARY: He has been named...Jesus.

END

TV CHRISTMAS STORY

ANNOUNCER: Stay tuned for the VBS Evening News with Barnabas Rather with the latest on a strange sighting in the sky; Martha Waltersberg from downtown Bethlehem where a huge crowd is gathering for the tax enrollment, Dr. Ben Hadad with reports about a new cold front moving in. That's the VBS news coming up next.

COMMERCIAL: Taxes. Taxes. Taxes. No one likes to pay taxes. Especially when H & R Blockberg can help you pay the least taxes possible. H & R Blockberg is the only tax consulting service authorized by the Roman Government and each and every consultant has tax collecting experience. Yes, you can trust H & R Blockberg for all your tax related problems. H & R Blockberg, 700 Appian Way.

ANNOUNCER: The VBS Evening News with Barnabas Rather in Jerusalem, Martha Waltersberg in Bethlehem and Dr. Ben Hadad on Mt. Ararat. Now...Barnabas Rather.

BARNABAS: Good Evening. There has been a new development on the strange light that has been sighted in the eastern sky for the last few nights. Correspondent Moshe Smith reports...

MOSHE: For the past few nights a bright light or star-like phenomena has been appearing in the sky. At first it was thought to be a meteor or an optical illusion, but tonight Dr. Ishmael Streisand confirmed that what everyone is seeing is, in fact, a star. The question is where did this star come from and what does it mean. Officials close to the situation are speculating that the star is not an isolated incident and that more strange occurrences may be expected. Concerned government officials are monitoring the situation closely and reliable sources have told VBS that other incidents have not been made public. This is Correspondent Moshe Smith in Jerusalem.

BARNABAS: VBS news has learned that an incident did occur near Bethlehem and we now switch to our mini-cam live in the hills of Bethlehem. David Saul reports.

DAVID: Barnabas, approximately 10 minutes ago a group of shepherds told me that they saw some kind of an angel accompanied by music and bright lights. Normally, stories from shepherds are discounted because of the fact that they are a strange breed...and tend to hit the sauce...but government officials here seem strangely concerned. From my discussions with the shepherds apparently they think this has something to do with a Messiah promised years ago. The mention of the Messiah seems to be what has government officials so concerned. From the hills of Bethlehem, this has been David Saul reporting.

BARNABAS: Last month Ceasar Augustus issued a decree requiring all citizens to return to their cities of birth in order to attain an accurate enrollment for taxing. Martha Waltersberg is in Bethlehem for the story.

MARTHA: I'm standing here at the No Room Inn on the outskirts of Bethlehem. Thousands of people are swarming into the city now and every available facility is full. Just a few minutes ago a woman who is about to have a baby was almost turned away. Finally, after protests from her husband, they were allowed to stay with the animals. We just finished talking with the head of the Best Eastern Lodge Association and he suggests that anyone heading for Bethlehem attempt to find lodging outside of town. The head of the Roman Government here in Bethlehem is deeply concerned about crowd control. So far, there have not been any major incidents. The question is, can this uneasy quiet continue? Martha Waltersberg at the No Room Inn in Bethlehem.

BARNABAS: A group of highly respected astrologers has begun a significant journey. Correspondent Mort Solomon reports from Peking.

MORT: Barnabas, a large party of wealthy astrologers are traveling toward Israel to observe a strange light.

Apparently it is the same strange light seen over Israel the past few weeks. Informed sources have told us that these men believe there is some relation between the light and the Messiah. Although there has been no official recognition by the Roman government it is believed that when the astrologers arrive within Roman territory they will be summoned before government officials. Reporters here, Barnabas, are baffled as to this sudden concern on the part of Roman officials for this promised Messiah. Why, we just will have to wait and see. Mort Solomon from China.

COMMERCIAL: The VBS News will continue in just a moment. Ladies, now is the time to order your hooded capes and robes. The Good Hood company has an incredible selection now. These hooded capes and robes are all one piece of material and the good cannot be lost nor can it become entangled in water jugs being carried on the head. The Good Hood Company—where we also have a clearance on beautiful sheepskin swimming suits. Come by and see us soon.

BARNABAS: Eric Rosen has been watching with interest the increasing speculation about a coming Messiah. Eric.

ERIC: The reason there is so much concern about a Messiah, of course, is the popular notion by the Jews that such a Messiah will become a political force and overthrow the Romans. This is a hope that Jews have had for years and we have seen potential "messiahs" come and go. We have a feeling that the strange light in the East is nothing more than a passing phenomena that those who are overly religious and mystical can cling to or, worse yet, use to mount a revolutionary movement. I have done some research on this matter of a Messiah and I am not so sure that if and when such a Savior were to appear, it would be a political leader. I am sure I will get a lot of mail about this, but I think it would be much more profitable if those who are so anxiously awaiting a Messiah would start living like they believed in the God they say they do. I guess it is always easier and less threatening to hope in the future than to live like the future were now. Eric Rosen...VBS News.

BARNABAS: Jerusalem has been the home of the National Open Spear Throwing Olympics. Stud Barjonas reports.

STUD: Coming off of major upset victories, two Hebrews will be facing each other in the finals to be held next Friday. Friday's match between Philip of Caesarea and Simion of Bethany has already been sold out. There is some concern that Philip of Caesarea may have trouble keeping his feet within the specified boundaries on his approach. He refused comment on the two warnings he received today. However, sources close to Philip confirm that he will be wearing a new imported brand of sandal to give him additional footing. Should be quite a match. In chariot racing today, Fireball Jonah narrowly escaped serious injury when his vehicle turned over in the northwest turn at the Hippodrome. This turn is considered one of the most hazardous in racing. In spite of the mishap, Jonah went on to win the main event.

BARNABAS: Dr. Ben Hadad has been standing by on Mt. Ararat for the weather report, but we have just received a bulletin from Bethlehem. Martha Waltersberg is there.

MARTHA: Barnabus, as you know from my earlier report I am at the No Room Inn here in Bethlehem. Just as we were getting ready to leave, we were told of a commotion at the back of the inn. We found a young girl who had just given birth to a baby where they keep the animals. Normally, we would have ignored the story, but, Barnabas, something strange is occurring here. A huge crowd is gathering and a number of shepherds and others almost seem to be worshipping the baby. We have been unable to get any comment from anyone here, but there is one thing else. That strange light in the sky seems to be much brighter now and almost seems to be directly above us. This is Martha Waltersberg in a stable in Bethlehem.

BARNABAS: And that's the way it is. Barnabas Rather for the VBS Evening News. Good Night.

END

WHOSE BIRTHDAY IS IT?

CHARACTERS
Mom
Dad
Ken (son)
Pam (daughter)

The setting is a typical living room on Christmas morning.

PAM: *(complaining)* No birthday present again! Why did I have to be born on Christmas Day? Did you know that nobody has ever remembered my birthday?

KEN: Considering the time of year, who's going to remember a mere birthday? It's Christmas!

PAM: *(complaining even more)* You get birthday presents every year and so do Dad and Mom. But all I ever get is combination birthday/Christmas presents. It's not fair!

(Dad and Mom enter.)

Dad: Merry Christmas, Pam. Merry Christmas, Ken.

KEN: Merry Christmas, Dad, Mom.

PAM: It's also my birthday, you know.

MOM: We know, dear. Merry Christmas.

DAD: Well, let's all open presents, shall we?

MOM: I wonder what I got from Santa this year!

KEN: Here, Dad! *(handing him a gift)* Open this one!

(Let characters ad lib their parts as they enthusiastically open their gifts, except for Pam who is becoming more upset that her birthday is being ignored. Eventually Pam bursts into tears and leaves the room. The others act surprised and annoyed that Pam is making such a big deal over such a little thing.)

KEN: I wonder what's gotten into her. What a Scrooge!

END

OTHER
HOLIDAYS

How are you fixed for Super Bowl Sunday, April Fool's Day programs, Mother's and Father's Day celebrations, and graduation ideas? Relax— we've got you covered. You'll find some of the coolest ideas ever for these holidays.

SUPER BOWL

GAME
SUPER BOWL PROPHECIES

No wagering here—just no-risk guessing at some of the innumerable details of pro football's climax. For next year's Super Bowl party, print up a quiz like the one found on page 184 and pass it out before the game. The point values are in parentheses. Tally points after the game and award creative or humorous prizes. *Sam Vernon*

APRIL FOOLS' DAY

GAME
APRIL FOOLS

As students enter the room, give them each a clear plastic clip-on badge cover. Inside each badge cover is the card shown on page 185.

Give no verbal instructions to the kids—simply give them the badges as they enter. During the allotted time, each student who fools another player may take the losing player's badges and attach it to his current string of badges. *Jay Firebaugh*

MOTHERS' DAY

PARTY
MOTHERS' NIGHT

Celebrate a moms' night by inviting all your kids' moms to attend a special program for them during your Sunday-night youth meeting on Mother's Day. (For those students who come without moms, have some surrogate moms ready—female sponsors, other women from your congregation, etc.)
• As kids arrive, supply them with construction

SUPERBOWL PROPHECIES

1. Winner _____(1) **By how much** _____(2) **Exact score** _____(3)

2. The first team to miss a field goal (circle one): (1)

   Bills   **Redskins**   **No misses**

3. The first team penalized in the fourth quarter (circle one): (1)

   Bills   **Redskins**   **No penalties**

4. Which player will score first? (1)

   Kelly   **Lofton**   **Thomas**   **Reed**   **Norwood**

   Rypien   **Monk**   **Clark**   **Riggs**   **Lohmiller**

5. How many commercials during halftime? (exact count 3; closest count 2)

6. First team to score: _____(1)

   Last team to score: _____(1)

7. Total points (circle one): (1)

   More than 40   **Less than 40**

8. Who will have the ball at the first-half two-minute warning? (1)

9. How many punts will there be in the game? (2)

10. Game length (circle one): (1)

    Less than three hours   **Less than three-and-a-half hours**

    Less than four hours   **Overtime**

11. Will there be any missed extra points? (1)

12. Which team will have the ball on last snap of game? (1)

Wear this badge where everyone can easily see it. Your assignment is to pull an April Fool's trick on as many people as you can. (Tell someone his fly is open, there's a phone call for her, his shoe is untied, etc.). Players who fall for the trick (look down to check, go to the phone, and so on) must give you any badges they are wearing. AFTER YOU LOSE YOUR BADGES, YOU CAN'T PLAY ANY MORE. Whoever has the most badges at the end wins.

Wear this badge where everyone can easily see it. Your assignment is to pull an April Fool's trick on as many people as you can. (Tell someone his fly is open, there's a phone call for her, his shoe is untied, etc.). Players who fall for the trick (look down to check, go to the phone, and so on) must give you any badges they are wearing. AFTER YOU LOSE YOUR BADGES, YOU CAN'T PLAY ANY MORE. Whoever has the most badges at the end wins.

Wear this badge where everyone can easily see it. Your assignment is to pull an April Fool's trick on as many people as you can. (Tell someone his fly is open, there's a phone call for her, his shoe is untied, etc.). Players who fall for the trick (look down to check, go to the phone, and so on) must give you any badges they are wearing. AFTER YOU LOSE YOUR BADGES, YOU CAN'T PLAY ANY MORE. Whoever has the most badges at the end wins.

Wear this badge where everyone can easily see it. Your assignment is to pull an April Fool's trick on as many people as you can. (Tell someone his fly is open, there's a phone call for her, his shoe is untied, etc.). Players who fall for the trick (look down to check, go to the phone, and so on) must give you any badges they are wearing. AFTER YOU LOSE YOUR BADGES, YOU CAN'T PLAY ANY MORE. Whoever has the most badges at the end wins.

Wear this badge where everyone can easily see it. Your assignment is to pull an April Fool's trick on as many people as you can. (Tell someone his fly is open, there's a phone call for her, his shoe is untied, etc.). Players who fall for the trick (look down to check, go to the phone, and so on) must give you any badges they are wearing. AFTER YOU LOSE YOUR BADGES, YOU CAN'T PLAY ANY MORE. Whoever has the most badges at the end wins.

Wear this badge where everyone can easily see it. Your assignment is to pull an April Fool's trick on as many people as you can. (Tell someone his fly is open, there's a phone call for her, his shoe is untied, etc.). Players who fall for the trick (look down to check, go to the phone, and so on) must give you any badges they are wearing. AFTER YOU LOSE YOUR BADGES, YOU CAN'T PLAY ANY MORE. Whoever has the most badges at the end wins.

Wear this badge where everyone can easily see it. Your assignment is to pull an April Fool's trick on as many people as you can. (Tell someone his fly is open, there's a phone call for her, his shoe is untied, etc.). Players who fall for the trick (look down to check, go to the phone, and so on) must give you any badges they are wearing. AFTER YOU LOSE YOUR BADGES, YOU CAN'T PLAY ANY MORE. Whoever has the most badges at the end wins.

Wear this badge where everyone can easily see it. Your assignment is to pull an April Fool's trick on as many people as you can. (Tell someone his fly is open, there's a phone call for her, his shoe is untied, etc.). Players who fall for the trick (look down to check, go to the phone, and so on) must give you any badges they are wearing. AFTER YOU LOSE YOUR BADGES, YOU CAN'T PLAY ANY MORE. Whoever has the most badges at the end wins.

paper and have them make matching or coordinated name tags for themselves and their moms. The more creative, the better.

•Next, a word game—in three minutes each

mother-kid team writes as many words as they can find in the phrase "Happy Mother's Day" (moth, math, prom, story, etc.).

•For an active game, try the old balloon-stomp game (in which players with balloons tied to their ankles try to stomp others' balloons while protecting their own), though with a Mother's Day twist—students must protect their own mothers. If a mom's balloon is popped, her child is out even if his balloon is still intact. If a kid's balloon gets popped first, however, the mom has to fend for herself against terrible odds.

•Entertainment? Try a short, improvisational skit that includes both moms and kids.

•Finally, the icing on the cake: The Mother-Teen Game, a Mother's Day version of the old "Newlywed Game." It's a fun game that helps kids and moms see how well they know each other, and the audience will thoroughly enjoy it, too. Here are some sample questions. Again, be sensitive to kids' parental situations; adjust the wording of some questions if you need to.

Sample Questions for Mothers

1. Who is your child's best friend?
2. What was the last movie you watched at the theater together?
3. You are sometimes heard to say, "Your room looks like _____."
4. What was your favorite Mother's Day present your child ever gave you?

Sample Questions for Teens

1. What is your mother's maiden name?
2. What is your most prized possession?
3. If you could name a food that is most like your mother, what would it be?
4. How many times in the last week has your mother told you to pick up your room? a) Not even once. b) Once or twice. c) Daily. d) She never stops telling me to.

Kenneth Lane

FATHERS' DAY

EVENT

FATHERS' DAY FUN

Here are some ideas for a Fathers' Day or father/son event.

• **Necktie Tie.** Fashion experts say that the tip of the properly tied necktie should come to the middle of one's belt buckle. Yet everyone knows how difficult it is to get a tie to do what you want it to do. Pick a few fathers and sons from the crowd and give each a necktie (if they don't already have one). Give them one (only one) chance to tie the thing around each other's neck, using the knot of their choice. The person whose tie tip comes closest to the belt buckle wins. Award prizes in different age categories.

• **Car Keys, Please?** Divide into teams of four or five people, and give each team five minutes to come up with snappy answers to the question, "May I borrow the car keys, Dad?" Have each team read their best answers to the crowd. Award prizes to the team with the most answers and the team with the one best answer.

• **Prairie Home Dad.** Get a few of your better storytellers (dads as well as sons) to prepare five-minute stories (à la Garrison Keillor) about lessons they learned from their dads or poignant memories of "life with father." Intersperse these stories throughout the event. *David M. Shaw*

GRADUATION IDEAS

THE BEARDED PROPHETS' PROPHECIES

This is a spin-off of the old "Most likely to..." sections in high school year-

---

The Bearded Prophets do hereby, forthwith, and even so prophesy that

Deb Kizer

shall in all likelihood and with great probability be known as the all new:

First ever Field & Stream cover girl

Complete with Bass Masters official dress and life jacket, cover girl Deb Kizer will sport the latest in fishery's finest. You'll see her wearing the latest in fishhook earrings, wader-hosiery, and Bass Masters headgear. Should you have the unfortunate opportunity to run into Deb in public, you may get a whiff of her ever popular new cologne, "Eau de Fisherie."

The Bearded Prophets do hereby, forthwith, and even so prophesy that

John "Okie" Mires

shall in all likelihood and with great probability be known as the all new:

Army Recruitment Poster Child

John, soon to be "Okie," Mires will adorn the walls of recruiting offices nationwide. After years of searching high and low for the new image Army man, John was selected on the basis of his bona fide "red-neck" pick up truck driving ability. Picture, if you will, Juan John Mires pointing a finger at you proclaiming, "Uncle Sam wants you." Once again, the Selective Service draft will be abandoned due to the overwhelming response brought on by the new Army recruitment Poster Child.

---

books. In conjunction with whatever else you plan to do to honor your graduates, present them with their own Bearded Prophets' Prophecies (it helps if one of your pastors or elders is bearded). Penned in calligraphy, the humorous prophecies describe a well-known idiosyncrasy or characteristic trait of each graduate. *Greg Fiebig*

NOT SO TRIVIAL

At your next graduation event, introduce your group's graduating seniors with year-of-birth trivia that is relevant to each student. For instance, introduce a musically inclined boy by playing snippets of the top 10 hits from his birth year. For a girl who lettered in softball, tell an anecdote about a baseball star from her birth year.

Find the trivia in encyclopedia year books, library files, back issues of *Rolling Stone* or other trendy magazines, or old almanacs purchased at a used bookstore. (Remember that an almanac dated 1973 will

contain information from 1972.) If you want to personalize it further, dig up facts for their birth month and day. Or make life real easy by ordering from a card shop a mock-up newspaper for a student's actual birth date. *Len Cuthbert*

SENIOR BLESS

Though high schoolers find it hard to say goodbye when seniors graduate, they yearn to tell each other how they feel. Give them a format for sharing their feelings by holding a Senior Bless. Once you've had a Senior Bless, your freshmen and sophomores will look forward to their turn.

Invite your seniors by phone or written invitation to come to a special meeting to honor them. At the last meeting before the seniors graduate, bring them up front one at a time and invite the rest of the group to tell things they like about each senior. Then ask kids to tell blessings they hope will be in each senior's future. As each compliment and blessing is spoken, write it in a super-size card to be presented to that senior. Bless seniors in order by birth date.

Some actual blessings bestowed by teenagers on seniors:
• "I hope people are as good to you as you have been to me."
• "I hope you can always see God clearly no matter how murky things get."
• "I pray you'll build a marriage that brings strength and joy to both you and your spouse."
• "I hope your job is awesome."

After all seniors have received their blessings, invite them to say anything they'd like to the group. It's not uncommon for some seniors to be too moved to speak. Others will add comments like, "Thanks for my blessing," "I really appreciate this group because you've shown me that God is real and he makes the world beautiful," "I'll miss you," "I'm glad I'll always be welcomed here." *Karen Dockrey*

GRAD RECOGNITION

PARTING SHOTS

Your seniors can have the parting shot with this idea. On an audiocassette record their answers to various questions that deal with high school, youth group, favorite magazines, TV shows, teachers, musicians, etc.

Using a dual deck that has a microphone jack, edit bits and pieces of their answers to make a hilarious spoof interview. Build different stories around each youth's supposed experiences—dating a current rock star, stealing vital information from the space shuttle, advising the vice president of the United States.

Put all the interviews on one tape and play it for the whole group. With effort and creativity, this idea can be a smash. The tape is also an appreciated memento for the students to remember their classmates. *David Flavin*

CRAFT

GALLERY OF GRADUATES

A month in advance of graduation Sunday at your church, ask your seniors to bring in items that represent them, their school and community activities, and their accomplishments—for example, 5x7-inch

senior portraits, graduation announcements, varsity letters, athletic equipment, photos, ribbons, awards, plaques, certificates, programs from plays and concerts, yearbooks, and anything with their school logo on it.

Make an individual display for each grad, using colored mat board as a background (available from art supply stores). Write the name of the honored graduate across the top in calligraphy. Use photo-mounting corners to mount photos, certificates, programs, and awards. Rubber cement or masking tape is fine for mounting letters, ribbons, and such. Place large items—yearbooks, athletic equipment, etc.—in front of each display.

On graduation Sunday, exhibit the individualized displays in the church lobby, then move them to where you'll hold the reception. *Tom Lytle*

CRAFT

GRAD PLACEMATS

For next June's graduation banquet, adorn the placemats with your graduates' photos, their names, their alma mater, poems, senior wills, or your congratulatory comments.

Check out what's available at your local quick-print/copy store, or if you have access to a scanner and computer or a color photocopier, create your own. For a lasting keepsake, cover the placemats with clear contact paper or have them laminated. *Mike Duggan*

BANQUET

GRADUATION ROAST

When you announce this Sunday afternoon cookout and senior roast, explain that people only roast those they love, care for, and deeply respect.

In the weeks before graduation, dig up all the dirt you can on your seniors by talking to parents, brothers and sisters, other relatives, youth group members, and other friends. Gather moderately embarrassing photos, slides, and movies of the seniors when they were much younger. Plan some funny remarks about each senior and some transitional comments that keep up the momentum between roasts.

On a Sunday near graduation and in the worship service just prior to the roast, have your graduating seniors come to the front of the sanctuary. Briefly extol their virtues and recount their ministry in the life of the church. Present them with a Bible or helpful devotional book. Deliver a brief charge and pray for the grads.

That afternoon begin the fellowship activities with a cookout—followed by the roast. One at a time have the seniors come forward and sit facing the group. Proceed to roast them—and watch the fun unfold. Give each of them a gag gift related to one or more of the anecdotes you tell on them. *Vernon Edington*

Professional Resources

Administration, Publicity, & Fundraising (Ideas Library)
Developing Student Leaders
Equipped to Serve: Volunteer Youth Worker Training Course
Help! I'm a Junior High Youth Worker!
Help! I'm a Sunday School Teacher!
Help! I'm a Volunteer Youth Worker!
How to Expand Your Youth Ministry
How to Speak to Youth...and Keep Them Awake at the Same Time
One Kid at a Time: Reaching Youth through Mentoring
A Youth Ministry Crash Course
The Youth Worker's Handbook to Family Ministry

Youth Ministry Programming

Camps, Retreats, Missions, & Service Ideas (Ideas Library)
Compassionate Kids: Practical Ways to Involve Your Students in Mission and Service
Creative Bible Lessons in John: Encounters with Jesus
Creative Bible Lessons in Romans: Faith on Fire!
Creative Bible Lessons on the Life of Christ
Creative Junior High Programs from A to Z, Vol. 1 (A-M)
Creative Meetings, Bible Lessons, & Worship Ideas (Ideas Library)
Crowd Breakers & Mixers (Ideas Library)
Drama, Skits, & Sketches (Ideas Library)
Dramatic Pauses
Facing Your Future: Graduating Youth Group with a Faith That Lasts
Games (Ideas Library)

Games 2 (Ideas Library)
Great Fundraising Ideas for Youth Groups
More Great Fundraising Ideas for Youth Groups
Great Retreats for Youth Groups
Greatest Skits on Earth
Greatest Skits on Earth, Vol. 2
Holiday Ideas (Ideas Library)
Hot Illustrations for Youth Talks
More Hot Illustrations for Youth Talks
Incredible Questionnaires for Youth Ministry
Junior High Game Nights
Kickstarters: 101 Ingenious Intros to Just about Any Bible Lesson
Memory Makers
More Junior High Game Nights
Play It! Great Games for Groups
Play It Again! More Great Games for Groups
Special Events (Ideas Library)
Spontaneous Melodramas
Super Sketches for Youth Ministry
Teaching the Bible Creatively
Up Close and Personal: How to Build Community in Your Youth Group
Wild Truth Bible Lessons
Worship Services for Youth Groups

Discussion Starter Resources

Discussion & Lesson Starters (Ideas Library)
Discussion & Lesson Starters 2 (Ideas Library)
4th-6th Grade TalkSheets
Get 'Em Talking
High School TalkSheets
High School TalkSheets: Psalms and Proverbs
Junior High TalkSheets
Junior High TalkSheets: Psalms and Proverbs
Keep 'Em Talking!
More High School TalkSheets

More Junior High TalkSheets
What If...? 450 Thought-Provoking Questions to Get Teenagers Talking, Laughing, and Thinking
Would You Rather...? 465 Provocative Questions to Get Teenagers Talking

Clip Art

ArtSource Vol. 1—Fantastic Activities
ArtSource Vol. 2—Borders, Symbols, Holidays, and Attention Getters
ArtSource Vol. 3—Sports
ArtSource Vol. 4—Phrases and Verses
ArtSource Vol. 5—Amazing Oddities and Appalling Images
ArtSource Vol. 6—Spiritual Topics
ArtSource Vol. 7—Variety Pack
ArtSource Vol. 8—Stark Raving Clip Art
ArtSource CD-ROM (contains Vols. 1–7)

Videos

EdgeTV
The Heart of Youth Ministry: A Morning with Mike Yaconelli
Next Time I Fall in Love Video Curriculum
Understanding Your Teenager Video Curriculum

Student Books

Grow For It Journal
Grow For It Journal through the Scriptures
Wild Truth Journal for Junior Highers